ST. MARTIN'S PRESS ❧ NEW YORK

VERTIGO

THE MAKING OF A HITCHCOCK CLASSIC

DAN AUILER

FOREWORD BY MARTIN SCORSESE

Book design by Gretchen Achilles
Composition by Pixel Press

Library of Congress Cataloging-in-Publication Data
Auiler, Dan.
    Vertigo: the making of a Hitchcock classic / Dan Auiler; foreword by Martin Scorsese.
      p. cm.
    Includes index.
    ISBN 0-312-16915-9
    1. Vertigo (Motion picture) I. Title.
  PN1997.V479A84   1998   97-31654
  791.43'72—dc21   CIP

FIRST EDITION: June 1998

10 9 8 7 6 5 4 3

TO ROSE AND MAYA

CONTENTS

ACKNOWLEDGMENTS

This book could not have been written without the gracious support of Leland Faust, Patricia Hitchcock O'Connell, and Tere O'Connell Carruba. In addition to the Hitchcock trust, I must thank the dedicated Faye Thompson and the staff at the Margaret Herrick Library of the Academy of Motion Picture Arts and Sciences, without whom I would have been lost in a sea of files. I also owe an enormous debt to the creative team behind *Vertigo,* who were always gracious with their time: the late Peggy Robertson, C. O. "Doc" Erikson, Henry Bumstead, Herbert Coleman, Herb Steinberg, Leonard South, Samuel Taylor, and Polly Burson. Thanks also to: Robert A. Harris, James C. Katz, and Marlene Noble from the restoration team and the late Pete Comandini at YCM labs who helped explain VistaVision and film processing to me; Brad Roberts and Elaine Bass provided help and information on Saul Bass; the artists Chris Marker, Cindy Bernard, and Chris Marclay for spending time discussing their work and its connection to *Vertigo;* John Whitney, Jr., and Michael Friend, film archivist at the Herrick Library, for help on Whitney's designs for the title sequence; Martin Scorsese for providing the foreword and being the "Godfather" of film history; A. C. Lyles for history on Paramount; and Rae Ferren for information on the film's dream sequence.

An enormous debt is owed to my agent Christy Fletcher and my editor Calvert Morgan, Jr., who held this first-time writer's hand and believed in the project from the beginning. Larry Kronish, Sean Stratton, George Turner, Laurent Bouterean, Ken Mogg, and Harrison Engle assisted me with the manuscript and made many important contributions. Harrison was also very kind and sharing with his own research on *Vertigo* for his American Movie Classics documentary on the restoration of *Vertigo.*

Finally, I must thank a number of people who helped in other ways (like putting up with long absences or providing much-needed comfort): Barbara Sturges, Katherine Dustin, Susan Madrid-Simon and the students at Upward Bound–Occidental College, Evan Ramstad, my play production students at Eagle Rock Jr./Sr. High School, the Shorb family of San Francisco, Cindy Chang, Bob Morris, and Andrew Morrison.

And, of course, none of this would be possible without the support of my family.

It's difficult to put into words exactly what *Vertigo* means to me as both a film lover and as a filmmaker. As is the case with all great films, truly great films, no matter how much has been said and written about them, the dialogue about it will always continue. Because any film as great as *Vertigo* demands more than just a sense of admiration—it demands a personal response.

A good place to start is its complete singularity. *Vertigo* stands alone as a Hitchcock film, as a Hollywood film. In fact, it just stands alone—period. For such a personal work with such a uniquely disturbing vision of the world to come out of the studio system when it did was not just unusual—it was

nearly unthinkable. *Vertigo* was and continues to be a real example to me and to many of my contemporaries, in the sense that it demonstrates to us that it's possible to function within a system and do work that's deeply personal at the same time.

Vertigo is also important to me—essential would be more like it—because it has a hero driven purely by obsession. I've always been attracted in my own work to heroes motivated by obsession, and on that level *Vertigo* strikes a deep chord in me every time I see it. Morality, decency, kindness, intelligence, wisdom—all the qualities that we think heroes are supposed to possess—desert Jimmy Stewart's character little by little, until he is left alone on that church tower with the bells tolling behind him and nothing to show but his humanity.

Whole books could be written about so many individual aspects of *Vertigo*—its extraordinary visual precision, which cuts to the soul of its characters like a razor; its many mysteries and moments of subtle poetry; its unsettling and exquisite use of color; its extraordinary performances by Stewart and Kim Novak—whose work is so brave and emotionally immediate—as well as the very underrated work of Barbara Bel Geddes. And that's not to mention its astonishing title sequence by Saul Bass or its tragically beautiful score by Bernard Herrmann, both absolutely essential to the spirit, the functioning, and the power of *Vertigo*.

Of course, we can now hear Herrmann's score with a clarity and breadth that it's never had before, thanks to Bob Harris and Jim Katz, the men who worked on the beautiful, painstaking restoration of *Vertigo*. I'm happy that the Film Foundation was able to play a part in making this important work possible, and I'd like to thank Universal and Tom Pollock for allowing it to go forward and, of course, I'd like to thank the American Film Institute for their invaluable contributions.

—MARTIN SCORSESE

Why does *Vertigo* affect us so deeply? Why isn't Alfred Hitchcock's 1958 psychological thriller, just coming off its third major rerelease in four decades, and available in gorgeously restored home-video editions, just another "Hitchcock and bull story," as *Time* callously described it upon its initial release? Doesn't that description better fit the other films Hitchcock created during his last great period?

Why? Because *Vertigo*, like other films that reach somewhere within us and grab us firmly by the entrails, is not the typical Hitchcock film, even as it represents the highest realization of so many of the director's career preoccupations. Seen today,

Vertigo can seem like the best of films and the worst of films: At moments throughout, its images shimmer with an incandescent beauty that few films in history could pretend to match, even as other moments—awkwardnesses in the script, longueurs in the storytelling—induce discomforts not originally intended by the director or his crew. *Vertigo* is not the perfect, pure cinema of *Rear Window.* Yet who is haunted, dogged, pursued by *Rear Window*?

If Hitchcock, as the critic Robin Wood has argued, is the cinema's Shakespeare, then *Vertigo* is his *Macbeth.* Not in theme, plot, or structure, perhaps, but in its status as a flawed gem—whose imperfections somehow make the work all the more effective. *Macbeth* does not possess the perfect unity and exquisite poetry of *A Midsummer Night's Dream,* but surely this terrible couple's anguish moves us far more deeply than the foolish lover's lament.

Vertigo is a classic of the heart—Hitchcock's and ours. It is a film that writes directly on our souls. Who knows the consequences ultimately of such art? I don't feel damaged after watching the film, as Scottie so painfully and permanently is at its conclusion. What I do know is that I've seen and felt something painfully true.

Those final moments in the tower: Scottie confronting his own illusion, his face leaning out of the shadows as its textures seem to ripple and convulse in

deep torment. "Oh, Madeleine, Madeleine, I loved you so—oh, Madeleine." This quiet moment, following the Sturm und Drang of the famous tower-climbing scene, is the Lear howl of the film. Scottie has loved and lost—and loved and lost again.

That final, shocking image of Scottie alone in the tower is what seals the heart and our fate—what binds us to the film, brings us back to countless screenings, drags us to the locations to walk their steps like hungry ghosts, what compels the writing of essay after essay and batters us in each new audience with question after unanswerable question.

Hitchcock sizes up San Francisco's Mission Dolores.

Readers of this book, paradoxically, will have a different kind of surprise in store for them: What many *Vertigo* aficionados will find perplexing are the systematic, businesslike, matter-of-fact circumstances under which this odd, obsessional, very un-matter-of-fact film was created. This is the nature of nearly all great films: They seem more accident than purposeful creation. As Martin Scorsese notes in his foreword, it is almost astonishing that so idiosyncratic and personal a work could be crafted within the confines of a studio system that, by the late 1950s, had come to seem monolithic, even prehistoric.

By nature, Alfred Hitchcock preferred smooth surfaces to rough. He preferred people to believe that his films were the easy, casual exercises of a genius. Yet the truths behind Hitchcock's glittery storytelling are more complicated. Peering into the written record left behind by Hitchcock, and into the memories of those who worked with him, we come to see a different filmmaker: Not the mad Svengali of Donald Spoto's biography, but the troubled artist at work.

Was it coincidence that Hitchcock should choose this more irresolvable of all his stories just as he and his wife had begun to confront their first serious health problems? Would anyone still attempt to argue that the film's fascination with shaping the image of a woman has nothing to do with Hitchcock's own failed attempts to re-create Grace Kelly in another actress, or with the idea, so widely discussed at the time, of creating competing blond bombshells—the very process that had molded Kim Novak?

Yes, there is all of this in *Vertigo,* and much more. Great works of art are by nature mysterious and provocative. We go back to the Mona Lisa not because she provides answers, but for the questions she provokes.

We can sense on fundamental levels that in *Vertigo* can be found the sum of Hitchcock's contradictions—romance and disconnection, the face and the mask, the director and his legend. If we start to pull away the layers that make *Vertigo,* what is the personality of the filmmaker we find at its heart? The dark figure of Spoto's biography, or the enigma of his official biographer, John Russell Taylor?

For, surely, what lies beneath the layers of creation that necessarily go into the making of any work of art is a heart—not a force of cold cruelty, but one of passion and unresolved longing. A heart, in other words, like our own.

CHAPTER 1 | THE POWER AND THE FREEDOM

ELSTER

San Francisco's changed. The things that spell San Francisco to me are changing fast.

(Scottie smiles at the old prints on the wall.)

SCOTTIE

Like all this.

ELSTER
(nodding)

I'd like to have lived here then. The color and excitement . . . the power . . . the freedom.

(Scene 22, Taylor script)

POP LIEBEL

. . . He kept the child and threw her away. Men could do that in those days. They had the power . . . and the freedom. . . .

(Scene 120, Taylor script)

SCOTTIE

Oh, Judy!! When he had all her money, and the freedom and the power . . . He ditched you? What a shame!

(Scene 269, Taylor script)

The drive from Alfred Hitchcock's mansion in Bel Air to the famous gates of the Paramount studios on Melrose Avenue—about twenty or thirty minutes east on Sunset to Gower—would have been long enough to give the director time to sort through the day ahead of him as he traveled to work on one spring morning in 1956. Hitchcock lived near the end of the circular Bellagio Road, and his house was adjacent to the eighteenth hole of the Bel Air Country Club's golf course; art director Henry Bumstead, who visited Hitch's house often during their days together at Paramount, remembers the director proudly displaying a box of broken glass—all the result of errant golf balls. After each window strike, the country club sent someone over to replace the glass. His wife, Alma, returned the favor, collecting the balls and returning them to the club in buckets at the end of each month.

Africa was on the director's mind that morning. Paramount had purchased two new properties for Hitchcock—one that he had wanted, and one that Paramount had wanted for him. The latter was a big international thriller, adapted from the novel *Flamingo Feather* by Laurens van der Post, to be shot on location in South Africa. The other was a new novel by a pair of French novelists whose previous book had been turned into a very successful, and rather Hitchcockian, film—*Les Diaboliques*—a few years before. *Flamingo Feather* would be produced by Paramount, and it would mean another African trip for the director who had made *The Man Who Knew Too Much*. The French story, on the other hand, he planned to transplant to San Francisco, and it was a film he would make himself—an Alfred J. Hitchcock Production.

From Among the Dead—a literal English translation of the French title *D'Entre les Morts*—was the Hitchcock production. Hitchcock received no up-front salary for his own productions, and he was obliged to share the development costs, but then after eight years, the picture's rights would revert to him. With his successful television series—a blessing he'd been talked into by his friend and agent Lew Wasserman—now a year into its successful run, money had never been more plentiful for him.

With cash only a minor issue, then, Hitch had the luxury of judging which of the two films he really wanted to spend a year making. Back to Africa? He had enjoyed his time there with Alma and the Stewarts during *The Man Who Knew Too Much.* Or would he confront the French story, which had much more personal resonance for him?

The limo drove through the DeMille gates and pulled in front of the Administration Building. Hitchcock walked to his large office on the ground floor, nearly dead center in the building. The office of Herbert Coleman, his associate producer, adjoined his; the two shared secretaries and assistants who worked in a small foyer between. Coleman, who had first worked with Hitchcock as an assistant director on 1954's *Rear Window,* had worked at Paramount's Hollywood studios since the days when Hitchcock was getting his start at Famous Players–Lasky in London, which was affiliated with Paramount. Friendly, competent, and efficient, Coleman handled most of the producer's tasks at Hitchcock Productions—without, and this was most important, getting in the Master's way when it came to final decisions.

Hitchcock's time had been divided recently between Paramount and Warner Bros. *The Wrong Man,* a disturbing, black-and-white Henry Fonda picture, was now in postproduction—and no one, except perhaps Hitch himself, was thrilled with the product. A stark documentary-style film based on the true story of a Stork Club musician wrongly accused of murder, it was considered grim and unsettling fare from the director who had made millions from glossy Technicolor suspense fantasies such as *To Catch a Thief* and *The Man Who Knew Too Much.*

The buzz in the office had turned to the two new projects, which had already been announced in the trades. Paramount, with characteristic politesse, was urging Hitchcock to take up the South African *Flamingo Feather* next. Pleased with the box-office receipts on *The Man Who Knew Too Much,* the studio was eager to keep Hitchcock in the *39 Steps* international-thriller genre and away from the more introspective films that *The Wrong Man* typified.

As Hitchcock settled in that morning, he buzzed Coleman, telling him to make arrangements for a tour of locations in Africa. Coleman was pleased: He wasn't sure about the French novel, but, just as important, he knew that location work meant more opportunities for creative input from him. Even today, when asked about his favorite films, Coleman begins with Hitchcock's earlier, sunnier European travelogue *To Catch a Thief*—not only because of the beautiful locations but also because Hitchcock had let Coleman handle the direction of the second-unit photography on that picture.

Hitchcock would inform Alma of his decision later. She preferred the French novel, but there would be time for that after Africa. They were getting older—both were fifty-six now—and a difficult location like Africa would one day be impossible for them. And he would never travel anywhere, certainly not to make a film, without Alma. It was in a tossing boat, while returning from working at the German film studio UFA in the mid-1920s, that he had asked Alma to marry him. She had been with him from the beginning—since a time when, as she occasionally liked to remind him, hers was the more successful of their careers.

Alfred Hitchcock and Alma Reville had gotten to know each other on the set of Graham Cutts's silent film *Woman to Woman* in 1923. She was the film's editor. Hitchcock had been hired to design titles for the picture, but he managed to become its art director and, ultimately, its assistant director.

Alma Reville began her career in the British film industry at the age of sixteen, as an assistant editor whose principal job was to rewind the film. By the time she knew of Hitchcock and he of her, she had cut several features. As assistant director, it was Hitch who offered her the job as editor on *Woman to Woman*. As she told John Russell Taylor, Hitchcock's first biographer, years later, "Since it is unthinkable for a British male to admit that a woman has a job more important than his, Hitch had waited to speak to me until he had a higher position."

Of course, the Hitch Alma knew in the early 1920s was a far different man from the Hitchcock of legend. The droll, still, Buddha-like image Hitchcock cultivated into an icon in the 1950s and thereafter is such a powerful one that it's difficult to reconcile him with the figure Alma Reville met and married—the plump comic who was captured running about in front of the camera in home movies from the twenties. Hitchcock the auteur was, in the beginning, England's boy genius.

Hitchcock told Peter Bogdanovich that he was originally hired by the London branch of the U.S. company Famous Players–Lasky (which would later be merged with Paramount) after he impressed the studio heads by designing title cards for a picture that they had been planning to film, *The Sorrows of Satan*. With much planning, the energetic young Hitchcock prepared thoroughly for the job interview, and his skill as an artist landed him a job as a title-card designer. The work was part-time at first (with proceeds shared with his supervisor at his day job, Henley Telegraph, who allowed Hitch the flexible work schedule), but soon Famous Players–Lasky awarded him with a full-time job in the title department. In the nascent industry, the work of a title-card designer involved not only lettering and graphic design but story editing—and, as Hitchcock's case proved, it could even lead to directing.

Hitchcock's first moments as a director were for Famous Players–Lasky. Now lost, his first effort, *Number Thirteen*, was never completed. A victim of the extremely unstable British film industry, the British branch of Famous Players–Lasky was forced to close after only three years, right in the middle of filming *Number Thirteen*.

Hitchcock would find work just a few doors down in industrial Islington, near Alma's hometown of Twickenham. After apprenticing with Graham Cutts (Britain's leading director at the time), followed by an influential stint at UFA, the progressive German film company located in Berlin, Hitchcock would assume the mantle of "Master of Suspense" with his silent film *The Lodger* (1926). What followed, of course, is history: *Blackmail, Murder, The Man Who Knew Too Much, The 39 Steps, The Secret Agent, Sabotage, Young and Innocent, The Lady Vanishes*—a decade's string of commercial and artistic successes that led straight to Hollywood as a member of the David O. Selznick team.

All this distant history may seem difficult to relate to *Vertigo*, a picture made more than a quarter of a century after Hitchcock's debut. Yet many of the later film's important roots are easily traced to these early times. It was Kay

Brown, who met the Hitchcocks in New York when they first arrived under Selznick's aegis in the late 1930s, who would suggest Sam Taylor, the film's final writer. Angus MacPhail, a longtime Hitchcock friend and coworker during the British years, would also briefly work on the *Vertigo* screenplay. An even more visible carryover from Hitchcock's early working days was Tom Helmore, who worked with the director in *The Ring* (a successful early Hitchcock silent film); in 1950s Hollywood, he once again stepped before the Master's camera to take the minor role of *Vertigo*'s sophisticated villain.

To appreciate *Vertigo* fully as Hitchcock's most personal film, it is with his formative years—his time of power and freedom as Britain's premiere film-maker—that we must begin.

Only one short story written by Hitchcock—from the days before his film career, when he worked as a senior estimator for the Henley Telegraph Company—is known to exist. It was written for the company's social club newsletter:

GAS

She had never been in this part of Paris before, only reading of it in the novels of Duvain: or seeing it at the Grand Guignol. So this was the Montmartre? That horror where danger lurked under cover of night, where innocent souls perished without warning—where doom confronted the unwary—where the Apache revelled.

She moved cautiously in the shadow of the high wall, looking furtively backward for the hidden menace that might be dogging her steps. Suddenly she darted into an alley way, little heeding where it led—groping her way on in the inky blackness, the one thought of eluding the pursuit firmly fixed in her mind—on she went—Oh! when would it end?—Then a doorway from which a light streamed lent itself to her vision—in here—anywhere, she thought.

The door stood at the head of a flight of stairs—stairs that creaked with age, as she endeavoured to creep down—then she heard the sound of drunken laughter and shuddered—surely this was—No, not that! Anything but that! She reached the foot of the stairs and saw an evil-smelling wine bar, with wrecks of what were once men and women indulging in a drunken orgy—then they saw her, a vision of affrighted purity. Half a dozen men rushed towards her amid the encouraging shouts of the rest. She was seized. She screamed with terror—better had she been caught by her pursuer, was her one fleeting thought, as they dragged her roughly across the room. The fiends lost no time in settling her fate. They would share her belongings—and she—why! Was not this the heart of Montmartre? She should go—the rats should feast. Then they bound her and carried her down the dark passage.

Up a flight of stairs to the riverside. The water rats should feast, they said. And then—then swinging her bound body to and fro, dropped her with a splash into the dark, swirling waters. Down she went, down down; Conscious only of a choking sensation, this was death

then

"It's out Madam," said the dentist. "Half a crown please."

Hitch

It is a revealing vignette. The nineteen-year-old Hitchcock certainly demonstrated his love for Poe, whose combination of melodrama and dark comedy he imitated wryly. The literary style of "Gas" is more highblown than the cinematic style he would later develop, but the content reveals elements that would dominate Hitchcock's work for the next fifty years—in setting, imagery, and theme.

[SETTING]

Hitchcock set the story in Paris, and specifically Montmartre, the notoriously dangerous neighborhood dominated by the Sacré-Coeur. The director never exploited this darkly romantic side of France in his films (with the possible exception of *Topaz; To Catch a Thief* is a postcard valentine to the area); nor did he ever make a film based on Poe. But he did find a reasonable facsimile in San Francisco, one of America's richest and most romantic settings—dominated by religious buildings, and an atmosphere haunted by the past—when he came to make *Vertigo*.

[IMAGERY]

The story is filled with what would become classic images of the Hitchcockian filmscape—all of which make appearances in *Vertigo:*

- **FLIGHTS OF STAIRS**: A climactic image in *Vertigo,* they recur in all but two of Hitchcock's films—*Rope,* set entirely in one room, and the bucolic *The Trouble with Harry.*

- **DOORWAYS**: Light streaming through a doorway—a classic image for both Hitchcock and Edward Hopper—is an image that recurs in almost every Hitchcock film.

- **DRAGGED BODIES**: A particularly disturbing image, it is used with great effect in his two most disturbing films—*Vertigo* and *Psycho.*

- **DARK, SWIRLING WATERS**: The swirling image is a consistent Hitchcock preoccupation, and water is the preferred choice for women wishing a premature end—Kate in *The Manxman,* Madeleine in *Vertigo,* and Marnie in the film of the same name all are rescued after plunging into deep waters.

The final draft of *Vertigo*'s memorable dream sequence has substantial resonances with the style and imagery of "Gas":

We see Scottie approaching the grave. . . . It is open; there is a great black abyss, with the headstone to mark it. . . . The black depths of the grave fill the screen, and now, suddenly we start to fall . . . at the moment of impact the picture clears, and Scottie is sitting up in bed, staring ahead in horror, awakened by the sound of his own scream. The scream is echoed by a fog horn in the distance.

[THEME]

The roots of Hitchcock's thematic sensibility are even more apparent in "Gas." Even before he was working in film, this early work demonstrates, Hitchcock had already set upon his most famous theme: the guiltless victim chased by an unknown pursuer. And—as would be true in so many of his films—it is not the pursuer whom the pursued has to fear as much as the circumstances into which he or she must run to escape. The innocent wrongly pursued is perhaps Hitchcock's most consistent and enduring character, one of his real contributions to cinema.

In addition to the "wrong man" theme, the story features another common Hitchcockian gesture: the overwhelming sense that his character is being watched. The voyeur may be Hitchcock's second most significant theme—a theme made explicit in *Rear Window,* then brought to a kind of culmination in *Vertigo.*

Also important is that Hitchcock chose a woman as the party to be pursued and, eventually, abased. The character may have been gleaned from the popular penny dreadfuls of the times, but in retrospect it is interesting to see the young Hitchcock hitting upon this idea so early—even in the context of a story that is, after all, meant to be a joke. In *Vertigo,* Hitchcock deftly softens the sobering abuse of his female protagonist, Kim Novak's Judy, by focusing on the passion and torment of her lover, Scottie (and casting James Stewart in his role). Consider the scenario, though, from Judy's perspective: She's picked

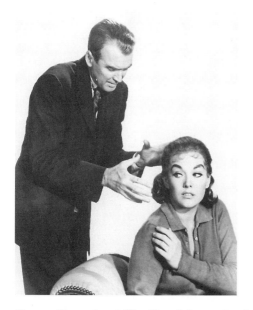 

Jimmy Stewart and Kim Novak in a pair of posed publicity shots for **Vertigo**—*shots resembling nothing in the finished film.*

up by one significantly older man, Gavin Elster (Tom Helmore's character), who gives her a new persona (Madeleine) and then involves her in the original Madeleine's murder. He promises her a deeper attachment, only to dump her unceremoniously after the deed is done. Then she finds the process repeated with Scottie—yet, despite his earnestness, his behavior is doubly humiliating, as it carries an implicit rejection of Judy's own self in favor of the fantasy of Madeleine. In *Vertigo,* the figure of the woman pursued—first explored in "Gas"—found its paradoxical culmination.

The oft-told story in which the young Hitchcock suffered a daylong incarceration for an unknown crime fits a little too neatly to be fully believed. The story has become as ubiquitous as Washington's cherry tree, and probably carries no more or less truth than that national legend. But there are deeper truths at play here: Alfred Hitchcock felt a need to explain his creative obsession with guilt. That the story should involve an innocent child betrayed by a most trusted figure (his father, who died when Hitch was young) is suggestive.

Another incident, which Hitchcock described to John Russell Taylor, may have deeper connections to Hitchcock's creative work. Both Taylor and Donald Spoto, his second biographer, maintain that Hitchcock was a sexual novice well into his twenties; Alma herself apparently had to explain the menstrual cycle to him while on location, which certainly indicates a general ignorance of the opposite sex. Here is how Taylor recounts Hitch's remarkable story:

> . . . On at least one occasion he discovered that Weimar Germany featured some diversions undreamed of in Leytonstone (as far as he knew, anyway). One evening he and Cutts were invited out by the family of one of their UFA bosses. To their surprise, after dinner they were taken to a night-club where men danced with men and women with women. Eventually, two German girls in the party, one of them still in her teens, the other thirtyish, offered to drive them back to their lodgings. But there was a little diversion: on the way they stopped at a hotel and the two Englishmen and their party were dragged in. In the room the girls made various propositions, which perhaps fortunately the terrified Hitch did not understand too exactly; he thought the safest thing to do was to keep saying *"Nein,*

nein" until they got discouraged. At this point, perhaps suspecting that the Englishmen were united by some special interest of their own, the two girls got into bed together. Hitchcock was surprised but fairly uncomprehending. . . .

Uncomprehending? John Russell Taylor submits that this scene had little effect on Hitchcock, but the director himself had told Taylor that it sparked his interest in abnormal psychology and inspired a scene in *The Pleasure Garden*.

Taylor's interpretation notwithstanding, the German hotel incident had a real effect on Hitchcock—one that echoed throughout his work. The master-works from the fifties period are filled with voyeurism, a subject whose ulti-mate meditations were *Rear Window* and *Vertigo*. *Rear Window* concerns a man trapped in a room—like Hitch among the Germans—with nothing to do but watch his neighbors, whose windows frame scenes of varying degrees of sexual content: young newlyweds, a dancer sunbathing, a woman the observer calls Miss Lonelyhearts. *Vertigo,* a few years later, is a long romantic poem to voyeurism that leads the viewer through lengthy specific sequences of silent pursuit, and through the much darker and broader story of one man's pur-suit—to unthinkable extremes—of his chosen romantic ideal.

To be sure, nothing in his life story suggests that that late-evening live sex show created in Hitchcock a man who preferred to observe; a man who crafted five decades' worth of extraordinary films could hardly be accused of a life of mere passive observation. But an interest and an identification with the trapped watcher—of that, there can be no doubt. More than thirty years after that night in a German hotel room, Hitchcock would find himself sitting in an-other hotel room—this one on a soundstage conjured at his command—watch-ing another couple make love, creating a scene with an intensity that continues to trap us, too, watching in the dark.

A flashing sign—TO-NITE GOLDEN CURLS—was among the first memorable im-ages Alfred Hitchcock would mount on screen. And its light reaches across thirty years to the vision of golden Madeleine, aglow against the red velvet walls of Ernie's. It's impossible to see what Hitchcock called the first true "Hitchcock" film—his 1926 silent *The Lodger*—without perceiving connections to the masterpiece of 1958.

Hitchcock had hardly been in a position of freedom or power in early 1926, when he began work on *The Lodger*. His prime motivation was fear—fear that the movie would not be the first true Hitchcock film, but the last. His first feature, *The Pleasure Garden,* was screened for the producers and shelved. His second, *The Mountain Eagle,* was a disaster. With no control over the production, Hitchcock was saddled with an unremarkable story set in the hills of Kentucky, and a then-famous Hollywood vamp as his leading lady. When it disappointed the producers, they shelved this film too. His next chance, then, would be his last.

The Lodger was a project first pursued, then adapted, and finally directed by Hitchcock, whose fiancée, Alma, was the assistant director. They had fallen in love during the filming of *Woman to Woman.* The young couple waited nervously outside the studio while the producers screened the finished film. They had poured everything that they knew about film into the production; though they were devotees of film art (a relatively new movement that considered film something more than a commodity), they were nevertheless middle-class enough in their needs and desires to want to make a commercially successful film. What they had created together, as it turned out, was a groundbreaking mix of European art cinema and commercial American cinema styles. But it left the producers confused.

The Lodger, like his first two films, was temporarily shelved; Ivor Montagu was brought in to help Hitchcock reshape the film. Later, though, both would admit that little was changed before the film's release. The producers, like most British companies of the time, hardly had enough product to keep *The Lodger* out of circulation for long. Reluctantly, they released the film—and it was a smash, firmly establishing Hitchcock as Britain's premiere director and giving the young upstart carte blanche to choose his own product.

The film's story line is classic Hitchcock material. Like so many of his future films, the story is one of mistaken identity: The lodger of the title, played by British heartthrob Ivor Novello, is mistaken for the Avenger, a Jack the Ripper–style murderer whose obsession is for golden-haired girls. In reality, the Novello character's sister was one of the Avenger's first victims; his suspicious behavior at the middle-class boardinghouse where he lives is the result of his own attempt to catch the Avenger. Hitchcock, notably, was already in command of the visual demands of the medium: Shadows and surrealistic images are wielded with an editing and storytelling sensibility that seems distinctly American. The film has few intertitles (the original cut may have had even fewer) and, despite Novello's theatrical overplaying, is still provocative today.

Vertigo is not one of Hitchcock's "wrong man" films; there are few links between the two films' plots. But the visual links are compelling: The lodger's fixation on golden hair, in particular, certainly presages Scottie Ferguson's fetishes. The characters' disturbing obsessions with the past are what haunt a viewer well after watching the films. The flashing neon sign that opens *The Lodger* appears again in the lower left-hand corner of the window in the film's final moments—framing the image of the former lodger embracing Daisy, then staring at her golden hair. The moment is unnerving and odd—and directly reminiscent of the fixation of Scottie Ferguson in *Vertigo,* especially in the instant in the later film when, during their famous 360-degree kiss, Scottie stops kissing Madeleine just long enough to steal a look at her newly blond hair.

Also connecting the films is a sense of helplessness native to both protagonists' characters. Each of these men has been overwhelmed by the events of the past and looks to a female figure to comfort him, resting his head on the woman in a position that suggests maternal comfort. In *The Lodger,* Novello's character escapes from the police and meets Daisy beneath a lamppost; handcuffed and exhausted, he collapses on her shoulder. In *Vertigo,* the moment comes much earlier—during Scottie's first attempt to cure himself of acrophobia, when he collapses on his friend Midge's shoulder after mounting a stepladder and glancing out the window of her apartment, which reawakens his fear of heights.

The films, too, share ambiguous endings. The police had suspected the wrong man once—might Novello indeed be the Avenger? Though it has the construction of a traditional, and very commercial, American "happy" ending, the conclusion of *The Lodger* is far from settling. *Vertigo* is the only other Hitchcock film that ends with such abject irresolution (although Anthony Perkins's frightening leer in *Psycho* is hardly comforting). Indeed, as the earlier film closes, Daisy is faced with the one dilemma—how to live up to the memory of the woman her lover is obsessed with—from which *Vertigo*'s Judy was, in essence, spared; in *The Lodger,* though, the question hangs in the air as the film closes.

The Lodger is shamefully overlooked in most retrospectives on the silent era. Tom Ryall, in his excellent work on Hitchcock's British films, is justified in complaining at the film's diminution to a footnote in Hitchcock's career. It is undoubtedly one of the ten or so great films of the silent era, and certainly one of the best from Britain (rivaled only by Hitchcock's later, more polished silents *The Ring* and *The Manxman*). If *Vertigo* is Hitchcock's highest achievement, then *The Lodger* is its more than worthy forebear, dated only by the wages of time—a fate that *Vertigo,* too, has had to battle.

Hitchcock and Alma would continue to work in England until early 1939, when they left to join the Hollywood studio system he admired so much. The films of his early British career are generally discounted as period pieces by critics and audiences, even by Hitchcock himself. Yet they are some of his finest films—and in them can be found the genesis and first exploration of his themes, his style, and his art.

In the United States, Hitchcock found his producer David O. Selznick's domination overbearing. Despite the success of their initial project together, *Rebecca,* Selznick was far too intrusive for Hitchcock's taste. The notion that he was owned by Selznick and could be loaned at whim to other studios like a prize stallion did not sit well with him. Thus, Alfred Hitchcock's quest for freedom and power recommenced soon after he arrived on American soil.

It had been simpler in Britain, where he had been a large fish in a small pond. In 1946, Hitchcock formed a production company with Sidney Bernstein—Transatlantic Pictures—but the results were not financially rewarding. The films *Rope* and *Under Capricorn* opened to sparse audiences. The company's distribution and production deal with Warner Bros. rescued him. The films made for Warner Bros. reflected his need to prove himself artistically and financially. Hitch wanted the security that a studio provided, but also the ability to choose his own stories and production teams—without an annoying producer second-guessing his decisions. The success of *Strangers on a Train* and *Dial M for Murder* led to yet another new contract, this one at Paramount. The commitment from Paramount was rather modest on its face: The studio shared production costs and risks with Hitchcock, and his salary was dependent on the profits of the films. As his films' fortunes fared, so would he.

He fared well. The first Hitchcock/Paramount production was the enormous box-office and critical success *Rear Window*. It was the beginning of the multimillion-dollar business that Hitchcock would become.

James Stewart had blazed the trail for such profit-sharing deals (called "back-end" deals, since the person in question is paid from profits after a picture's release, not by salary beforehand) some time before. Both Hitchcock and Stewart were represented by Lew Wasserman, and Hitchcock followed suit, becoming one of the first directors to make profit-sharing part of his contract with Paramount.

Stewart and Hitchcock's first work together, the single-room drama *Rope,* had been something of a trial. The first Transatlantic film and Hitchcock's first color film, the film was made as an experiment in technique: The entire script was shot in sequence, in a series of ten-minute (full-reel) uninterrupted takes, creating a huge challenge for everyone involved. The single-take gimmick had stopped being an amusing novelty during production and had become an actor's nightmare. The pressure for an accurate performance was almost unbearable. With each take lasting at least ten minutes, the tension ratcheted upward every passing minute. A gaffe in the first few moments was meaningless—little time and money was lost—but an error near the end of a ten-minute take was devastating to everyone involved, especially the poor soul responsible. Other problems with the set and the complicated Technicolor process caused entire weeks to be wasted; the demands of the production were crushing.

If he'd been asked at the time if he would work with the British wonder again, even Jimmy Stewart might have been less than gracious. But over time, as Hitchcock's reputation began to rebuild and their mutual representation by Wasserman kept the Stewarts and Hitchcocks in the same professional circles, their reunion must have begun to seem more plausible. Considering the problems generated by the single-set *Rope* shoot, though, it's ironic that their next film together, six years later, was another single-set drama. Perhaps it was some consolation to Stewart that this time the one set would be one of the largest Paramount had ever constructed on a soundstage: The courtyard-apartments set for *Rear Window*.

Hitchcock wasn't the only attraction at Paramount that brought Stewart back. That the young, glamorous, and charismatic Grace Kelly had signed to costar in the film was another. Stewart might never have made *Rear Window* if Grace Kelly had not been involved. And Hitchcock, by many accounts, would never be the same after she signed on.

Grace Kelly and Alfred Hitchcock had a special relationship. Hitchcock was attracted to Kelly—who wasn't?—but there was also an immediate closeness and likeness of mind between the two that had a great effect on the director. Kelly made only three films with the director, but she came to represent the ideal Hitchcock woman; her pictures with Hitchcock were her best work, and had fate not intervened in the person of Prince Rainier of Monaco, both her career and Hitchcock's might well have taken far different paths. Indeed, *Vertigo*— easily taken as a fable about the loss of Hitchcock's own ideal—might never have been made.

Before he encountered Grace Kelly, Hitchcock had worked with a number of actresses both cool and hot—Madeleine Carroll in the thirties and Ingrid Bergman in the forties memorable among them. Kelly, who was twenty-five at the time she was making *Rear Window,* combined the smart, crisp, cold beauty of Carroll and the smoldering eroticism of Bergman. The director's passion for his blond star was noticeable on screen. The luminous, dreamlike appearance of Kelly as she leans in to kiss Stewart in *Rear Window,* and the extraordinary costume work by Edith Head on Kelly's two Hitchcock films for Paramount are visual proof of his affection.

Her arrival on the scene certainly brought about the brightest of Hitchcock projects, the light but critically underestimated *To Catch a Thief.* Contrary to myth, it wasn't on the original shoot that Kelly met her future husband—it was on a return trip—but whatever the couple's origins, Hitchcock could hardly have avoided sorrow over the actress's choice of life as a princess over life as an actress. In the 1960s, Princess Grace momentarily agreed to return to the screen in Hitchcock's *Marnie,* but the citizens of Monaco were so incensed that she was forced to retract her offer. Yet the two remained friends; their families met often, and the director and his onetime star corresponded into the 1970s. According to John Russell Taylor, Kelly and her family were the only visitors to Hitchcock's Bel Air home who dined with the Hitchcocks, in the kitchen, as family.

Her departure in the mid-1950s was offset for Hitchcock by the discovery of Vera Miles, whose passing resemblance to Kelly convinced Hitchcock that he could shape her into the next Hitchcock blonde. After signing an exclusive contract with Hitchcock, Miles costarred in his 1956 film *The Wrong Man*. Tucked between the blockbuster remake of *The Man Who Knew Too Much* and the unnerving beauty of *Vertigo,* this black-and-white gem is often overlooked as a Hitchcock achievement, and its documentary look seems to set it apart from his other

work of the period. Yet here, too, links with *Vertigo*'s plot are evident: Manny in *The Wrong Man*—played by Henry Fonda, Jimmy Stewart's closest friend and a comparable screen presence—experiences a terror that shares much with what Scottie endures. Everymen of a type, both Manny and Scottie experience nearly identical losses of equilibrium when their respective views of reality are ripped from them.

Surprisingly, a careful examination reveals that *The Wrong Man* is also the film closest in style to *Vertigo*. Long tracking shots, uninterrupted even by the opening and closing of doors, predominate. The use of elaborate spinning camera movements to evoke internal confusion and loss of control is common to both films. And apart from *Vertigo*, *The Wrong Man* is certainly Hitch's darkest film. Despite the miracle that saves Manny from perdition, *The Wrong Man* leaves us just as unsure of our blind justice system—just as uncertain of the guilt or innocence of the man arrested in Manny's stead.

Most filmgoers preferred the light touch that was associated with *To Catch a Thief,* and the box-office performance of *The Wrong Man* could have done little to persuade the director otherwise. Hitchcock always claimed to be unhappy with *The Wrong Man*, but in truth he may have been unhappy only with its low returns and poor critical reception. Hitchcock was only just beginning to understand the small print in the Faustian bargain he had made with the public through his television series: His jocular introductions to the TV shows created a humorous image of Hitchcock that the audience, in turn, expected to be reflected in his film work, as well. Hitchcock felt that television gave him a forum for his lighter work—after all, his lightest film, the pre-TV *The Trouble with Harry,* hadn't proven strong enough to lure sizable audiences—so that he could devote his motion pictures to more profound, even uncommercial stories. But he had played the popular filmmaker for too long to change course that easily.

Perhaps it was a moment of doubt about just that change of course that led Hitchcock to consider filming the Laurens van der Post novel *Flamingo Feather* before getting down to work on the French novel. Yet something else was clearly at work within him—the artistic compulsion that led him to eschew future travelogues in favor of the more significant cycle of films that would follow. *The Wrong Man* and *Vertigo* both offer evidence that Hitchcock was articulating themes he felt were important enough to gamble box office and reputation.

Hitchcock's roots were in the art-film movement of the twenties, a movement concerned with experimentation and with the use of boldly symbolic imagery. One of the dramatic arcs of his subsequent career was the constant struggle for the kind of independence that allowed him to mix commerce with work that was true to the art-film vision. *Vertigo, North by Northwest, Psycho,* and *The Birds* would be the final films Hitchcock would make with the kind of overarching power traditionally ascribed to auteurs—and power that allowed him to realize that combination of art and commerce. These films put him in an enviable position, as he signed a long-term contract with Universal, newly run by his former agent, Lew Wasserman. But the power and freedom he had assumed would follow were as illusory as Scottie Ferguson's Madeleine.

But that loss is another story. The making of *Vertigo* is the story of Alfred Hitchcock at his peak: the master manipulator experimenting with a rhapsody of obsession. "Men could do that in those days."

According to Donald Dewey's biography of James Stewart, Lew Wasserman negotiated Stewart's first profit-sharing deal at a party. The then head of Universal, William Goetz, was interested in getting Stewart to make a Western for the studio. Stewart wanted to put the play *Harvey* on screen for Universal, but

Goetz could not afford Stewart's current $200,000 salary. "Depending on the source, it was then either the studio head or the agent who proposed the idea of Stewart doing both *Harvey* and the western, *Winchester '73,* for a percentage of the profits instead of a straight salary," Dewey writes.

Despite the fact that many actors had participated in their film's profits over the years, Stewart's well-publicized deal seemed to popularize the practice. Stewart would rarely work for a straight salary again. The earnings on *Harvey* and *Winchester '73* were enormous and conveniently spread out over the life of each film, which helped avoid the taxes of the time—which could cut an actor's salary in half.

Hitchcock's deal three years later with Paramount was formed in the mold of Wasserman's deal for Stewart. Both men participated in their films' profits and were proportionally enriched by their films' successes.

Even during the murderous production of *Rope,* Stewart liked the fact that Hitchcock allowed actors to shape their own performances. He also admired the director's loyalty to a consistent crew from film to film, and, according to Dewey, was reassured when he knew Hitchcock would be surrounded by a familiar and professional team on *Rear Window.* By all accounts, there was a certain sympathy between the two men, but their relationship seemed to be principally professional; the two men dined together on occasion, but their real connection had more to do with their joint professional guru, Lew Wasserman, and with a mutual professional respect. They seldom spoke at length about character, and Hitchcock was rarely seen giving Stewart direction.

Hitchcock saw in Stewart an American different from the George Bailey of *It's a Wonderful Life*—or, perhaps, an American derived from the troubled, guilt-ridden innocent Bailey becomes well into that film. His Stewart was not the dark opposite of Stewart's usual character, as some critics have written, but a much more complex figure—a George Bailey whose guilt and confusion were uniquely Hitchcock's creation. The Hitchcock male was complex—the hero, yet reluctant; the lover, yet confused and restrained; the innocent, yet menaced as if guilty. They were men drawn reluctantly to women—Cary Grant in *Notorious* and *To Catch a Thief* and Jimmy Stewart in *Rear Window* and *Vertigo.*

"I look for a man . . . it is an effort to get along with in life," Stewart explained once, "whose judgment is not always too good and who makes mistakes. I think human frailty is a very nice thing to portray." Frailty is certainly a dominant trait in the Stewart characters. In the fifties, the move by the actor into grittier parts was deliberate. His profit participation made him an active participant in preproduction, and all three (*Rear Window, The Man Who Knew Too Much,* and *Vertigo*) of the Paramount films required Stewart's approval before they could move forward. It was a fact that may have driven the two men apart as the decade came to a close: Hitchcock pointedly crafted *North by Northwest* for Cary Grant, despite promising his next film to Stewart.

Stewart's films of the fifties offer an extraordinary array of characters: the engaging simplicity of Elwood P. Dowd in *Harvey,* the vengeful, brutal McAdam of *Winchester '73,* the curiously restrained icon Glenn Miller, and the haunted, obsessed Scottie Ferguson.

Few people realize that the majority of the films made at Stewart's peak were directed by only two men—Anthony Mann in a series of pictures through 1955, and Alfred Hitchcock through 1958. These close collaborations allowed Stewart a consistency and control over his image that few other stars have had.

Yet the role of Scottie Ferguson is so complex and ambiguous that it must have tested even his proven judgment: What made Stewart want to make the film? There is no certain answer. Stewart liked the original story; he had problems with early scripts but was ecstatic with Samuel Taylor's final version. But just as his admiration for Grace Kelly had been a part of Stewart's decision to make *Rear Window,* here again the actress who would become his costar seemed to be crucial: Stewart—indeed, like Hitchcock himself—did seem to have become more interested in the picture when, at the last moment, the original female lead stepped down. Legend has it that Hitchcock was furious when Vera Miles became pregnant and dropped out of *Vertigo.* Perhaps a more realistic assessment, though, is that Hitchcock and Stewart had been having their own doubts about Miles as a star.

Hitchcock had discovered Vera Miles during casting for his television series, and he was impressed enough to place her under personal contract; yet according to Samuel Taylor, though secure about her acting ability, Hitchcock felt she didn't yet possess that luminous quality that made a star. By placing her under exclusive contract, he hoped to create that quality in her.

From the onset, though, Miles was reluctant to be shaped by anyone—even a director she respected as much as Hitchcock. Her first feature with Hitchcock was not exactly a showcase for the new blonde. *The Wrong Man's* microscopic focus on the justice process left little screen time for Manny's wife. Dressed down and psychologically shattered by Manny's unjustified arrest,

Miles's character is never fully developed. Hitchcock seemed impatient with the wife's story line, and his indifference shows on screen. The film's sanitarium scenes are similar to the scenes in *Vertigo,* with the same overwhelming sense of helplessness in the face of psychological crisis; yet there was little occasion for Vera Miles to do much else on-screen to make an impact.

This film, and the role in *Vertigo* that was intended to follow, dominate the Vera Miles story. There is much more, though, to the full picture. Her career had begun with small roles in 1951 in *Two Tickets to Broadway* and in 1952 in *For Men Only;* Miles effectively used her television performances as audition pieces for Hitchcock—and for John Ford, who cast her in *The Searchers* a year before she filmed *The Wrong Man. Vertigo* was intended as Miles's big break— but even before her first screen tests in November of 1956, there were signs of doubt from Hitchcock. A few weeks before Miles reported to Stage 5 at Paramount for hair, costume, and makeup tests, Hitchcock screened *The Eddy Duchin Story,* a biopic featuring an actress who was being molded by one of Hitchcock's crosstown rivals.

Kim Novak promised an autobiography some years ago, then became entangled in legal actions when it was never delivered; she seems reluctant to have anyone else digging into her background, even threatening to sue when one publisher released a tame examination of the star's life that included personal comments from her at the conclusion of each chapter.

She has spoken often, and with some contradiction, about her experience with Alfred Hitchcock: Critical for most of the sixties, indifferent during the seventies, she became finally reverent after the film's restoration and rerelease. In her most recent public interviews about the film, there are signs that the bumps in her road to *Vertigo* have been smoothed by time.

Despite her reluctance to write or tell her own story in a book, Novak has never been reluctant to give interviews to magazines. Novak, the star, was the problematic creation of Harry Cohn, the head of Columbia Pictures. The Marilyn Monroe explosion of the fifties had given studio heads the notion that they could take any woman with the right dimensions and create a sensation, and so Cohn began grooming Novak to replace Rita Hayworth as Columbia's leading lady. Novak had the shape, but Cohn had trouble taming the Chicago girl, who seemed to find scandal at every turn.

VERTIGO: The Making of a Hitchcock Classic

But Harry Cohn, who had earned a reputation as the most feared and hated man in Hollywood, was shrewd—and Novak had more than a shape. She had that certain something, that aura that generates what execs call "heat" at the box office. And Miss Novak's burgeoning heat could not have been missed by Hitchcock and Stewart as they were putting together the *Vertigo* production.

Hitchcock never worked with Columbia—it was the only major studio for whom he never worked in his long career—and the only apparent encounter between Hitchcock and the Cohns seems to have been one recounted by screenwriter Ernest Lehman to Donald Spoto. Hitchcock had told Lehman (who wrote the screenplays for *North by Northwest* and *Family Plot*) that during his visit to the United States in 1937 "we were on the *Super-Chief* and a man introduced himself to me. He was Jack Cohn, head of Columbia Pictures in New York and the brother of Harry Cohn. He sat down, had a drink with us, and asked if I knew any of his products—Ann Harding films, and so forth. He named three films and I said I didn't see any of them. And then he asked, 'Well, don't you ever see movies?' I answered no, not very often. He then said, 'If you don't see movies, where do you get your ideas from?'"

But Hitchcock did see movies—quite a few, according to his appointment books. And the timing of the *Duchin* screening is too suggestive to be ignored. Hitchcock himself claimed that he often watched movies for casting purposes, a claim confirmed by his associates. The record tends to suggest that he spent a certain amount of time checking out the competition, as well. Hitchcock did not create in a vacuum, and there are many signs that he often turned to other people's movies when he was grasping around for ideas.

Was Hitchcock casting *From Among the Dead* when he screened *The Eddy Duchin Story,* starring Kim Novak, on October 25, 1956? And what was the substance of the meeting he had with Vera Miles five days later, on October thirtieth? These are the facts: Hitchcock screen-tested Miles in November; after requesting delays for personal reasons in January and February, Miles pulled out of the production in March because she was pregnant. Kim Novak was almost immediately named as her replacement. No other names were floated; despite claims to the contrary that have been made over the years, there is no evidence that screen tests were performed (except for Miles) on *any* actress, including Novak, for the role.

Novak became the lead actress in what was then being called *From Among the Dead* for a large fee and a trade: Stewart agreed to make another film with Novak, for Columbia (*Bell, Book and Candle*), after *Vertigo.* Peter Brown claims in his book on Novak that Miles was never seriously considered for the role. Wasserman wanted Novak from the beginning, he contends, and pushed Hitchcock to accept Novak even as they were testing Miles. But nothing in the Paramount or Hitchcock files at the Academy of Motion Picture Arts and Sciences Library shows any pressure on Hitchcock from Paramount; Herbert Coleman admits Novak was the studio's first choice, but he recalls no explicit pressure from Paramount. Considering the amount of control in his contract, moreover, any such pressure would have been meaningless. (Advice from Wasserman, though, would have been another matter.) A plausible scenario is that all agreed Novak was the better choice after Vera Miles drew such tepid critical and box-office response in *The Wrong Man,* and the actress's pregnancy provided an easy out. Hitchcock was famous for finding ways to end relationships without ruffling feathers.

In retrospect, it's odd that there was even a serious competition between the two women. Novak meant big box office, while Miles never registered. Would Stewart agree to costar in a major Hitchcock thriller with an unknown after costarring with Grace Kelly and Doris Day? And, finally, hindsight suggests that Novak brought a multilayered performance to the film that Miles might not have been able to pull off. Novak, after all, had had plenty of experience being told how to dress and act by an older man.

Her screen test for Columbia was a scene from *The Moon Is Blue*—the play, coincidentally, that had made her *Vertigo* costar Barbara Bel Geddes famous on Broadway. According to Bob Thomas's biography of Cohn, the studio chief was unimpressed—"She can't act!" Cohn yelled—but her agent, Max Arnow, pointed out her other attributes, and Cohn must have seen something, for soon thereafter he began investing a great deal in Novak. The young girl who was discovered while touring the country as "Miss Deepfreeze" was intimidated but not cowed by the aggressive Cohn. She was never afraid to argue with him; she even used her loan-out to Hitchcock to renegotiate her salary.

Cohn cast her in important films and orchestrated a smart publicity campaign that made Novak an all-American box-office favorite; by 1957, she had appeared on the cover of *Time* magazine. So why wouldn't Hitchcock want to work with her? She was difficult, and Hitchcock preferred to avoid difficulties. But the deal was brokered by Wasserman, and as soon as Miles was out, Novak was in.

For Novak, the role took on a personal significance. She identified immediately with the Madeleine/Judy character. "When I read the lines, 'I want you
to love me for me,' I just identified with it so much," Novak recalled recently. "It
was what I felt when I came to Hollywood as a young girl. You know, they want
to make you over completely. They do your hair and makeup and it was always
like I was fighting to show some of my real self. So I related to the resentment
of being made over and to the need for approval and the desire to be loved. I
really identified with the story because to me it was saying, Please, see who
I am. Fall in love with me, not a fantasy."

Back in May 1956, Hitch and Alma went to the federal building downtown to
take yellow fever shots in preparation for their tour of Africa. He had already
begun preliminary work on a screenplay for the Van der Post book *Flamingo
Feather.* An old coworker and family friend, Angus MacPhail, had begun working up a treatment of the book. MacPhail had recently helped with *The Wrong
Man,* and Hitch had promised him another project, despite his concern over

MacPhail's drinking problem. He also wanted to work with Maxwell Anderson (the principal writer on *The Wrong Man*), so he passed on his translation of *From Among the Dead* to Anderson.

Hitchcock had intended to pursue both stories just long enough to see which worked first, and when he left for South Africa in July, he was certain *Flamingo Feather* would be his next film. The San Francisco film, ultimately more important to him, could wait—*should* wait. He had discussed his options with Wasserman at a meeting in June; Wasserman was concerned that he was committing to both at the same time, and just as concerned about the dark quality of the French novel. Yet it may have been just those qualities that kept the director interested, and the project started to take on a deeper significance for Hitchcock as the screenplay began taking shape.

| # WORDS FROM THE DARK: WRITING THE SCREENPLAY

Hitchcock had some big writers on his films, but you would never know it.

—*John Michael Hayes to Pat McGilligan in* Backstory: Interviews with Screenwriters of the 1960s and 70s

A love-hate relationship developed between Alfred Hitchcock and almost every one of his writers. Few directors were as involved in the writing process as he was; many writers felt he deserved cowriter status on their screenplays. He rarely took screenplay credit, yet his overwhelming control over the final shape of a production sometimes antagonized writers, who felt slighted when critics ignored their contributions—and rather more so when Hitchcock himself failed to point out their contributions in interviews.

Hitchcock made few films that were not based on another source. Early in his career, he cowrote two screenplays for Graham Cutts, *The White Shadow* (1923) and *The Passionate Adventure* (1924), and wrote two others for Cutts, *The Blackguard* and *The Prude's Fall* (both 1925), himself.

As a director, he wrote the scenario for *The Ring* (1927) and Alma wrote the screenplay. After this film, one of his finest silents, Hitchcock based only one other film on a story of his own devise: *Notorious* (1946), reworked into a full screenplay by Ben Hecht. For the rest of his oeuvre, he drew on whatever other sources were available to him—and, very often, from previously published fiction.

[THE NOVEL]

Since the publication of François Truffaut's historic interviews with Hitchcock in the 1960s, it has been widely accepted that the authors of *D'Entre les Morts* knew that Hitchcock had bid unsuccessfully for their first novel, and that envy of the resulting Clouzot film's success had left him wanting another story from them.

But according to Thomas Narcejac, one of the book's authors, this was never the case. He admits that Hitchcock and their writing team shared common interests, but in an interview conducted for this book, he maintained firmly that he and his collaborator never had any intention of writing a book especially for Hitchcock. The genesis of the idea for their second novel actually took place, much more provocatively, in a French cinema. As Narcejac was watching a newsreel, he felt he distinctly recognized a friend he had lost touch with during the war; the idea of discovering a lost acquaintance in such a way stayed with him, and it suggested to him the outline of a story. "After the war," he explains, "there were many displaced people and families—it was common to have 'lost' a friend. I began to think about the possibilities of recognizing someone like this. Maybe someone who was thought dead . . . and this is where *D'Entre les Morts* began to take shape."

Thomas Narcejac was born in a small French coastal village in 1908. He would have gone into the family seafaring business had he not lost the use of one eye in a childhood accident; his partial blindness led him instead to a philosophy degree from the French Société des Lettres and then to a teaching career. As a teacher, Narcejac became fascinated by the form and function of the mystery genre and began to write mystery fiction, most of which he threw away. Enough was kept, though, and published that he was awarded the Prix Roman d'Aventure in 1948. It was a study of the mystery genre that he published in 1948 that caught the attention of his colleague in crime, Pierre Boileau.

Boileau was born in the Montmartre neighborhood of Paris in 1906. After working for years at the kinds of jobs that are often quaintly referred to as opportunities to gather experience, Boileau had begun writing in the 1930s. His novel *Les Repos de Bacchus* had won the Prix Roman d'Aventure ten years before Narcejac's, in 1938. Yet the glory would be short-lived: Considered anti-Nazi, Boileau was immediately arrested in 1939 with the German occupation.

He was sent to work as a member of the French welfare department. The experience proved rewarding, as it required Boileau to spend his time interviewing criminals at various penal colonies—an ideal experience for a mystery writer. When he was released in 1942, he returned to his writing; six years later, while browsing in a Paris bookshop, he came across Narcejac's book about the genre, and he was intrigued enough to contact the author.

Boileau and Narcejac held similar views on the way mysteries should be structured, and soon they had developed a successful working relationship: "I was more the person who developed the character, the internal, emotional logic of the story," Narcejac recalls, "and Boileau was definitely best at the plot, the external logic of the story. We would meet and discuss an idea. Then, from only a few notes, I would have to go away and start the novel, giving Boileau the pages a few at a time. These he would correct—pointing out inconsistencies, contradictions. Some things I would lose track of, as I was following the emotion of the story and not the plot."

Their first novel, *The Woman Who Was No More* (1952), was successful in France, England, and the United States. Throughout their partnership, the two produced novels that were puzzles requiring close attention, each combining startling twists of plot with characters at their wit's end, grasping at any opportunity to find meaning.

It was *Les Diaboliques* (1955), the Clouzot film of their first novel, that brought the team to the attention of Paramount and Hitchcock. *Les Diaboliques* was an outstanding success, and the style and story of the film were certainly Hitchcockian—a fact that could not have been lost on either the director or his studio.

Paramount recorded its first reading of the team's next novel in 1954, before it was even translated into English. The strength of reader Edward Doyle's November 1954 synopsis, and the French writers' reputation, sold Hitchcock on the novel. Paramount purchased the rights to *From Among the Dead* on April 20, 1955, for $25,275.

A memo from Paramount executive John Mock reveals that *Flamingo Feather* and *From Among the Dead* were bought with the agreement that each would be made by Hitchcock for Paramount. *Flamingo Feather*, it suggests, was not so much a project Hitchcock wanted as one Paramount wanted for him. The French novel appears to have been a trade—the studio would buy Hitchcock that novel if he'd make the adventure story.

The novel begins with the meeting of two old friends:

> "Here's what I mean," said Gévigne. "I want you to keep watch on my wife."
>> "Good God! Is she being unfaithful?"
>> "No."
>> "Well?"
>> "It's not easy to explain. She's queer. . . . I'm worried about her."
>> "What exactly are you afraid of?"
>> (from the Denny translation of *From Among the Dead*—1955)

According to associate producer Herbert Coleman, it was Lew Wasserman who brought the French novelists to the attention of Hitchcock. The evidence suggests that it was Hitchcock himself who requested the coverage on the book from Paramount. This 1955 report by Allida Allen is a straightforward summary:

> ROGER FLAVIERES, Paris advocate, is asked by a former school-fellow, GEVIGNE, for help in a delicate personal matter. Gevigne, prosperous shipbuilder—particularly now with France and Germany at war—explains he's concerned over the sudden odd behavior of his wife, MADELEINE. They have been happily married for 4 years, but in the last few months she has been acting strangely—suddenly falling into deep meditations or trance-like withdrawals to a world

where he cannot reach her. The doctors can find nothing wrong with her, either physically or mentally. But Gevigne fears for her and, extremely busy with his war time contracts, he cannot spend much time with her. That is why he is asking Flavieres to keep watch over Madeleine for him. Flavieres's questions bring out the fact that Madeleine seems obsessed—in some occult way—by the spirit of her great-grandmother, Pauline Lagerlac, whom she resembles. Pauline was considered queer and died young. Flavieres accepts the unusual assignment and for several weeks follows Madeleine wherever she goes, observing her actions—but taking care she does not see him. They have never met. She possesses a strange beauty that enchants Flavieres so that, before a week is out, he is hopelessly in love with her. Then one day he saves her from the Seine, and from then on they become friends. He does not mention knowing her husband. They form the habit of rambling about Paris and the countryside together and Madeleine, who on several occasions falls into a trance-like meditation, gradually confides to Flavieres she is certain she has lived before—she can recall scenes—a town which Flavieres later ascertains from Gevigne she's never been to. But Pauline Lagerlac had! The more he sees of Madeleine the greater grows the mystery and his love, which he confesses to her. Then one day she insists on their driving to a small town some distance from Paris and climbing an old church tower—though Flavieres, who suffers from vertigo, cannot follow her to the top. To his horror, he sees her body come hurtling to the ground. Dazed by grief and shock, he cannot bring himself to go near the body and flees to Paris. He says nothing to Gevigne about being with Madeleine. When her body is found, Gevigne seems distracted with grief. Still in a daze, Flavieres leaves Paris—and a sudden German advance blocks his return. The war is over when Flavieres returns to Paris. He has been unable to forget his love for Madeleine. Inquiry reveals Gevigne, upset when police questioned him about his wife's death, fled from Paris—only to be killed in a German air raid. War has even obliterated Madeleine's grave. Flavieres however cannot believe she is really dead. He is certain she lives again. Then a newsreel sends him hurrying to Marseilles in search of a woman he saw in it. He knows she is Madeleine—but when he finds her, she denies it. She is RENEE SOURANGE and is living with ALMARYAN, a black market operator. But Flavieres, having gotten Renee to leave Almaryan for him, stubbornly persists in trying to make her admit that she is Madeleine. She finally does confess she is the Madeleine he knew, but her name is really Renee Sourange. He never saw Gevigne's wife—the real Madeleine! It was a plot of Gevigne's—with the aid of Renee, then his mistress—to rid himself of his wealthy wife without being suspected. It was the real Madeleine who fell from the tower—Gevigne having taken her there before Flavieres and the supposed Madeleine (Renee) arrived. Flavieres's testimony about Madeleine's strange trances was to mislead the police. But Flavieres's flight upset things—Stunned, Flavieres seizes Renee in his anger—and not realizing what he is doing, strangles her. Then, horrified and remorseful over what he has done he surrenders to the police.

Allen's synopsis is complete, with the exception of one remarkable touch she omits: At the end of the novel, as the police take him away, Flavières kisses the dead Renée. Though latter-day writers have claimed that Hitchcock's film was so complete a transformation as to render its origins unrecognizable, anyone familiar with *Vertigo* will find it easy to perceive the roots of the film in the Boileau-Narcejac original. Many of the basic elements are there, down to the vertigo itself—mentioned only in passing in the synopsis—which would become the center of Hitchcock's psychological drama.

[THE SCREENPLAY]

Hitchcock turned to the distinguished playwright Maxwell Anderson on June 14, 1956, to transform the French novel into a first-draft screenplay for a flat rate of $65,000. The novel and Allen's summary were shipped to Anderson at his home in Stamford, Connecticut, along with airline tickets for Anderson and his wife to visit San Francisco. In the record that survives in the Hitchcock files, there are undated interlinear notes indicating the location change to San Francisco and Mission San Juan Bautista. It is not possible to tell whether these are Hitchcock's annotations, but they indicate that San Francisco and the Spanish mission to its south were selected early in October as the film's locations.

The following month, Hitchcock left for his extensive African trip, scouting *Flamingo Feather* locations with his wife and associate producer, Herbert Coleman. *Feather* was an elaborate story involving a secret concentration camp of South Africans who were being trained for evil purposes—and, as Hitchcock and his traveling team soon found out, if the preposterous story wasn't enough to kill the project, the inevitable difficulties of filming in Africa would be. While Anderson began work on *From Among the Dead,* Angus MacPhail tried in vain to make some sense of *Feather* for Hitchcock. But by the end of the summer, the African project was scrapped, placing a great deal more importance on whatever Anderson had managed to accomplish in the interim.

Fellow playwright Samuel Taylor remembered Maxwell Anderson as "bluff and hardy, a perfectly nice man" known principally for his great plays *What Price Glory?* and *Winterset.* He had worked sporadically as a screenwriter since 1930, when he cowrote the screenplay for Lewis Milestone's film adaptation of the Erich Maria Remarque novel *All Quiet on the Western Front* (1930); for Milestone he also wrote *Rain* (1932), then cowrote *Death Takes a Holiday* (1934) for director Mitchell Leisen—a short but exemplary list of films. His collaboration with Hitchcock on this film would be his last film work: He died in February 1959.

A writer of great prestige, Anderson was known and trusted to work quickly on his own. After his weekend in San Francisco, Anderson toiled away at the screenplay for *From Among the Dead* at his Stamford home. His agent, Irving "Swifty" Lazar, wired Herbert Coleman in Nairobi that Anderson would have fifty pages for Hitchcock to see when he stopped in New York City on his way back from the African tour.

The two lunched and spoke at length at the St. Regis Hotel in New York upon the director's return to the States, but it would be their last optimistic meeting. It's unclear whether Hitchcock could have done more than glance at Anderson's work before the two met—more likely, he read the pages on his flight back to California—and in any event, it would have been unlike Hitchcock to say anything negative to Anderson about the work he'd done. But whatever the case, the collaboration was doomed: He wouldn't fire Anderson immediately but upon his arrival home, Alfred Hitchcock immediately began looking at other screenwriters.

"Darkling, I Listen," the September 1956 draft Anderson submitted to Hitchcock, is a standard B detective picture that would have seemed creaky during the late forties. The feel of the Anderson script is similar to *The Wrong Man,* sacrificing the atmosphere and imagination of the original novel by staying too close to its plot points and detective-story details. Anderson was interpreting the French novel using the same realistic vocabulary of *The Wrong Man*—and for the vertiginous nightmare vision the novelists (and, no doubt, Hitchcock) had in mind, this style would not do.

The Anderson script opens, like the novel, with the meeting between Flavières and Gévigne (whom he renames Kilrain and Elder). Kilrain reluctantly agrees to follow Elder's wife; his first opportunity to see her is at an opera that evening. There are fellow detectives in this first version who serve to provide the needed exposition on Kilrain's acrophobia—caused somewhat implausibly by an unfortunate accident atop the Golden Gate Bridge.

Madeleine sings and paints in this first draft; her character is haunting, but in a clichéd way. The romantic side of the story line develops rather quickly: Kilrain has an affair with Madeleine; he confronts Elder, and is fired by him, before Madeleine leaps from the top of Pigeon Lighthouse, near San Mateo.

The second half of the screenplay concerns Kilrain's obsession with the dead Madeleine. The denouement is not at the lighthouse or a tower, but, once again, atop Golden Gate Bridge. Renée turns to Kilrain—"Dying is easy," she says—before leaping into San Francisco Bay. There is one nice touch: Kilrain had a cigarette lighter inscribed *Eurydice,* after the ill-fated wife of Orpheus. But Anderson's dialogue is awful, his set pieces overworked. The sequence on the Golden Gate is a good example of how not to write a Hitchcock scene. And yet, buried among the overwhelming inadequacies, Anderson contributed important elements to the story that would remain through the final film: The Mission Dolores sequence is in this first draft, as well as a scene that would evolve into the first encounter between Scottie Ferguson and Madeleine Elster.

Dissatisfied with Anderson's work, Hitchcock turned next to his old comrade Angus MacPhail. MacPhail had been a fellow editor with Alma at Gaumont-British; he was responsible for coining the term *MacGuffin* in Hitchcock's work—the item in so many Hitchcock screenplays that drives the action but actually has little to do with the film's characters and the creation of suspense. (The secret airplane plans in *The 39 Steps* and the uranium ore in *Notorious* are among Hitchcock's famous MacGuffins.) As a team in the thirties, MacPhail and Hitchcock worked on *The Man Who Knew Too Much* (MacPhail co-wrote the 1950s remake), and during the war MacPhail worked with Hitchcock on two films about the French Resistance. Throughout, Mac-Phail battled alcoholism; by the 1950s, Hitchcock had sent a letter to MacPhail's friends in an effort to create a monetary fund to help support him during his "illnesses."

After *Flamingo Feather* collapsed, MacPhail was depending on Hitchcock to come through with another assignment. In early August, while working on the African script, MacPhail had written Coleman: "How is Hitch? How is the San Francisco story? I have a new idea about the story, that it should be told from the start, from the lady's own angle. Indeed, I keep having crazy ideas." Hitchcock must have been glad to hear that someone was having new ideas about the story, since Anderson's work hadn't been panning out.

But in late August of 1956, MacPhail wrote to Coleman from the Westwood Manor Hotel that his planned start on *From Among the Dead* the following Tuesday would have to be canceled. "It's no use my trying to kid either you or myself," he wrote: The drinking had been getting to him, and he had decided his only course of action was to take the open-air cure. "You can imagine what I feel like, missing this splendid assignment. But it's better to miss it than to fall down on it."

But the MacPhail story wasn't over. On the morning of September fourth, Coleman would sign MacPhail after all—only to have another note arrive later the same day:

Herbie:

Terribly sorry to let you down like this, but I'm in bed again. Over did my attempt to get well quick.

It's a fascinating story of course [*From Among the Dead*]—but it needs a real big imaginative contribution—which I simply couldn't provide just now.

Incidently, it ought to be a woman working on this subject.

Signed *Angus.*

Coleman canceled the note signing MacPhail.

Before his departure from the project, MacPhail did complete fifteen pages of an opening scene for the story: the long conversation between Flavières and Gévigne (or Roger Dane and Carl Garron, as MacPhail calls them). His version plays much longer than Anderson's, with constant inexplicable interruptions by Garron's secretary. But he provided no more, and he may not have been paid for his work; his name does not appear in the film's final budget.

During this time, MacPhail wrote the director an amusing note, the message of which might have been seconded by many of Hitchcock's writers. "The chap at Jurgensens [a grocery store] said to me yesterday, 'I saw *The Man Who Knew Too Much*. Swell picture. Does Mr. Hitchcock write a lot of his films himself?' I replied, 'More than somewhat—but don't report my word to the writer's guild or I shall be extradited.'"

His flirtation with work on *From Among the Dead* and the work he completed on *Flamingo Feather* would be the last film work MacPhail would attempt. He died, at age fifty-six, in 1961.

Hitchcock signed the virtually unknown Alec Coppel to the San Francisco project on September twenty-first, at a salary of fifteen hundred dollars per week. There's no compelling evidence to suggest why Hitchcock chose Coppel. According to Coleman, he was under contract to Paramount; perhaps the studio offered Coppel. Perhaps it was a recommendation from Alec Guinness, who had starred in Coppel's only previous film work—*The Captain's Paradise* (1953—Anthony Kimmins, director), based on his original story of a sea captain who changes his personality for a different girl in every port. Coppel had written three books of light fiction—*A Man About a Dog* (1947), *Mr. Denning Drives North* (1950), and *The Last Parade* (1953)—as well as one stage play, 1953's *I Killed the Count*. But his work on *Vertigo* would be of a different order altogether.

From September twenty-first until the end of 1956, Hitchcock would work intensively with Alec Coppel on the script. Hitchcock's usual manner was to meet daily. His greatest concerns in crafting any film had to do with structure—with the shape and order of the sequences that would become the film's skeleton, providing a sound structure on which to build dialogue and characterization. Charles Bennett, who worked with Hitchcock on many of his first series of great films in Britain (from *Blackmail* to *Young and Innocent*), recalled that Hitchcock preferred to talk over lunch or dinner, often at a favorite club or restaurant: "Sometimes the conversation appeared to have nothing to do with the film until Hitchcock would suddenly say, 'That reminds me, in the scene . . .' That's how he preferred to work—often an indirect approach."

Hitchcock admitted to this penchant for taking breaks. "Certain writers want to work every hour of the day—they're very facile. I'm not that way. I want to say, 'Let's lay off for several hours—let's play.' And then, we get down to it again."

In his first meeting with Coppel, Hitchcock outlined the picture in nineteen scenes—Coppel's handwritten notes, among the *Vertigo* files that survive, give each scene's basic action. Many of the essential moments from the film are present in these notes, dated "9/27/56," including an intriguing character study of Renée, the character who would become Judy in the final film. In a portrait quite different from what we'd expect, she is described in these notes as being "from a wealthy family back East—and ultimately very disturbed by the murder." Renée met Gavin Elster (a slight twist on Anderson's Elder), he notes, on a cruise to Europe.

The description of Gavin Elster, on the other hand, is consistent with the character in the final film, and in these notes a few details about his life are established for the first time—among them his impressive office and his profession as a shipbuilder. Also included in these notes are ideas for another beginning for the film. The book and Anderson's screenplay had begun with the meeting between Gévigne (Elster) and Flavières (Kilrain). Hitchcock and Coppel create a new scene—a police chase on the rooftops of San Francisco.

A production sketch of Gavin Elster's office, made when the film was still known as "From Among the Dead."

NEW OPENING

Picture to open with chase over San Francisco roof tops with 2 policemen chasing a suspect. They are armed and one of them is in uniform. The climax of the chase comes when the uniformed man slips and the plain clothes detective fails to rescue him from a perilous hanging position.

Would like to discuss with Henry Bumstead in order that he can figure out some sketches showing how this could work.

Also, we should work out how we can put over in a pictorial way the effect of a man suffering from vertigo. (Herbie Coleman has some preliminary sketches on this idea which must be done optically.)

There is one difference here from the scene that made it to the screen: Here it is the uniformed policeman who slips first, and the plainclothes detective who fails to help him; in the film, it is the opposite way around. But ultimately more important is this early mention of the need to translate the effects of vertigo to the screen: Hitchcock's desire to convey the condition visually was one of the major technical challenges of the motion picture.

Anderson's draft had included a number of plot turns Hitchcock and Coppel disliked. In Anderson's script, for example, the Elster character is shot; but Hitchcock pointed out that this was not necessary—in fact, it was important that "the husband should stay alive so that when our detective returns a year later he finds a distraught man who has lost his wife and who refuses to accept the detective's confession of guilt for allowing his wife to throw herself from the tower.

"This scene could take place at a time when the husband, now a broken man over his wife's death, is leaving San Francisco for good. He will go to Europe and will probably live there for good—where he is not sure, he will let his old friend know when he has settled down.

The Academy of Motion Picture Arts and Sciences preserves dozens of storyboard sequences for individual scenes in the film—revealing how carefully Hitchcock and his crew mapped out each shot long before cameras began rolling. Here, in seventeen frames, the rooftop chase conceived by Hitchcock and Alec Coppel was rendered in pencil sketches that mirror closely the final film.

▶

"The reason for the husband being alone now and that Renée is no longer with him is because the witnessing of the murder was such a shock to her and the brutality and clumsiness of it sent her away from him."

The September twenty-seven notes also contain the first extensive discussion of the tower scene at San Juan Bautista—not the lighthouse, as Anderson had envisioned it in his first draft, but a far more picturesque and old-world setting. In later production notes, it's pointed out that the actual lighthouse would not be available for filming—and, in any case, was normally locked to the public, making it impossible for Kilrain and Madeleine to enter. Yet this must have been the production crew just doing their duty: Hitchcock had settled on the church at San Juan Bautista after the first location trip.

According to the notes, it was important to Hitchcock and Coppel's vision that San Juan Bautista be fairly deserted in the film. The Spanish mission is slightly off the tourist's path; the charm of the period buildings and the peacefulness of the beautiful mission attract tourists nonetheless, but it was that charm—not the tourists who craved it—that the filmmakers wanted to capture on-camera.

Hitchcock noted that at the top of the tower

when Madeleine continues to the very highest landing, she should not lock the door on Kilrain because this would indicate that they are not using his acrophobia at all. After all, if she was going up to a tower she could even elude a normal man and lock the door.

When he looks out and sees the body falling, we should create again the same effect as at the beginning of the picture. In fact, we should show it twice in the tower—once when he is deterred from following Madeleine and again when the body falls.

After the body has fallen and he is staring down we should quickly lap dissolve to a reprise of the shot when the policeman fell at the beginning so that we are able to photograph his terrible guilt and his reason for hiding and running away.

In notes dated October seventeenth through October twenty-third, further details emerge—typical of the continual evolution that occurred as Hitchcock worked with his screenwriters. In a gesture that later proved unnecessary, Hitchcock noted that a NO PARKING sign should be added outside of

Mission Dolores to give Madeleine a reason to enter at the rear of the mission. Other locations were changed altogether in the course of this week of meetings—from Golden Gate Park to Lincoln Park; from the DeYoung Museum to the Palace of the Legion of Honor.

By the end of October, the script had begun to take on a recognizable shape. Much of what Hitchcock and Coppel had come up with together would remain in the final draft. Yet there are exceptions, among them a persistent sequence that takes place in the moments after Madeleine's suicide attempt. Adding detail—and a modicum of suspense—Hitchcock and Coppel had a fisherman rush to Kilrain's aid. Kilrain puts him off and takes Madeleine to his apartment, where the scene progresses much as it does in the final version.

A more notable scene eventually lost in subsequent drafts takes place at Coit Tower, where Madeleine tries to cure Kilrain's acrophobia—an episode apparently intended to demonstrate that Gavin Elster is testing the severity of Kilrain's fear of heights. As Madeleine goes to the top of Coit, Kilrain waits anxiously at the base, watching for her to emerge from the elevator at the top. She does, but then she disappears. He circles the base, terrified that she has plunged to her death. Madeleine emerges from the elevator at the base and says, "What were you afraid of—that I was going to fall? That's only because you have the fear."

Early in November, Coppel and Hitchcock penned an interesting initial version of the first kiss—the first draft of a remarkable moment of passion.

Inside the car, Madeleine is in the middle of describing a dream to Jimmy. She says that it is a recurrent dream and this bothers her in some way. She feels there is something very important about this dream but the importance eludes and mystifies her. Jimmy tries to laugh this off telling her that we all have our own recurrent dreams—they are quite common and one shouldn't worry about them. Madeleine continues telling him of the substance of the dream. She sees very distinctly and in great detail a scene which seems to be set in Spain. There is an old Spanish church with cloisters. There is a monastery with a square outside and buildings surrounding it. As Jimmy listens he watches her with growing concern at her intensity, because she seems to be slipping back into one of her odd moods again. He then very gently asks her about the possibility of her ever trying to commit suicide again. She replies that she doesn't think he really understands her. He presses her but she tries to avoid continuing the discussion. She opens the door of the car and moves away to the rocks at the edge of the sea. Jimmy follows her, concerned and alert. Surprisingly she turns and stretches out a hand to him—she asks him to hold onto her, as though she is fighting against some compulsion. Jimmy moves closer to her. Suddenly she flings herself into his arms pressing herself close to him holding him tightly as though for support. She is on the borderline of hysteria—apparently from fear. With her head turned away from him she begs him to hold her—not to let her go. We can see from Jimmy's face that not only is he moved by this, but that he is desperately in love with her. He quietly reassures her and lifts her face to him and kisses her. Still in a wild mood and with the wind whirling around them, she passionately returns his kiss. FADE OUT.

Among the intriguing details this passage reveals, one is paramount: Hitchcock and Coppel are no longer referring to their protagonist as Kilrain or Flavières, but with the unmistakable name of their leading actor: Jimmy.

In the following days (through November thirteenth), another major sequence was solidified; Hitchcock's interlinear comments are written on Coppel's typed notes. Describing Madeleine's dream, Hitchcock wrote that Jimmy says, "It is preserved just in the way she describes, the old hotel, the livery stables—all kept intact as a sort of museum." Coppel wanted Jimmy to sign in at San Juan Bautista's visitor's book. Hitchcock struck this and wrote "Why?" in the margin.

A new sequence that would survive to the final draft is Scottie's dream sequence after Madeleine's suicide attempt.

INT. JIMMY'S BEDROOM—NIGHT—FADE IN. We see a restless figure lying asleep. A BIG HEAD [extreme closeup] of him fills the screen as he turns from side to side. There is a SLOW DISSOLVE—but the head of the restless Jimmy is still on screen. Coming into focus and super-imposed as it gets closer is the head and shoulders of painted Pauline [Carlotta in the final film]. The camera pans down until it comes to the posy held by a skeletal hand. The picture clears from

the screen and a new image super-imposes itself. It is the final scene at the inquest when Madeleine's husband is reassuring Jimmy. But this time though it is not too well lit, a woman's head can be seen buried in his shoulder. The husband says, "Tell him it wasn't his fault. Tell him." The woman moves her head and turns with an enigmatic smile to Jimmy. It is the face of Pauline Lagerlac dressed in the costume she wore in the painting and wearing the ruby necklace. This picture FADES AWAY and a new image comes over the scene. It is the graveyard at Mission Dolores. The camera is moving nearer to the grave of Pauline Lagerlac. We see a CU of Jimmy approaching it. Then we reverse and show the camera approaching the grave—it is open and there is a black abyss but the headstone is still there. CU of Jimmy coming to a stop as he stares down. Now we show the black depths of the grave filling the screen. Suddenly we are falling, in the same spot that Jimmy saw his policeman colleague fall. BIG HEAD CU of Jimmy—hair windswept—staring down in horror as he falls. Reverse angle—he is still falling but this time he is falling into the roof of the Mission and when he reaches spot where Madeleine fell, the picture clears and Jimmy sits up in bed in alarm staring up into camera.
FADE OUT.

Later, contemporary artist John Ferren, who had worked with Hitchcock on *The Trouble with Harry,* would provide a detailed description and story-board for the dream sequence—and the final sequence would remain true in almost every detail to this earliest draft of the nightmare.

By late November, the script was nearly complete. In the second half of the Coppel screenplay, "Jimmy" searches madly for a Madeleine look-alike he has spotted outside of the McKittrick Hotel. Tracing her through the Department of Motor Vehicles, he learns that the car is rented to a Mr. Howard Joslin at the Clift Hotel—a boorish businessman who is "keeping" the girl, Renée. After Jimmy picks Renée up in the hotel's bar, there is a confrontation between Joslin and Jimmy, with Joslin ultimately abandoning Renée. She ultimately moves to Jimmy's apartment and the screenplay begins the sequence we recognize, the makeover of Renée (Judy in the final version) into Madeleine.

The script dated November fifteenth describes the second famous kiss:

Quite silently, she turns and takes a step towards him. Jimmy moves over and takes her in his arms. BIG HEADS of the two of them together. At Last. The camera moves around the big heads. We see Jimmy holding her tighter and tighter. He looks past her shoulder and we see that his eyes are closed, because he now has Madeleine in his arms. He opens his eyes—the camera swims around the room. We are now in the livery stables at San Juan Bautista. We see it only for the briefest moment and it DISSOLVES away. Jimmy kisses her once more as he did then. The camera PULLS BACK slowly and their two figures are held in the center of the room—one of the beds is brought into foreground of picture.
DISSOLVE.

The notes from this period produce countless examples of Hitchcock and Coppel trying out solutions to little story problems—devices often later discarded for more elegant solutions. Renée's involvement with Gavin Elster is discovered, for example, when the hotel receptionist produces a necklace belonging to Pauline Lagerlac, Madeleine's doomed antecedent. Renée denies that it is hers, but the receptionist is insistent—producing the signed envelope in which Renée had enclosed the necklace when she gave it to the receptionist. The revelation leads directly to their confrontation in San Juan Bautista's tower—where, in Coppel's draft, Renée jumps to her death unprompted by any sudden fright.

Coppel completed his first draft of *From Among the Dead* at the end of November. The script is recognizable as a nascent *Vertigo,* with several of its major sequences in place. But Hitchcock was still unhappy—enough that he wrote to Maxwell Anderson on December fourth to discuss the problems. Hoping that Anderson would be able to solve these problems by tackling a new draft of the screenplay, the director offered an excellent demonstration—perhaps the only one that survives in writing—of the extent of his involvement in the construction of a Hitchcock screenplay:

> *My dear Max,*
> A voice from Nether regions. In the words of the Duke of Windsor, "At last I am able to lay down my burden." In other words, Max the new story outline is complete. . . .

Before I go on to tell you what has been done, I think I should admit to you that after all this time it might have been better for me to have followed your original suggestion to have completed the structural layout even as far as a temporary script before you did the dialogue. I can only apologize for putting you to "double trouble." (Wouldn't this be a good title for this picture?) . . .

First of all, I should make it clear that the structure has been organized on the basis of telling two stories. First the "front" story, which is the one that the audience is looking at and second the big story which, in other words, is the conspiracy and which is only revealed to the audience in the final scene.

The element that has given constant trouble throughout the telling of the front story is the fact that we seemed to be coasting along until we reach a specific climax. For example: once the central character of the ex-detective meets up with the strange behaving woman we actually had nothing specific to develop until she threw herself from the height and "apparently" committed suicide. Now, of course, we knew what we were leading to, but the audience did not. So the question arose what apparent story was being told on the surface after the man and woman met?

As you will see when you read the suggested story line, the only thing we have to tell is a love story between a man who is being entrusted by a husband to take care of his wife, but by falling in love with her betrays that trust. Naturally, this is a situation that he cannot help. Nevertheless, it was important to develop this man's infatuation for the woman, which up to the suicide was never consummated. The value of this I am sure you will see, would show how justified his obsession was of her even after death. So that the consummation finally occurs when he has completed the reconstruction of her in the person of Renee as she is called in the book.

So you see, Max, an audience sitting there looking at this picture has no idea at all that this is a murder story. In fact, this film, up until the final scene, should be a strange mood love story with perhaps the same feeling of Daphne Du Maurier's REBECCA, which as you know, I made many years ago.

Now let me tell you about some very important changes concerning the characters. One. Our central character's emotions and purposes throughout the story are pretty clear except for one important change, and that is this: in order to avoid his appearing a completely and utter foolish victim of a conspiracy, we have made a change at the end whereby he discovers a flaw in their scheme and this will come after he has reached the climax of his emotional binge with the reconstructed Madeleine. This flaw which I won't go into here because you will be able to read it in the bare outline which I am enclosing in this letter. It enables him to behave like a smart detective again, and solve a good part of the mystery without a full confession by the character Renee.

You will also note that the effect of the woman's "suicide" upon him is extremely devastating. He has a nervous breakdown as a result of it, and when he seems to be recovered from it, he continues to wander around the city and apparently "seeing" Madeleine in every woman who is more like her than any of the others. This one he pursues.

Now, Max, the reason for this change is this. We had a feeling that, for example in the book, he sees a woman who looks like the dead Madeleine and goes on a journey to another city in search of her. This gave one a very strong feeling from the audience's point of view that something very definite was going to emerge from this and I had the feeling that would almost be tipping off the audience ahead of time. Whereas, with the present idea of drifting into the situation, the audience would not be aware of what was to come. One final thing about the man's character. I don't know how far it is necessary to account for his phobia, but you will read in a suggested scene a little idea concerning his going through a parachute jump experience. However, we have been doing a bit of psychiatric research on this, which we will send to you.

Now concerning the girl. The major change suggested here, that she fall in love with our central male character. The emotional climax is reached just prior to the suicide. Although we do not learn of this until the end of the story it does provide us with one very vital behavior pattern on her part in the second half of the story. You have to realize one very important fact. Here is a woman who has been an accessory to a murder, she has let herself revert back physically to her original color and style. And yet, she allows a man to recreate her in the image of the dead woman. Here, as you will see, she is taking a terrible risk. After all, she is a woman virtually in hiding. When she renews her association with the ex-detective she would love to pursue their old relationship in her current physical appearance, but naturally, he will have none of this. It is only as Madeleine he wants her. So you see, Max, the woman must be desperately in love with him to allow him to do this. And this she tells him at the end of the story.

You can see what a chance she is taking because as Renee, she is safe both within her identification and being able to stand up to any probe into her background. Because remember, that she was Renee before she was turned into a blonde, and was dressed as nearly as possible like Gavin's wife. So again, Max, you see the woman falling in love with him is of the utmost importance to justify her behavior in section two.

It is this section that you will also notice that we have only used the one man with Renee who gets rid of her because, I think, we get a better mood with her alone rather than a lot of extraneous characters who, I feel, destroy this emotional line we are trying to draw . . .

Now, Max, one final thing. I am really anxious to get mood, but not necessarily somber mood, into this love story. I don't want us to get heavy handed with it. After all, Barrie's MARY ROSE had some of the elements of the first part of this story and, as you know, this quality was quite a fey one.

Also, while I think of it, I don't want to make Renee—Judy, as we are going to call her, too cheap a character. Because the contrast will become too stagey. It is my intention in directing the picture to have the voice of Madeleine be quite a soft one, and the voice of Renee a sharper more nasal one. The first voice can be justified by the fact that Renee is assuming the characteristics of a mysterious person in the story. (I don't know if we have to justify her as having been an actress.) . . .

Incidentally, you will notice in this batch of material that there is no reference made by the husband in the first office scene of the mystery of the character of Pauline. This was deliberately omitted because following this springboard scene we proceed to show the visit to the churchyard and the old ancestral home of the Lagerlacs. This would have come out as anti-climactic, for we would have been telling something, and then showing it. Now, of course, with the husband simply telling him to follow her, it naturally works out that when the ex-detective reports to him, that the husband explains the character of Pauline Lagerlac. As you will see, the ex-detective then says, "Well, that's understandable if she is living in the past." Whereupon, the husband can tell him that there is no possible reason for his wife having knowledge of Pauline Lagerlac, and then proceed to explain why.

Please, Max, forgive me for being so long-winded about this, but this construction has taken many weeks of work between Mr. Coppel and myself, and I still wonder that after all the years of one's experience why construction is such a hard job. . . .

Besides revealing some of Hitchcock's touchstones—including his long-standing love for *Mary Rose, Peter Pan* creator J. M. Barrie's 1920 play—this remarkable letter throws into relief Hitchcock's abiding concern with character and motivation, and with the importance of structure to suspense. It was his hope that Anderson would bring his talents to bear on such issues in a new draft.

But it wasn't to be. Coppel's involvement, and the duo's major changes to the story, may have led to some consternation on Anderson's part; he never returned a new draft, and he negotiated to complete his contract in February 1957 for a reduced fee of fifty thousand dollars—an eye-opening sum, considering how little of his version would end up on the screen. Herbert Coleman hints that the relationship's end wasn't amicable, but there are no letters or notes in either Anderson's or Hitchcock's papers to substantiate this—only a complete silence after December 1956.

At the end of the year, Hitchcock was distracted by publicity demands for *The Wrong Man,* which Warner Bros. had rushed into a New York theater in late December, according to Spoto, in vain hopes of an Academy Award nomination. In a much-publicized incident, the film did attract a "mad bomber":

A pipe bomb was planted at the theater. No one was hurt, and the incident even elicited some amusing remarks from Hitchcock. But in the end, nothing would help this detailed, thoughtful, and bleak film.

After spending the holidays at his Bellagio Road home, Hitchcock returned to work in January, to find Wasserman and Stewart as unhappy with the Coppel script as he was. Another writer was needed, and into the hat was thrown a new name: Samuel Taylor. Taylor's agent, Kay Brown, had recommended him to Hitchcock because of his native knowledge of San Francisco. After directing the *Alfred Hitchcock Presents* episode "One More Mile to Go," Hitchcock decided on January twelfth to give Taylor a try. He was signed on January sixteenth at a fee of twenty thousand dollars for six weeks' work. Taylor was given the Coppel script and notes. But fate would keep the new screenwriter from working directly with Hitchcock.

After a long and successful career on both coasts, Taylor now lives outside of Bangor, Maine. He recalls how he became involved with *Vertigo:* "Hitchcock called my agent one day and said, 'I'm having a bad time. I can't use my screenplay. Who do you suggest?' And she probably said, 'Sam Taylor can do anything.' So he sent me the script and I read it and I said to Kay Brown, 'This is an awful screenplay.'" Taylor cannot recall the exact time line, but he probably received the Coppel screenplay just before the end of the year.

Certain that the script was beyond repair, Taylor at first was leery of taking the assignment. "She said to have a go at it because she'd like me to know Hitchcock. So I said all right and I studied the screenplay on the train going out, because in those days you almost always traveled by train. By the time I got there I had a pretty good idea what I could do with it."

In their first meeting at Hitchcock's Paramount office, Taylor recalls, he told the director how he felt about the screenplay. Hitchcock told Taylor, "Well, to be honest, it's unshootable and that's why I asked you to come. Jimmy Stewart won't do it."

"We had a talk and I said the first thing we have to do is make these people real. He said, 'That's what Jimmy Stewart said.' The whole story is so unreal and so fantasized and you never touch reality at all. Therefore I have to create somebody who is completely in the real world who can test you, the man, so that you can come back to reality and say to the audience, 'Is this a real world?'"

He described what he wanted to do and Hitchcock said, "Fine, go ahead and do it."

"It's hard to remember if I went to work on the script right there or if he sent me to San Francisco with my wife. Because I'm a San Franciscan—I think he sent us there first, together, to look at the locations that he had already picked. Some of the locations were not picked and he said, 'You go and see what you can find,' and we did."

It was just as well. Just after signing him, Hitchcock had taken ill. After five days of intense pain, in January the director was diagnosed by doctors at Cedars-Sinai (then Cedars of Lebanon) with a hernia and colitus. After minor surgery, he stayed at home until the end of the month.

The illness—and a second one that would follow some weeks later— marked a watershed in Hitchcock's career and life. The hernia episode brought him his very first trip to the hospital, and the operation and recovery took a toll on his energy. And that made for a significant difference between Alec Coppel's experience and Samuel Taylor's: Though at first they worked together closely, Taylor's efforts would get much less of the day-to-day attention than Coppel had received.

Taylor worked out of his office at Paramount, in the famous row of two-story offices that appear in Billy Wilder's *Sunset Boulevard*. Before the onset of his illness, Taylor and Hitchcock followed a routine that was familiar to any writer who had worked with Hitchcock.

"Hitchcock and I would sit and talk, sometimes at his office, quite often at his home in Bel Air. We would just sit and talk about scenes, and I would say what I thought I could do, and he would join in with me and we would discuss things."

Taylor never remembered Hitchcock losing his calm or being concerned during his first illness. "He was in good form and we were having a very happy time writing. We really were.

"It was pure serendipity. We discovered as soon as we met that our minds worked alike and that we had a rapport. It seemed to be a rapport that didn't have to be announced. So, when we worked, especially at his house, we would sit and talk. We would talk about all sorts of things—talk about food, talk about wives, talk about travel.

"We'd talk about the picture and there would be a long silence and we'd just sit and contemplate each other and Hitchcock would say, 'Well, the motor is still running.' And then all of a sudden we would pick up again and talk some more."

It was not always work. "We'd have lunch and sometimes, especially in those days, he would retire and take a nap and rest, because naturally he needed it. I would return to the studio and work. There was a complete rapport."

The first Taylor draft, dated February twenty-first, carried the whimsical title *From the Dead or There'll Never Be Another You,* by Samuel Taylor and Ambrose Bierce. "All the titles were Hitch's," Taylor recalls. "The Ambrose Bierce was just a joke. The only title I can remember suggesting was *To Lay a Ghost.*"

In this first Taylor installment—a rewrite of the film's first half—much of the Coppel-Hitchcock structure remains intact. But the lightness of Taylor's dialogue, and the depth of his characterization, demonstrate the real talent he was bringing to the project. The character's names now appeared in their final form: Kilrain had become John "Scottie" Ferguson; Gévigne was now Gavin Elster; Renée, the girl who becomes Madeleine, was renamed Judy; and the ghost, Pauline Lagerlac, was now Carlotta Valdes.

Taylor didn't yet add a death plunge to the opening rooftop sequence, but what he did add may have been far more important to making the people real: a brand-new character, Midge. The exposition scene among Scottie's fellow detectives remains, but all of the previous establishing work is now accomplished in conversation between Scottie and Midge in her apartment.

Taylor admitted that he had the young actress Barbara Bel Geddes—a friend and a Broadway actress he admired—in mind when he created Midge. Bel Geddes has had a fascinating, eclectic career. Her father was the famed stage designer Norman Bel Geddes; her first stage appearance, at the age of ten, was in her father's production of *Dead End.* Her debut on Broadway in *Out of the Frying Pan* and her Academy Award nomination for *I Remember Mama* warranted the attention they garnered: She was a self-described perfectionist and was a member of Elia Kazan's Actors Studio in New York. Great fanfare marked her debuts on Broadway and in Hollywood—like Kim Novak, she was also featured on the cover of *Time* magazine, in 1951—but she never played along with the publicity machinery.

When Bel Geddes signed for *From Among the Dead* in 1957, Hedda Hopper marked the event in her column:

After almost seven years Barbara Bel Geddes is coming back to Hollywood October 10 for one of the top roles in Amongst the Dead for Paramount. She will play Kim Novak's rival and that will put Kim on the mettle because Barbara never gives a bad performance.

Barbara has been living in Ireland with Windsor Lewis, her husband, and has been refusing all offers for stage and screen. Her last big stage play was *Cat on a Hot Tin Roof* (1955!) on Broadway and before that *The Moon is Blue*.

Barbara Bel Geddes took a very different tack in her life from that of Kim Novak, and the difference extended to their work on *Vertigo:* Throughout the production of the film, the two never met.

The first half of Samuel Taylor's screenplay also introduced several notes of San Francisco color to the script, including the famed restaurant Ernie's (Hitchcock's choice), as well as the character of Pop Liebel and the darkening bookstore. Taylor recalls the genesis of the Argosy Book Shop: "People are always amazed because there was a thing in some magazine about trying to find all the locations and they couldn't find the bookshop. Finally fans decided that we had made it up and it was right in the middle of Union Square.

"They were very close, because when I was growing up, there was a sort of a new-and-used bookshop, mostly used, right on the corner of Stockton Street and Maiden Lane. I was in college. I used to work at the City of Paris Bookshop, which was right down the street. I used to wander up at lunchtime to this shop up on the corner of Maiden Lane and browse around and talk to people."

Of the bookstore owner, he recalls: "The character was not a bookshop character. Pop Liebel was a man who ran the corner candy store when I was a little boy. And Hitchcock cast him just right."

When the first fifty-nine pages of Taylor's list were distributed for review, the circulation list included all of the key production staff, along with Jimmy Stewart and Vera Miles. Everyone was relieved that the picture was coming to life.

But medical disaster struck again. In the early hours of March 9, 1957, Hitchcock was again rushed to the hospital with severe abdominal pains. He was diagnosed with a diseased gallbladder and obstructing gallstones. An operation—the second and most serious of Hitchcock's life—took place two days later. The director would be forced to stay in the hospital and then at home, recuperating, through all of March and April.

While Hitch recovered, Taylor worked in New York, corresponding with Herbert Coleman. He completed his first full draft on April third. It would be a month before Hitchcock would be well enough to meet to discuss it.

Hitchcock and Taylor did not correspond during his recuperation. Taylor continued to send pages to Coleman, who would then relay them on to Hitchcock. Little serious work was completed until their next meeting in early May, when Hitchcock returned to work. Before that May meeting, Taylor and Coleman discussed various plot points: the pros and cons of having Midge helping Scottie with the investigation; whether Judy should stay at the McKittrick Hotel, as Madeleine had. When Taylor doubted the wisdom of having Judy stay there, Coleman wrote in reply, "I don't agree. She might very well have tried [it] on the manageress to see if she could get away with it."

During Hitchcock's convalescence Coleman had enlisted other production staff, along with Jimmy Stewart, in evaluating Taylor's script. Hitchcock's own involvement was minimal: An April letter from Coleman to Taylor says that Hitchcock was again showing interest in the project, suggesting that his condition must at least for some time have been diverting his attention.

During the May sixth meeting with Hitchcock, several issues were addressed. Most important was Taylor's desire to reveal Judy's secret to the audience two-thirds of the way through the film, rather than at the conclusion. His argument rested on the assumption that the audience's suspense would be doubled if they knew Judy was in on the crime, leading them to wonder when Scottie would learn.

"That's a matter of my expertise as a playwright," Taylor recalled, "and I had kept saying to Hitchcock that there's something missing. Then one day I said to him, 'I know exactly what's missing'—I said, 'It's really a Hitchcockian thing.' I was naturally being Hitchcock with him. I said, 'This is not pure Hitchcock unless the audience knows what has happened,' and he agreed.

"The trouble was, I didn't know exactly how to write it because I thought originally of [having a] scene between Judy and Elster, in which he is preparing to go east and she is saying, 'What will become of me?' That would've revealed it to the audience, but I came to the conclusion—not I alone, but Hitch and I talking about it—we came to the conclusion that would strangely rob Scottie. It was just an instinct with us both.

"We finally fastened on what we did, which is the writing of the letter and the flashback. I always felt that it was a weakness that we had to do it that way, but there was no other way to do it."

With that final element agreed upon—at least for the moment—Taylor began making his final script revisions late in May, while Hitchcock and his production team finalized the film's locations. By the end of May, Hitchcock's full-time involvement in the writing of *From Among the Dead* was more or less completed, and he began a daily involvement with writer Ernest Lehman in preparation for his next film, *North by Northwest*. In June, however, the director provided Taylor with a new set of notes, suggesting various fine-tunings in Taylor's newest version.

By July, Taylor had tightened the script, added the Judy revelation, and dropped all of the expositional, early detective scenes. But Hitchcock still had concerns: He felt that playing the acrophobia test in Midge's apartment "straight" might get a laugh. "Suggest," he advised, "that he is just doing it for fun."

Such revisions suggest an early awareness of a delicate issue of concern to both *Vertigo*'s filmmakers and its latter-day fans: its modulations between high tragedy and light comedy. Asked about another moment in the film that can elicit uneasy laughter today—the scene where Scottie implores Judy to dye her hair ("It can't matter to you")—Taylor maintains that humor was hardly what the filmmakers had in mind. "No, that was Hitchcock's passion, you see. I guess Jimmy caught the fever. No, it was not meant to get a chuckle."

The calibrations continued, a parade of minor but significant adjustments of detail. Hitchcock was worried about the moment when Scottie sees Madeleine's necklace on Judy's neck. In his notes, he used Scottie's own voice to outline what would be going through his mind in this pivotal instant:

A. The necklace from the portrait definitely connects Judy with the past. Therefore I haven't created another Madeleine, Judy is Madeleine!

B. If I were to confront her now, she would deny everything, because I have already seen her identification as Judy.

C. If Judy is Madeleine, who was the woman who fell from the tower, dressed the same as Madeleine, with the same color hair?

D. Judy could not have been Elster's wife at the time because Elster's wife's maiden name was Valdes.

E. Elster's wife had money therefore she must have been the dead woman—murdered for her money.

F. Why was I brought into this thing? Madeleine pretended to have suicidal tendencies. I was fooled by her throwing herself into the water. I was fooled by the Carlotta Valdes nonsense. But why me? Because I was to be a witness of the suicide—a witness who could not climb to the top of the tower.

There is an additional note from Hitchcock, in his own hand: "She [Carlotta] could not be buried in a Catholic Mission after committing suicide unless found to be insane. If Protestant—can receive Christian burial under any circumstance."

The July revisions included changing Judy's hometown from Santa Rosa to Salina, Kansas. Although Salinas, California, is the city closest to San Juan Bautista, the parallel with Salina was never in the mind of the filmmakers. A note from Taylor to Hitchcock comments on another intended joke:

> You will note, in the lower depths of the pages, that I have made Judy a native of Salina, Kansas, this because I have a dear friend who is an Episcopal minister in Salina. Salina is pronounced as though it were saliva with an "n." Do I make myself clear?
>
> I anticipate that, because of the way I have constructed the scene, the words "Salina, Kansas" will get a laugh. I do not believe this is wrong. I hope you agree with me.

The final shooting script is dated September 12, 1957. It contains a final scene reminiscent of *Rear Window:* At Midge's apartment, a broken Scottie listens to a radio report on Gavin Elster's arrest. (Spoto says that there is an annotation to the final page of the script concerning the 360-degree kiss—yet the kiss scene was originally written with Coppel nearly a year earlier, and the scripts contained in the Hitchcock *Vertigo* archives contain no such note.)

The final script follows the story that we are familiar with as the film *Vertigo.* It begins with a rooftop chase that introduces Scottie as the very opposite of a hero: Clinging desperately to a gutter, he watches as a fellow officer falls to his death. The story then leaps in time to the day before he is to have his brace removed—a brace he wears as a result of injuries sustained during the initial chase. As he visits with his only close friend in the film, his old flame Midge, we learn that Scottie has resigned from the police force because of his fear of heights. We also learn that he plans to meet with an old college acquaintance, Gavin Elster, the next day. At the end of this scene, Scottie attempts a make-shift cure for his vertigo by climbing the rungs of a stepladder—a plan that fails when he looks out the apartment window from the top of the ladder and collapses into Midge's arms.

Scottie meets with Elster in his elegant office, which overlooks his ship-building business. Appealing to their old college ties, he asks Scottie to follow his wife, Madeleine, who he fears has become possessed by the spirit of her dead great-grandmother, Carlotta Valdes. He describes strange trances and mysterious wanderings. Scottie at first refuses the case but then agrees at least to consider helping Elster after he is encouraged to see her when the couple goes to dine at Ernie's.

There Scottie sees Madeleine, and he is immediately attracted to her. He takes the case.

Scottie then spends a day trailing the entranced, mysterious Madeleine around the city; she drives her green Jaguar from her home at the Brocklebank Apartments to Podesta Baldocchi, a florist, to purchase a bouquet, and then to the Palace of the Legion of Honor, where she sits for some time before the portrait of Carlotta as if in a trance. In this portrait, Scottie finds the reason for

A more primitive set of sketches outlines the brief scene at the McKittrick Hotel.

VERTIGO: The Making of a Hitchcock Classic

the visit to the florist: Carlotta holds a bouquet exactly like the one Madeleine had purchased there. He also notices that Madeleine's hair is done in the same swirling pattern as Carlotta's.

She leaves the Palace and drives to an old hotel, the McKittrick, on Eddy and Gough streets. She enters, and Scottie sees her raise the shade in a second-floor apartment. When he questions the manager about Madeleine (whom she knows as Carlotta Valdes), she denies that she has been there that day. When Scottie insists that she check, he is surprised to find the room empty—and her Jaguar missing from the front curb. He returns to the Brocklebank Apartments and sees the Jaguar has returned, the bouquet visible on the dash.

That afternoon, he returns to Midge's studio apartment and asks if she knows someone who is an expert on San Francisco history. Caught up in the promise of adventure, she dashes out the door to take him to Pop Liebel's bookstore before he can even finish his drink.

At the Argosy Book Shop, Liebel tells the sad Carlotta's story in the darkening twilight: She was a music-hall dancer who had become the lover of a rich and powerful man. He built her a mansion to live in—the house that became the McKittrick Hotel. She bore him a child, after which he abandoned her, keeping the child to raise himself. This broke Carlotta's spirit and she took her own life.

The next day, Scottie returns to Elster at his club to tell him the story; Elster acknowledges its details, then hits Scottie with an unsettling revelation: Madeleine has never heard of Carlotta Valdes, he claims. Her mother had kept the truth from her in an effort to protect her. Scottie is clearly affected by the news, which seems to defy rational explanation.

7

8

9

10

11

12

The next day, he follows her again. After returning to the Palace, she drives to Fort Point at the base of the Golden Gate Bridge. She stands by the water's edge, dropping petals from her bouquet into the surf. Then, unexpectedly, Madeleine jumps into the bay. Casting off his hat and coat, Scottie quickly dives in after her; he carries her to the Jaguar and takes her to his apartment.

The next scene opens there; Scottie has undressed Madeleine and put her to bed. We can hear her mumbling something about "my child." The phone rings—it is Elster, to whom Scottie utters a few quick words of reassurance before hanging up—and the sound wakes Madeleine, obviously somewhat taken aback to find herself awakening undressed in a stranger's bed. After donning Scottie's robe, she sits with him by the fireplace, drinking coffee and answering Scottie's questions. She has no recollection of her suicide attempt or how she got to Fort Point. She does not recall having ever entered the Palace of the Legion of Honor. Their hands brush accidentally as they reach for a coffee cup. Elster phones again, and Scottie takes the call in his bedroom, but when he hears the door close, he hurries back, just in time to see Madeleine driving away. Meanwhile, Midge, who has just driven up to his apartment, has also seen Madeleine drive off in the Jaguar. Assuming there was more to the visit than coffee by the fire, she drives away.

Scottie follows Madeleine again the next morning. They seem to be going nowhere—until he realizes that they are returning to his apartment. She has come back to drop off a thank-you note. Scottie suggests that they wander together. She agrees.

They drive out to Big Basin Redwoods State Park. Wandering through the ancient sequoia stands, they stop at a tree circle with dates on it. Madeleine, slipping into a trance, points to one of the rings, indicating where she was born and where she died—dates that clearly refer to Carlotta's life, not her own. She walks away from Scottie and seems to disappear. Scottie hurries after her and finds Madeleine pressed against a redwood, agitated, anxious to get somewhere in the light.

He takes her to Cypress Point. When she runs to the edge, Scottie hurries after her, telling her it's his job to protect her now. In a strange, almost-catatonic tone, she tells him of a nightmare that has beleaguered her; she breaks from him, and when he catches her farther down the rocky oceanside, he embraces her and they kiss.

That evening, he goes to Midge's apartment (at her request). She's waiting for him with a private joke: She has duplicated the painting of Carlotta but has superimposed her own face over the original. Scottie is not amused, and he leaves. We see him wandering in the early-morning hours on Union Square; later, Madeleine rings his bell as he slumbers on his couch. Panicked—she's had the nightmare again—she begins another trancelike recitation of its details: The dream takes place in a Spanish town with a mission that has a tower. Scottie recognizes the location as San Juan Bautista—"It's all there," he says—and promises to take her there later in the day.

At the mission, Scottie shows her the originals of the various images from her dream, but Madeleine is unsettled, and she seems unconvinced. They kiss, this time in the stable across from the mission. She again breaks from him and runs toward the church. He catches her, but after telling him that she loves him, she's able to break his grasp a final time. She runs into the church, and Scottie follows. She starts up the bell tower, but though Scottie continues his pursuit, he is soon overcome by his vertigo and cannot continue the climb. Then he hears a scream from above; from a window, he sees her fall. In shock, Scottie staggers out of the mission as some bystanders climb to the mission's roof to retrieve Madeleine's body.

Scottie's inability to stop Madeleine's suicide, and his confusing behavior after her death, are recited in pregnant tones by a coroner in the following scene, but he restricts his accusations to a withering parade of insinuations. The jury rules the death a suicide, and the still-dazed Scottie meets one last time with Gavin Elster, who tells him, "You and I know who killed Madeleine."

An unspecified period of time elapses. Again, we see the San Francisco skyline in the twilight. Scottie is sleeping restlessly; he's dreaming, and the nightmare opens before us—spinning flowers, images from the Carlotta painting, the Mission Dolores cemetery, all coalesce in a visual representation of a psychotic breakdown.

With Midge's help, Scottie is placed in a sanitarium. Midge leaves him there, knowing that even though he may someday be free of the hospital, he will never be free of Madeleine.

More time passes. Scottie returns to the city streets, but his obsession colors everything around him. He sees the likeness of Madeleine in all of their old places—the Brocklebank, Ernie's, the Palace of the Legion of Honor. Then, one afternoon in front of Podesta Baldocchi, he sees a woman who looks remarkably like Madeleine. He follows her home to the Empire Hotel, then upstairs to her room. He gets her to tell him her name—Judy—and after some uneasy conversation, Scottie asks her out on a date. Though suspicious, she agrees to go out with him. When he leaves, we can tell she's troubled. And then comes the revelation: We see in a flashback that Judy *was* Madeleine—that it was she who had gone up the tower, then hid in the shadows with Elster as he threw the real Madeleine from the window. She begins to write a note to Scottie explaining her complicity and her love for him, then decides to see him after all and tears up the note.

Scottie asks to see Judy often, and soon he is occupying all of her time. Within days it is clear to the audience that he intends to remake her into the Madeleine he longs for. He buys her outfits and shoes to duplicate those Madeleine wore. He has her dye her hair and style it in Madeleine's fashion. She's reluctant, but she ultimately consents in her desperate bid to regain Scottie's love. When she emerges from her bathroom, dressed and coiffed as the Madeleine he had known, the two kiss with passion; as the room seems to spin around them, Scottie is transported back to his final kiss with Madeleine.

In the next scene—there's an implication that they've made love. Madeleine has dressed again. Scottie waits patiently as she adds the finishing touches to her costume. She asks him to help with a necklace. Then, as he fastens it, he recognizes it as the necklace Carlotta wore in the painting—and suddenly the truth tumbles before him. Abruptly, instead of Ernie's, Scottie suggests going somewhere out of town for dinner.

They drive to San Juan Bautista, Judy growing more apprehensive with each mile. When they arrive at the mission, she struggles, but Scottie becomes forceful. He drags her up the tower stairs, conquering his vertigo; near the top, he confronts her with the truth, to which she confesses. He insists they return to the scene of the crime.

They enter the tower. Scottie knows now that the Madeleine he loved never existed. Judy, embracing him, trying once more to convince him that it's not too late, is frightened by a rising dark image. She backs away and falls to her death as a nun enters the bell tower.

This script's coda finds Midge in her apartment, listening to the radio. The announcer describes the search for Elster in Europe and his imminent arrest for murdering his wife. Scottie enters and crosses to her window. She goes to make him a drink. Fade out.

In such a collaboration as Taylor had with Hitchcock, who contributed the depth of emotion in Scottie Ferguson's story?

"I don't know. I honestly don't know," Taylor says. "You see, in working together, naturally I didn't write it. Sitting alone and writing a scene, I would naturally write the way I did. I think that the scenes indicate that Hitchcock felt pretty strongly about this terribly frustrated love, just the way that he thought out the scenes and how he shot them.

"I think you could say that Hitchcock had that kind of influence over the screenplay, without ever talking about it—we never talked about it."

After *Vertigo,* Hitchcock and Taylor would team up to write an unproduced film, *No Bail for the Judge;* Taylor was brought back in—this time, too late—to save *Topaz* (1969). To the end, the Taylors and Hitchcocks shared a special relationship. "We never lacked for conversation; we never lacked for quiet interludes, because they were so natural and normal. We were so comfortable with one another. This goes for wives, too. Never lacked for conversation, and very witty and humorous conversation and very sharply clashing conversation—very intellectual conversation.

"In public he made jokes and in private he made jokes, but in private, you know, we would talk about anything. We used to talk about everything. I think that people who were intelligent enough and talented enough to recognize that knew it. You know, he had a collection of George Bernard Shaw's short plays and the inscription on the title page was 'For Alma Hitchcock's husband.' There you are. He was marvelous. Marvelous."

Taylor considered *From Among the Dead* (as it was still called) his script, and he made a bid to have Alec Coppel's name removed from the screen credit. This brought a terse response from Coppel, who added a telling bit of criticism:

Sept. 16, 1957

Dear Hitch:
    Because of the publicity given to the fact that I was writing the screenplay of "From Among the Dead" with you, I must very reluc-

tantly fight for my right to a credit on the final script—and in fairness to me it must be agreed that a great deal of my construction remains. I am conscious of the new dialogue and the new character Midge (who doesn't amount to anything)—but if Sam Taylor had started with only the book as his guide he couldn't possibly have arrived with this latest script.

Next time we meet I would like very much to know why you jettisoned the entire mystery of the novel, and our script when I left you, by telling the audience on page 112 the truth about Judy? I'm sure you had reasons—but it seems to me that after that exposé you can reach for your hat.

Things are very busy here . . . .

Alec

At the time, Hitchcock still seemed confident about revealing Judy's identity to the audience before the film's ending; yet Coppel's reservations proved prescient—the issue would raise its head again, dramatically, before the film's opening.

As required in a credit dispute, the Hitchcock office turned over the script files on *From Among the Dead* to the Writers Guild. The letter from the Hitchcock office humorously explains that "this material consists of bits and pieces without any continuity or completion, which is pretty generally the method of work that Mr. Hitchcock enjoys with his writers until such time as a screenplay is actually launched."

The Writers Guild came back with the only response possible, considering the evidence: Samuel Taylor and Alec Coppel would receive shared credit on the screenplay.

A little more than a week after the completion of Taylor's final draft, shooting began on Paramount production 10344: *From Among the Dead.*

| # FILMING THE DREAM

Dreams are so much more beautiful than the stuff they call reality.

—*Pierre Boileau and Thomas Narcejac,* The Living and the Dead

Production of the film that would become *Vertigo*—separate from the preparation of its blueprint, the screenplay—began when the first coverage of the novel was submitted to Hitchcock in late 1954. At this point Danny McCauley, the assistant director, put together a list of locations for the novel; then, two years later, he prepared a list of locations for the Maxwell Anderson screenplay. Location visits began around the same time and continued for another year before actual filming commenced.

The project evolved quickly. After Hitchcock returned from South Africa in August 1956 with the realization that *Flamingo Feather* would be impossible, he met to discuss the next project over lunch with the unit production manager, Doc Erickson, and the director of photography, Robert Burks.

A month later, *From Among the Dead* was the subject of a lunch discussion among Hitchcock, Jimmy Stewart, and Lew Wasserman. The trio then spent the next two days watching *The Wrong Man* (due for release in December), *The Deep Blue Sea,* and Henri Clouzot's *Les Diaboliques,* the Boileau-Narcejac project that had first attracted Hitchcock's eye.

Maxwell Anderson's San Francisco visit during the summer of 1956 was followed by a visit from Hitchcock, Coleman, McCauley, Coppel, and Burks in October. It was during this visit that many of the final locations were determined: Mission Dolores (present in the earliest of drafts), the Palace of the Legion of Honor, Fort Point, and Big Basin Redwoods State Park (near Santa Cruz). Other locations were still up in the air. Mission San Carlos Borromeo in Carmel was originally slated as the site of the climactic church tower, but Coleman remembered that he and Burks had found the location too obviously pretty; Hitchcock wanted a location that looked abandoned, and the search would have to continue, or even be abandoned and a set on a soundstage used. Coleman was staying with his daughter, a teacher in the Salinas area, when she recommended the rather secluded San Juan Bautista.

Only a few miles from Highway 101, San Juan Bautista is approximately ninety miles south of San Francisco. The town and mission are truly a hundred years away from the city, remaining frozen in the mid-1800s—full of western storefronts and stables, a large courtyard flanked by the long cloistered mission, an old stage hotel and livery. Look at the images of San Juan Bautista in the film and you see the San Juan Bautista of both 1850 and 1998. The only thing missing, ironically, is a tower. This fact seemed to dash the scouting party's hopes; the mission had once had a tower, but it was lost to fire in the earthquake of 1906 (the mission offers a breathtaking view of the San Andreas Fault).

In spite of this drawback, though, the mood of the mission settlement was perfect for the film, and ultimately the decision was made to re-create the bell tower in a studio. This is an excellent example of why location scouting expeditions occur even before a script is finished: Not only do locations shape the finished screenplay but, more important to the studio, they shape the budget. The tower would be the most expensive set built for the production of *Vertigo.*

Hitchcock had found a trusted team when he joined Paramount. Coleman, art director Henry Bumstead, and editor George Tomasini were loyal members of

Mission San Juan Bautista, in a production sketch that adds the fateful tower.

the team. Bumstead later worked on *Topaz* and *Family Plot* and Tomasini edited *North by Northwest, Psycho, The Birds,* and *Marnie.* His cameramen, led by director of photography Robert Burks, were also loyal members, whom he had kept from Warner Bros. Together, they would create in *Vertigo* a film of dazzling technical virtuosity.

Robert Burks's first job as Hitchcock's director of photography was on 1951's *Strangers on a Train,* and he would shoot every Hitchcock film through *Marnie* with the exception of *Psycho.* Theirs was a long, trusted relationship; the trademark Burks lighting and camera setup defined the Hitchcock look at a critical time in the director's career, so much so that the style was duplicated for the television series to give the shows that Hitchcock look. The few cinematographers Hitchcock worked with after Burks's tragic death (he and his wife died in 1968 in a fire started by a smoldering cigarette) were compelled to try and re-create the Burks look; the only one who succeeded was Leonard South, Burks's camera operator for all of the Hitchcock films, who photographed Hitchcock's final film, *Family Plot.*

After returning from the *Vertigo* location shoot, Hitchcock sat down with Robert Burks to discuss just how the vertigo effect would be achieved. Hitchcock's notes during the writing of the screenplay suggest that Coleman had some early ideas for producing the effect, but it was an uncredited cameraman who thought up the technique. Combining a forward zoom with a reverse track, the cameraman instinctively came up with what became known as the "vertigo shot"—one of the most innovative and imitated effects in film history.

"I'll tell you who came up with that idea," Coleman remembered. "Irmin Roberts, who was always used as a second-unit cameraman—I was always the second-unit director on almost every one of the Hitchcock films [at Paramount] and we always used Roberts, but he didn't get screen credit on *Vertigo* because they gave the screen credit to another close friend of ours who did all the process work on the stage [Wallace Kelley]."

During this time, Vera Miles was having her hair, makeup, and costume tests shot for the dual role of Madeleine and Judy. Miles watched the test work with costumer Edith Head and makeup artist Wally Westmore on November twelfth in Paramount's Projection Room 5, while at the same time Everett Sloane (of Mercury Theatre fame) was being considered for the role of Gavin Elster. Miles reported to Stage 17 with Edith Head on November sixteenth for lens tests with Burks; from the end of November through the Christmas vacation, the production was on hold as Hitchcock found himself consumed with promotional activities for *The Wrong Man*—the film that may have helped to spell her downfall as the lead actress of *Vertigo*.

Hitchcock had given specific directions to Head for costuming, and he was confident that she would follow them to the letter. The two had first worked together ten years earlier, on *Notorious* (1946), and Head knew exactly what Hitchcock wanted: clothing that was stunning but simple, sexy but not too revealing. Her later work on *Rear Window* was perfect, though the task was daunting: What do you put on a girl who's a couture buyer? Grace Kelly never looked more beautiful—until *To Catch a Thief,* that is. Head was allowed to be more ostentatious in dressing this Kelly character, a rich young woman from the United States. The film had two costume-stopping moments: the bathing suit that gives the Carlton lobby pause, and the orgy of costumes in the party at the end. Head was capable of giving the full range to Hitchcock. And she appreciated his matter-of-fact, no-nonsense approach to business: The director made certain specific requests, and she was allowed to fill in the details.

The requests for *From Among the Dead* were quite specific: The gentleman indeed seemed to know what he wanted. A gray suit was designed for Miles that would later cause legendary problems for Novak. It is perhaps the most often told *Vertigo* production story, one that Hitchcock, Head, and Novak repeated on many occasions. Edith Head wrote about the incident in her memoir:

> . . . I remember her saying that she would wear any color except gray, and she must have thought that would give me full rein. Either she hadn't read the script or she had and wanted me to think she hadn't. I explained to her that Hitch paints a picture in his films, that color is as important to him as it is to any artist. . . .
>
> As soon as she left I was on the phone to Hitch, asking if that damn suit had to be gray and he explained to me that the simple gray suit and plain hairstyle were very important and represented the character's view of herself in the first half of the film. The character would go through a psychological change in the second half of the film and would then wear more colorful clothes to reflect the change.
>
> . . . "Handle it, Edith," I remembered him saying. "I don't care what she wears as long as it's a gray suit."
>
> When Kim came in for our next session, I was completely prepared. I had several swatches of gray fabric in various shades, textures, and weights. Before she had an opportunity to complain, I showed her the sketch and the fabrics and suggested that she choose the fabric she thought would be best on her. She immediately had a positive feeling and felt that we were designing together. Of course, I knew that any of the fabrics would work well for the suit silhouette I had designed, so I didn't care which one she chose.

Madeleine was given dark shoes to wear, which, in Novak's words, "anchored her to the earth." The actress took the limitations of her costume as a source of character development: "I can use that feeling when I play Judy. Judy is trapped into portraying Madeleine, and she doesn't want to. She wants to be loved as Judy. But she always has to go along with what someone else wants in order to get the love she wants. So I used that feeling of wearing someone else's shoes that didn't feel right, that made me feel out of place. The same thing with Madeleine's gray suit, which made me stand so straight and erect the way Edith Head built it. I hated that silly suit, to tell you the truth, but it helped me to be uncomfortable as Madeleine."

As the script was nearing completion in the summer of 1957, the front office began to express two concerns about the film: standard concerns in the legal department over Production Code problems, and a lingering dissatisfaction with the title.

The legal department raised a red flag in July 1957, informing Hitchcock that there could be legal problems with the character of the coroner at the inquest, and specifically with the condemning remarks he makes in his summation to the jurors. They felt that the speech "could not properly be made by the man presiding at the inquest. It is not judicial in tone or concept, and is more appropriate to an advocate or prosecutor than to a judicial officer. This is aggravated by the verbal description of him [later cut from the film] as a 'son of a bitch.'"

The concern was with libel; the real-life coroner in San Benito County was only one person, so any derogatory reference to him could be taken as a direct libel of that individual. Hitchcock apparently ignored the office's opinion, since the scene remains in the film, but some of its language seems to have been toned down.

Next, the office focused on the questionable morals of the film's characters. An August letter detailed problems with the early banter between Scottie and Midge about the brassiere and Midge's love of life. They recommended this should be eliminated, as well as any photography of "intimate garments hanging on the cord" in Scottie's kitchen after Madeleine's suicide attempt. They added, "If the present indication is to be approved that Scottie has completely undressed Madeleine and put her to bed, the evidence of embarrassment on her part will have to be played down. Also, on page 60, Scottie's broken line, 'Not at all, I enjoyed—talking to you' should be read without the break and also without any show of embarrassment." Geoffrey Shurlock, the man responsible for trying to keep Hitchcock "moral," went on to note five additional scenes that suggested illicit relations between Madeleine/Judy and Scottie.

Although most of the concerns focused on illicit sex, Shurlock also worried about a different kind of morality. His note would have an impact on the final draft: "It will, of course, be most important that the indication that Elster will be brought back for trial is sufficiently emphasized"—a note referring to the final script's original ending, in which Midge and Scottie together hear the radio report of Elster's imminent arrest.

A final letter from Shurlock, on September eighteenth, reflected Hitchcock's resistance to change. Of the ten original concerns, six remained in the screenplay. Shurlock must have given up on the brassiere and Midge's love life, as well as on the coroner's possible libel. These were no longer mentioned. Underwear and any implications of illicit sex were the final concerns. At one point, Shurlock's advice even seemed to stray into Hitchcock's own territory: In referring to the deep kiss by the ocean, Shurlock wrote that "while the camera angles of course are indicated, the scene should conclude on the couple and not pan away to the pounding waves." This sort of advice to avoid the cliché couldn't have pleased the master director.

From Among the Dead was the literal translation of the French novel's title—it was published in April 1957 in the United States as *The Living and the Dead*—and while filming cruised happily along under the working title, a nearly yearlong debate raged over what the final film should be called. As early as October 1956, Paramount executive Arthur Kram suggested the title "A Matter of Fact" to replace *From Among the Dead,* which many found awkward.

Another executive, Sam Frey, provided Hitchcock a list of seventeen title possibilities in September 1957, just before filming was to start. Of the seventeen—which included "Tonight Is Ours" and "The Mad Carlotta"—Hitchcock (according to a wire sent by Coleman) preferred "Face in the Shadow." This was one of six variations with the word *Face* as part of the title; all were thrown out on September eighteenth because of the Warner Bros.' film *A Face in the Crowd* and a novel with the same title by Peter Ordway. Hitchcock had wired New York only a couple of days before about his dislike for the title: "It's like a B picture and very cheap."

Hitchcock finally settled on *Vertigo* as a replacement title. His office wired the New York office of the decision, but a quick response came on September thirtieth: "Nobody here likes Vertigo as replacement for From Among the Dead. They prefer title Face in the Shadow to title Possessed by a Stranger." A return wire indicated Hitchcock's satisfaction with *Vertigo*. This would not be the end of the title war with the head office—for the moment, the production continued to work under *From Among the Dead*—but as far as Hitchcock was concerned, the battle was over.

[THE LOCATION SHOOTS: FEBRUARY 28—OCTOBER 15, 1957]

Photography for *Vertigo* began with second-unit location shoots in late February of 1957, long before any of the actors would report for work—indeed, some six months before the script itself had been entirely finalized. Second-unit work (usually involving undemanding background photography that requires the presence of neither actors nor director) rarely begins before the principal photography, but Hitchcock's illness and delays caused by Kim Novak reversed the order; forced to push back his own intended start date of late spring, Hitchcock was obliged to let the filming begin without him.

On February twenty-eighth, the second-unit team, under the direction of assistant director Danny McCauley, began their work with a series of window-view shots: The views from Scottie's apartment in the 900 block of Lombard Street; from the McKittrick Hotel; from Midge's apartment; and from the window of the Argosy Book Shop out onto Powell Street. They also did test shots at the Palace of the Legion of Honor.

McCauley, Burks, and South returned to San Francisco late in August to shoot some additional tests at Mission Dolores; they also shot all of the film's traveling-car footage, which would later be used in transparencies on Paramount's Stage 2—the domain of Farciot Edouart, the head of process photography at Paramount. Edouart had begun with Paramount before World War I, and he was considered the best in the business at the art of combining preshot footage with new scenes to transform their appearance; before commencing work on *Vertigo,* he had finished the extraordinary process work for Cecil B. DeMille's *The Ten Commandments.*

Just as they were leaving for San Francisco to begin principal photography in August 1957, the production was thwarted by another serious obstacle. Kim

Novak, who had already delayed production with a summer European vacation, now refused to show up for work on August thirtieth. She was holding out for more money—not from Hitchcock, but from Columbia, her home studio. Columbia immediately put her on suspension. The stakes were high—if the gamble by Novak and her agents didn't work, she would lose both *Vertigo* and *Bell, Book and Candle* with Stewart.

The trade papers in Hollywood loved the fight as much as Hitchcock must have hated it. *Variety*'s headline was characteristically jocular: KIM NOVAK DEFIANT; WILL BE "AMONGST" THE MISSING TILL COL RAISES HER SALARY. In *The Hollywood Reporter*'s "Trade Views" column, W. R. Wilkerson had this to say: "The Agency pulling of Kim Novak from the Paramount picture is, in our books, one of the most stinking agency maneuvers this business has had."

Harry Cohn's Columbia was paid $250,000 for Novak to do *Vertigo* and the next picture with Stewart—but Novak herself was still making $1,250 a week. Interviewed after the fracas was resolved, Novak explained that her actual take-home pay was even less—around $250. "I was unable to buy sufficient clothes for myself," she told Bob Thomas of the Associated Press. "When I wanted to go to a party, I'd have to borrow a dress that Rita Hayworth had worn in a picture. . . . The studio was making a great deal of money off me, and I was seeing very little of it."

As unnerving as her salary strike was for Hitchcock, Kim Novak's stunt worked. By September, Novak had renegotiated a two-step pay hike: Beginning with *From Among the Dead,* Novak would be bumped to $2,750 a week; at the start of 1958, the number would increase to more than $3,000. As Novak explained to Bob Thomas, "I don't like to have anyone take advantage of me."

As the finishing touches on the screenplay were being made in September, Kim Novak finally reported for work. She shot three days' worth of makeup and wardrobe tests on September thirteenth, sixteenth, and eighteenth (in the gray Madeleine suit, as well as Judy's more colorful wardrobe). Additional tests were shot just days before the crew left for San Francisco.

Hitchcock loved San Francisco. The family owned a ranch not far away, near the little town of Los Gatos in Scotts Valley. He had long dreamed of making a San Francisco movie. This dream may have roots in one of Hitchcock's favorite books, Wilde's *The Picture of Dorian Gray* (a book he read "many" times, according to Spoto). Wilde writes of San Francisco: "It's an odd thing, but everyone who disappears is said to be seen at San Francisco. It must be a delightful city, and possess all the attractions of the next world."

Despite his desire to make this film at this time, Hitchcock hated to be manipulated. The past year had been unbearable: His illness, the trouble with Miles, and finally the imbroglio over Novak—which he could only have seen as childish grandstanding—had all threatened to kill a project he wanted to make. He'd walked away from other problem productions; he could easily have scrapped this film and begun the project he'd been dreaming up with Ernest Lehman for MGM. Years later, he would advise François Truffaut repeatedly during their interviews never to be afraid of walking away from a project.

But this time, Hitchcock did not walk away.

Filming began September thirtieth in San Francisco. The first scene to be filmed was the haunting Mission Dolores sequence, in which Scottie trails Madeleine to the grave of Carlotta Valdes. It was a fitting passage with which to begin, as it had survived all of the screenplay drafts—it had been a part of the director's vision from the very start.

The scene lasts three minutes; it required more than twenty setups, eventually yielding twenty-eight linked pieces of film. An entire day and part of the next morning were spent at the location.

Detailed records of the filming exist, thanks to Peggy Robertson, who served as script supervisor—one of the most vital roles in a film production. Robertson had worked before with Hitchcock, during his brief return to England after the war. Her work on *Vertigo* was invaluable to the production, and remains so to the film historian: Her daily records chart the course of the film, describing each take in both story and technical terms (specifying, for example, what lenses, special filters, and camera movements were used for each shot). Along with these notes came a list of which takes were to be printed for the next day's rushes. Entrusted with this prodigious job, Robertson would become Hitchcock's trusted special assistant for the rest of his career.

The very first shots filmed with the actors were the exterior shots of Madeleine and Scottie entering the chapel of Mission Dolores. The first take of the first shot was filmed at 8:15 A.M.: Scene 58. Three takes were required; in fact, most of the shots filmed in the course of *Vertigo*'s production would require only one to three takes. An exception that first day was the complicated set of point-of-view (POV) shots in which Scottie watches Madeleine at the Carlotta headstone; these required a simple camera move, which complicated matters enough to require six takes on the average.

Novak remembers stumbling during the film's first takes. "When I tripped over a tombstone in the cemetery scene, Jimmy helped me up and said softly, with a small smile, 'You might try lifting your feet.'"

Mission Dolores is the oldest building in San Francisco, dedicated on October 9, 1776, and completed on August 2, 1791. There are three bells in its tower, provided between 1792 and 1797, and it is their actual sound we hear at the end of *Vertigo*'s mission sequence: One of the takes listed in the script supervisor's report is a sound recording of the tolling bells. The western writer Bret Harte wrote some verse upon hearing the Dolores's bells toll, lines that seem appropriate to the film as well:

> *Bells of the past, whose long-forgotten music*
> *   still fills the wide expanse,*
> *Tingeing the sober twilight of the present*
> *   with color of romance.*

The mission's cemetery contains a who's who of early Spanish California, from the first governor of northern California, Don Luis Antonio Arguello, to the far less noble James Yankee Sullivan—who either committed suicide in jail or was killed by an angry mob after caught stuffing ballots in a local election in 1856. A visit to the cemetery today reveals few changes from October 1957. Careful observers will notice that Hitchcock rearranged the entrance slightly. Visitors actually enter the mission, as did Stewart and Novak, from the left. There is only one exit, at the altar, to the right, which the film suggests leads straight into the cemetery. In reality, the cemetery is to the left of the altar, and visitors must enter the garden by walking to the end of the mission and entering through a small arch.

Today, the layout is still familiar, but changes have been made even in the last ten years. On the author's first pilgrimage to the site in 1986, the cemetery was virtually identical to what one sees in the film. Today, the low shrubs that framed the cemetery have all been removed, though the seemingly eternal English yews through which Stewart spies on Novak remain. The Our Lady grotto to the left of Carlotta's grave is now gone—replaced by a circular spot in the path to commemorate the thousands of Native Americans buried in the cemetery, once several city blocks in size.

Even the grassy spot where the Carlotta headstone was placed is gone—replaced by a concrete walkway between one of the few sizable gaps in the headstones. After a period of restoration and improvements, the cemetery has lost something of the slightly abandoned charm visible in *Vertigo*. What cannot be changed, however, is the remarkable light of the cemetery, an effect produced by the large whitewashed walls of the mission. The quality of this reflected light is impressive; its bluish, slightly fogged quality was captured in the film without resort to any special technique.

Mission Dolores today.

PRODUCTION "FROM AMONG THE DEAD" Tech: VV No. P.10333

Location.Ext: & Int: Dolores Mission. Ext:Graveyard DATE SHOT Monday 30 Sept:1957

115—N-67

SETUP No.	TAKES MADE	SLATES PRINTED	TIME FIRST SETUP GIVEN	TIME CAMERA READY	TIME FIRST TAKE	TIME SCENE COMPLETED	DESCRIPTION OF ANGLES, ACTION AND DIALOGUE
1	3	1X-3 50'	7.30	7.45	8.15	8.25 .15 sun	Sc:58. 50 mm. Ext:Dolores Mission.Day Madeleine gets out of Jaguar.PAN with her as she crosses pavement & enters Mission door.Camera L to R. L.S. shooting from camera car.Scottie's pov
2	1	2X-1 60'	8.35	8.55	8.57	8.58 .13 sun	Sc:60. 35 mm. Ext:Mission Dolores.Day Low shot.Scottie gets out of de Soto crosses pavement R to L & enters Mission. Reverse.
3	3	3X-3 50'	9 (Waiting for sun)	9.30	10.40	10.50 .27 sun	Sc:72 & 74. Ext: Graveyard.Day.Shootin from side of path. 40 mm. Scottie thru wall opening from Int:Mission. PAN JIB UP to C.S. Scottie. Turns anti-cl & exits camera R.
4	1	4X-1 30'	11 (Waiting for sun)	11.5	11.15	11.16 .9	Sc:76.Ext:Graveyard.Day.L.S. Madelein stands at tombstone.Shooting from side path.
5	2	5X-2 25'	11.20	11.30	11.35	11.40 sun	Sc:76.Ext:Graveyard.Day.Closer shot of 4X. Madeleine looking at tombstone 40 mm.
6	6	6X-6 20' T.2.Fair.T.4.Look short.T.5. slow.Flicker.	11.58	12	12.3	12.5 .10	Sc:83.84.Ext:Graveyard.Day.Scottie peers round rock.PAN L to R as he goes down path - taking out pencil& pan & goes to tombstone, in L.S.40
7	1	7X-1 30' Lunch 1.230 - 1.	1	1.15	1.20	1.25 .9 Sun	Sc:78.Ext:Graveyard.Day.40 mm.L.S. Mad:comes round bend camera R looks at tombstone
8 Light o pfox t	1½ pfox	8X-1 25'	1.30 (Waiting for sun)	1.40	2.10	2.11 .5 Sun	Sc:73.Ext:Graveyard.Day.40mm.L.S. Madeleine at tombstone - turns. (second camera)
-	1	PS3X-1 1000'					SOUND TRACK ONLY of Mission Bells. Sc:60-86.
9	1	9X-1 15'	1.30 (Waiting for sun)	1.40	2.15	2.16	Ext:Graveyard.Day.50 mm. Closer on Madeleine at tombstone. Turns.
10	2	10X-2 35' T.1.Slower.	2.20	2.30	2.35 .12	2.40 2x2	Sc:75.Ext:Graveyard.Scottie's pov. Track Forward along side path.Madelein stands looks camera R at tombstone.40m
11 Better quality	1	11X-1 40'	2.43	2.50	2.55	2.56 .20	Sc:75.40 mm.Ext:Graveyard.Day.Scottie' pov.Track forward along side path. Madeleine stands at tombstone.
12	2	12X-2 35'	2.58	3.	3.10	3.15 .18	Sc:75.Ext:Graveyard.Day.Scottie's pov Track forward on Madeleine at tombsto
13 (waiting for sun)	1	13X (Only 1 take - of bad light)	3.18	3.25 take - no pr	3.40 int because	3.41	Sc:75.Ext:Graveyard.shooting toward end wall.Scottie enters, coming roun bend.Track back as he comes down path (Hand on end tombstone)

The first full day wrapped at 6:30 P.M. Robertson logged the estimated first two minutes and forty-nine seconds of screen time completed—in a testament to Hitchcock's efficiency and planning, a time that is within seconds of the duration of the finished sequence. (The final film would run 127 minutes.) Hitchcock, the actors, and the crew returned to Mission Dolores the next morning to film additional close-ups of Stewart and Novak, never logging more than five takes on any shot. At 12:30, the crew broke for lunch and moved to the Brocklebank Apartments—conveniently located across the street from the Fairmont Hotel, where cast and crew were staying while in San Francisco. Nob Hill, where the Fairmont and Brocklebank buildings are located, is virtually unchanged today. Many tourists mistake the Mark Hopkins building as the home of Madeleine Elster—an easy mistake to make, since the building is practically a twin of the Brocklebank, located on the other side of the Fairmont at 2000 Mason. In fact, the Fairmont can be seen behind Scottie in the later shots at the Brocklebank after Madeleine's suicide. Lee Patrick played the older woman that Scottie mistakes for Madeleine in one of these later scenes; years before, the actress had a memorable role in another San Francisco classic—as Effie in John Huston's *The Maltese Falcon*. The day ended after 6:00 P.M.; another two minutes and thirty-seven seconds had been added to the tally of finished script time.

A production sketch of Madeleine's bedroom at the McKittrick Hotel.

The moment that started it all: **Vertigo's** *opening rooftop scene set the film's tone of mingled suspense and anguish.*

Early sketches for Kim Novak's Madeleine and Judy hairstyles . . .

. . . and the way she looked in the film.

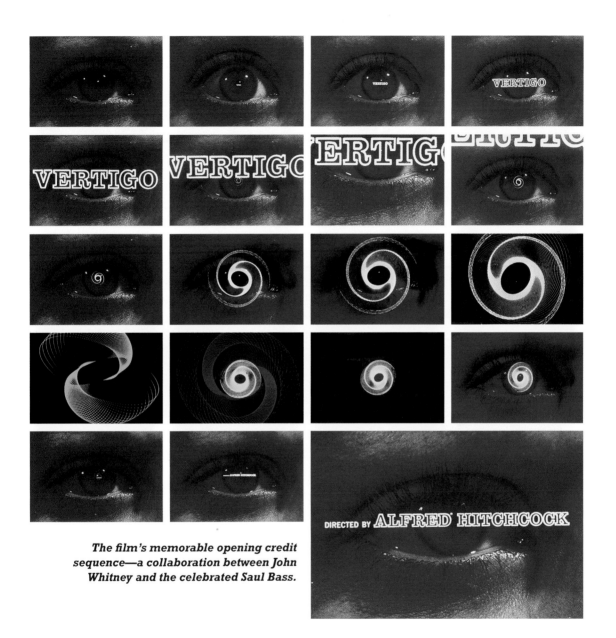

The film's memorable opening credit sequence—a collaboration between John Whitney and the celebrated Saul Bass.

*The love story at the heart of **Vertigo** was photographed by Alfred Hitchcock and his production team with such beauty and craftsmanship that many of the individual shots—here reproduced in the rich colors of the 1996 restoration—resemble carefully composed paintings.*

Kim Novak brought an ethereal quality to her portrait of Madeleine Elster, enhanced by the camera's lingering eye.

Cindy Bernard's 1990 photographic series Ask the Dust included a salute to Vertigo; its view of the Fort Point site was a remarkable echo of the original Hitchcock shot.

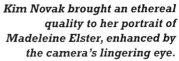

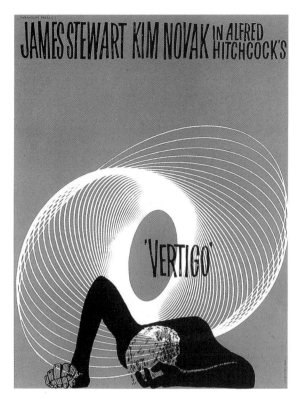

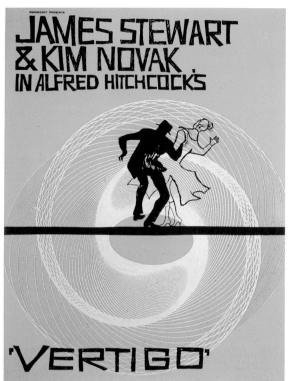

Alternative poster designs for the original release.

In 1996, Barneys New York devoted one of its famous window designs to the Vertigo look.

The best argument for restoration: a frame from an older, fading print of Vertigo, and the same scene from the 1996 Harris/Katz rerelease.

The next two days were routine. October second was spent at the now-demolished Mc-Kittrick Hotel. The only scene to require more than the few Hitchcock standard takes was the dialogue between Scottie and the hotel manager—played by Ellen Corby (who became well known as the grandmother on *The Waltons* in the 1970s)—which required five.

Part of Thursday, October third, was spent in the alley behind Podesta's (only in the film—in life, the alley was at Maiden Lane, not far away) and outside Scottie's apartment (900 Lombard Street, on the block beneath the most crooked street in the United States). Thursday also marked the first night shoot for the film—the scene where Midge drives up to Scottie's apartment and sees Madeleine leaving. The first take of the day was at 9:00 A.M. in the alley; the last at 10:45 P.M. outside the apartment—which means that most of the crew were involved from 7:00 A.M. until nearly midnight.

And the next day was not very restful. Three different locations: the exterior of Gump's, Fort Point, and Judy's hotel. The Gump's sequence was simple—the first take rolled at 10:00 A.M., and they were on their way to Fort Point by 11:30.

Herbert Coleman remembers that the scenes outside Gump's and Ranso-hoffs were shot with a hidden camera, so as not to attract onlookers. Yet in the film, both scenes appear to be shot from the sidewalk—not from inside a van, as Coleman recalls—and there is no indication in Peggy Robertson's notes that any special measures were taken.

Fort Point, the scene of Madeleine's suicide attempt, is one of the stunning locations most often associated with *Vertigo*. Located beneath the Golden Gate Bridge, it is one of the most dramatic locations in San Francisco from which to view the bridge, the bay, and the city.

On October fourth, Stewart and Novak were filmed arriving at the location. Madeleine would then drop petals from her Podesta flower arrangement

A twenty-one-frame storyboard of the famous Fort Point scene . . .

VERTIGO: The Making of a Hitchcock Classic

in the bay and then suddenly jump in. For the brief jumping shot, Novak was replaced by a double, who actually jumped onto a stretched parachute. This is the scene for which some have claimed that Novak was tormented by Hitchcock's demands for endless takes; Novak would eventually spend time in a tank on a Paramount soundstage, but

. . . along with four more detailed frames . . .

on this day the double endured only four takes—with the third and fourth printed for use in the finished film.

Fort Point was not without its complications. Unlike in the soundstage set used for the rescue scene, there are no steps to help in climbing out of the water; the double had to jump four times off the sheer edge and onto the parachute. Regardless of the weather, the waves are always high and the drop is dramatic. Jumping from the side onto anything would not have been easy.

. . . and the memorable (and nearly identical) shots from the film itself.

At 5:25, the crew packed up for a night shot of Judy entering the Empire Hotel. The Empire, located in the 900 block of Sutter, was chosen for its seediness and for its memorable green neon sign. Hitchcock wanted the green neon light to spill through Judy's window for two key scenes. The interiors would be duplicated back at Paramount, but the hotel would be used for several exterior shots of Judy arriving, and one shot of Judy opening her shades.

You can still visit what was once the Empire Hotel. Gone is its seedy, run-down quality—and, unfortunately, the large neon sign. In fact, the only indication that the building at 980 Sutter was once the Empire Hotel is the name Empire stamped in concrete above the hotel's bar, the Plush Room. Now called the York Hotel, the recently renovated building is decidedly more upscale than in the 1950s: Judy would have to shell out five to six hundred dollars a week for her room today.

Inside, though, a surprise: Though there have been substantial changes throughout the building—many of them designed to bring the building back to its pre-1950s splendor—a visitor to what is now room 501 will immediately recognize the room Hitchcock and art director Henry Bumstead re-created at Paramount. Still present is the armchair sitting in front of the bay window; the bathroom is still by the entrance, and the closet is now a built-in bureau.

Though it never appeared on film, the room is hauntingly familiar—permanent evidence of Hitchcock's amazing concern for authenticity. After all, few directors would have felt compelled to stick to the reality of the hotel room; only a handful of people in the world would know that he had made changes to the interior. But that handful mattered to Hitchcock. He told Truffaut that realism, even in the smallest details, was important to him—a sentiment borne out in a visit to the York Hotel.

It took about an hour to set up at the Empire; then, after only a few takes, another long day was wrapped at 7:45—bringing the total screen time filmed to just over twelve minutes in five days' work.

The York Hotel today.

Five days would be the end of a studio week (six-day weeks had ended earlier in the decade), but Hitchcock had begun *Vertigo* on location, which allowed weekend work to save money. And so they pressed on.

Saturday's lineup included three locations: the San Mateo cemetery for a simple shot of Scottie looking at Madeleine's grave; some additional exterior work at the Brocklebank Apartments; and an early-evening shot of Judy at the Empire Hotel. The evening shoot finished a little after six.

The early finish compensated for the 4:00 A.M. call at Union Square on Sunday. The scene in which Scottie walks the empty San Francisco streets is one of the more memorable moments in the film. The empty predawn Union Square is shot from a high angle, as Scottie crosses Stockton and walks east on Geary. The first take rolled at 5:00 A.M., and only three were required. They were ready to move to the flower shop, Podesta Baldocchi—only a few blocks away on Grant—by 5:30.

As in the case of the room at the Empire Hotel, the interior settings in a film are often reproduced in a studio, giving the filmmaker complete control over the environment. But art director Henry Bumstead honed in on a striking visual detail in the actual Podesta that he knew would add vivid verisimilitude to the scene—the shop's striking Italian tile floor—and recommended shooting the interior scene on location. (The back entrance into the flower shop was re-created later on a soundstage.)

Florists at Podesta recall having to change flowers several times because the hot studio lights were wilting them. What is amazing is how the crew managed to fit into such a small location. *Vertigo* was filmed in the 1950s VistaVision color process, and the camera and tripod for such a production are enormous, requiring a minimum of two or three people to operate them. At least three, and possibly four or five, lights would have been needed. On this Sunday, Burks and South were manning the camera; standing about would have been another half dozen or more crew members to help set up and break down the equipment; Hitchcock himself and script supervisor Peggy Robertson would have to have sat close enough to the camera to see the action—all of this in a tiny florist shop!

Room 501 as it appears today—a brighter image of its former self.

Podesta Baldocchi had occupied that space for nearly forty years—the previous tenant had been Tiffany's—but in the years since the production of

Madeleine at Podesta Baldocchi.

Vertigo, they have moved from the small shop at 224 Grant to new quarters on Fourth and Bryant. The site used for the filming has become a fashionable clothing shop, its striking tile flooring covered with wood.

October seventh and eighth were spent doing exterior work at a number of locations—Golden Gate Park, the McKittrick Hotel, Fort Point, and the Empire Hotel. The running total of completed film time was now at seventeen minutes, forty-seven seconds. The most extensive location work on these two days was done on the eighth, at the Palace of the Legion of Honor in Lincoln Park.

The scenes where Scottie observes Madeleine entranced by the portrait of Carlotta Valdes were filmed in the Palace's Gallery 6. William Eisner, a former registrar at the museum, recalls that the museum was turned "topsy-turvy" as Hitchcock waited for just the right light. "We didn't close the museum, but we were afraid people would trip on the cables. People watched the moviemaking more than the paintings," Eisner said. Bert Scully, the senior guard and later chief guard, was paid five hundred dollars for his small role: handing Jimmy Stewart the museum's catalog and identifying the painting.

The Palace of the Legion of Honor boasts an impressive site, on a hill overlooking the city and San Francisco Bay, but it was not always considered a first-rate museum by San Franciscans; recent renovations have increased its

As Scottie looks on (right), Madeleine is transfixed by the portrait of Carlotta Valdes at the Palace of the Legion of Honor.

gallery space significantly, though, giving the museum ample room to display an enormous collection, whose treasures include several Picassos. The Palace staff is often asked by tourists where the portrait of Carlotta Valdes is on display, but alas, the director's concern for authenticity did not extend this far: *Portrait of Carlotta* was painted by John Ferren especially for the film, and it may no longer exist (although an earlier version with Vera Miles's features hangs in Robert A. Harris and James C. Katz's office). But the other paintings seen in the hall, hanging behind Scottie, still hang in the Palace in Gallery 7: Nicolas de Largillière's *Portrait of a Gentleman* (1710) and Charles-André van Loo's *Allegories of the Arts: Architecture* (1752–1753).

On October ninth the crew returned to the gallery to continue, filming mostly interior work; they finished relatively early, at 3:05, anticipating the big move the next day to San Juan Bautista.

Perhaps there is no other location that is more closely linked to *Vertigo* than this sleepy town off Highway 101. Certainly the town is proud of its association with Hitchcock's masterpiece: The film is prominently mentioned in the chamber of commerce's literature, and the state park distributes a sheet offering a few general facts on the filming—the general date of the work and the fact that the tower did not exist at the mission, for example.

The *Vertigo* screenplay called for an extensive visual tour of San Juan Bautista, to emphasize the empty, abandoned atmosphere, but Hitchcock must have realized he could do it all in a few quick gestures: All the establishing footage that remains in the final version is a slow pan down on the livery as Scottie approaches Madeleine seated in the surrey. The livery is unchanged today, but the surrey and horse have been moved from the room on the right to the room on the left; the old horse, which gives Stewart one of his fleeting moments of comic relief in this haunting segment of the film, is tucked in the back, looking forgotten.

The *Vertigo* team spent two and a half days in San Juan Bautista. Many of the older members of the town remember Hitchcock's visit: In a recent interview, the current owner of the nearby Casa Rosa restaurant recounted the many visits Kim Novak has made to the restaurant over the years (and the many tourists from around the world who have eaten there after Spoto mentioned her fondness for it in his Hitchcock biography). Waitress Cheryl

Hagan remembered her parents telling her that she was held by Novak during the filming in the square. Only four or five at the time, Hagan doesn't remember Novak herself, but she does remember her parents' pride at being there when it all happened. Another local resident, Carmen Munoz, now a chamber of commerce representative, was only recently married when she visited the set one evening after dinner at her parents' house. "Of course, I wanted to see the stars—Jimmy Stewart or Kim Novak. I did see Hitchcock, but that didn't seem such a big deal at the time," Munoz remembered.

Leonard Caetano, owner of Mission Reality, had the most vivid recollections—among them a small revelation about the alterations Hitchcock's crew made to their historic site. Two of the arches on the cloisters, he recalls, had to be faked with plywood and paint. Caetano remembered the crew building the fake arches to cover square openings that had earlier been cut into the cloisters so that carriages could enter. The faked arches—the larger ones at the far ends of the cloister—restored what the crew must have seen as authenticity to the facade.

Caetano also remembers a large crane being brought in to film the body on the rooftop from the perspective of the tower. Caetano recalls the crew dropping a body dummy from a basket hanging from the crane, and camera operator Lenny South and production manager Doc Erickson recall filming a falling dummy from the crane. In the film, we do see Madeleine's fall, from two different angles: We watch from Scottie's point of view as she falls past a window at his eye level; later, during Judy's letter-writing flashback, we watch from above as she falls. (It is this latter viewpoint that is also used earlier in the film, during Scottie's nightmare sequence, when it is his body that falls, rather than hers.) But South and Erickson confirm what careful viewers will suspect. The body-dropping footage shot at the mission was never used in the film; it was fabricated later using process photography.

The first day in San Juan Bautista did not start until nearly noon, and the crew was forced to stop abruptly thereafter to wait out the sudden rain. The only material filmed that afternoon were two interior shots (without actors) of the Plaza Hotel Bar room and front parlor, and of Scottie entering the mission in pursuit of Madeleine; the shots were intended to convey the silent, deserted quality of San Juan Bautista, but they, too, failed to make it into the final cut.

Scene 207 reads:

INT. CHURCH. SAN JUAN BAUTISTA—DAY

Scottie runs in and looks around frantically. The church is empty. A moment, then he hears the sound of footsteps running up wooden steps. He turns in the direction of the sound, sees a door standing open at the side of the church, and through the door the beginning of a flight of steps. He runs to the open door and goes through.

Of that screen moment, only the shot of Scottie running into the mission and looking around frantically was filmed at San Juan Bautista; the doorway and stairs he sees were built back at Paramount and then edited in later. They finished filming these few scenes a little after 5:00 P.M.

The next day, October eleventh, was devoted to the events that take place in the courtyard between the mission and the livery—among them Scene 195, the difficult opening panorama of San Juan Bautista, which begins with the camera looking down the cloisters and then slowly pans to the right. Five takes were made on this pan, and the fifth one was printed; in the original directions, this is the lead-in to the Plaza Hotel interiors filmed the previous day, but in the finished film, the Plaza footage is eliminated, and the pan from the cloisters to the hotel dissolves into a pan down to the livery.

The next scene filmed was 199; since the two intervening scenes were omitted in the final cut, the crew essentially was shooting in sequence. This is the scene as it appeared in the script:

199. INT. LIVERY STABLE—DAY

(Madeleine's eyes are closed. Scottie, leaning against the surrey, looks up at her intently. After a moment he calls to her softly.)

SCOTTIE

Madeleine . . .?

(She opens her eyes and looks down at him.)

SCOTTIE

Where are you now?

(She smiles at him gently.)

MADELEINE
(softly)

Here with you.

SCOTTIE

And it's all real.

MADELEINE

Yes.

SCOTTIE
(firmly)

Not merely as it was a hundred years ago. As it was a year ago, or six months ago, whenever you were here to see it.

(pressing)

Madeleine, think of when you were here!

(She looks down at him with a worried, regretful smile, wishing she could help him. Then she looks away into the distance, and speaks almost irrelevantly.)

MADELEINE
(dreamily)

There were not so many carriages, then. And there were horses in the stalls; a bay, two black and grey. It was our favorite place. But we were forbidden to play here, and Sister Teresa would scold us. . . .

(Scottie looks up at her in desperation. Then looks about the stable for help. His look scans the carriages and wagons lined against the wall, goes past the old fire truck on which there is a placard proclaiming *the world's championship of 1884, and finally stops at a small buggy—a bike wagon—to which is hitched a full-size model of a handsome grey horse.)*

SCOTTIE

Well, now, here!

(He races to the horse. On it hangs a sign: "Greyhound World's Greatest Trotter.")

SCOTTIE

Here's your gray horse! Course he'd have a tough time getting in and out of a stall without being pushed, but still . . . You see? There's an answer for everything!

(He looks across to Madeleine eagerly. She is staring ahead, lost in the past.)

SCOTTIE

Madeleine! Try!

(No answer. The music is more insistent, now, a pulling wind, and the faint voices call more clearly. Madeleine slowly rises to her feet as though sensing the call. Scottie moves back to her and stands there, looking up. He raises his arms, she puts her hands on his shoulders and slips to the ground with his help, and he is holding her. Their heads are close together.)

SCOTTIE

Madeleine, try . . . for me. . . .

(With a small movement, their lips come together, and they kiss; not impulsively, as before, but with deep, sure love and hunger for each other. Their lips part, but he still holds her tightly, his head pressed down against hers, and she is looking past him, her eyes wide with anxiety. And a clock strikes the three-quarter hour.)

SCOTTIE

My love . . . because I love you . . .

MADELEINE
(whispering)

I love you, too . . . too late . . . too late.

SCOTTIE

No . . . we're together. . . .

MADELEINE

Too late . . . there's something I must do. . . .

(He holds her gently now; brushes his lips along her hair, to her eyes, down to her mouth.)

SCOTTIE
(murmuring)

Nothing you must do . . . no one possesses you . . . you're safe with me . . . my love . . .

(And they kiss again. As they part.)

MADELEINE

Too late . . .

(She looks up at him with deep regret and wonder in her eyes, then suddenly breaks from him and runs out the door. He stands still, startled for a moment, then runs after her.)

This scene, one of the most poetic and romantic in Hitchcock's canon, also offers a revealing window into the process by which a Hitchcock screenplay was turned into a film. The screenplay was written in great detail, as it should be directed—down to the camera directions and even the commentary on the music. The very specific visual detail Taylor wrote into the scene (none of which appears in the Coppel script) was ultimately revealed in a simple medium shot of the horse and carriage, rather than the long meandering pan he called for, but the careful attention to visual elements is characteristic of the best of Hitchcock's filmmaking.

"Too late": Scottie and Madeleine on the verge of tragedy.

Sc. 185A Scottie sits in car watching her.
She does not move. Transp. plus car.

1

Sc. 185B Madeleine slowly starts to walk
toward the sea. Location with double.

2

Sc. 185C Scottie opens car door and jumps out.
Transp. plus car.

3

Sc. 185D Madeleine has stopped and turned.
Scottie joins her. Location with doubles.

4

The kiss, as passionate and filled with longing as the Cypress Point kiss—part of which was filmed the next day—required the most takes of the day: six, with the last one printed.

The next morning, the crew returned to the livery stable to film the background for what Hitchcock called "the swimming shot"—the film's kiss (Scene 249), in which the room seems to spin and transform around Scottie and Judy as they kiss in her hotel room. This shot—to be used later as process photography—required six takes. The crew wrapped in San Juan Bautista early, to get to their next site, Cypress Point, on the famed 17-Mile Drive, by 12:15.

Hitchcock and his crew spent three hours filming at the austere coastal location, spending the bulk of their time capturing the drive up to the point and the footage of Scottie and Madeleine as they walk to the edge of the bluff. The run down the bluff was completed using doubles for Novak and Stewart; the love scene was finished on the transparency stage back at Paramount Studios. To make it easier to match the scene later in the studio, art director Bumstead decided to eschew the many twisted cypress trees that can still be seen today along the 17-Mile Drive, in favor of a single tree he transplanted to the location for the purpose.

The day was finished by 3:57, wrapping earlier than usual to allow time for the equipment to be transported to Big Basin Redwoods State Park. In two and a half days, Hitchcock had accomplished all of the location work at San Juan

THIS PAGE AND OPPOSITE: *A Cypress Point storyboard, with preliminary notes about the use of doubles and transparency shots.*

Bautista and the vicinity—committing the film's tragic dreamscape to film by creating a mix of realism and artifice. It was a measure of the production's values that for background footage of the long drives to the mission, the second unit filmed a picturesque passage of road braced by tall eucalyptus trees just *south* of San Juan Bautista on Highway 101; in the final film Scottie and Madeleine drive to the town as if coming from Los Angeles, not San Francisco!

Sc. 185E Madeleine and Scottie play scene at cypress tree. Transp. plus studio set. Madeleine turns and exits scene.

5

Sc. 185F Madeleine running toward the edge of the land. Scottie following. Location with doubles.

6

When cast and crew made the move from San Francisco to San Juan Bautista, the refined elegance of their Fairmont accommodations was abandoned for decidedly more humble surroundings. Hitchcock, James Stewart, Herbert Coleman, Doc Erickson, Robert Burks, and Peggy Robertson were all put up at Hitchcock's home in Los Gatos, according to Erickson; Novak stayed in nearby Watsonville with the crew.

Next on the agenda was the filming of the picture's dreamlike redwood-forest sequences. *Vertigo* aficionados have often assumed these were filmed at Muir Woods, close to San Francisco, especially since there is a reference to that location early on in the film's development; the scenes have even become known collectively as "the Muir Woods sequence." Muir Woods also features a dated redwood cross section as one of its exhibits, like the one used in the film. But the *Vertigo* sequence was filmed far away, in Big Basin Redwoods State Park.

The drive from Los Gatos or Watsonville to Big Basin is a long one: As the crow flies, Big Basin is thirty or forty miles away, but the twist-

Sc. 185G Scottie catches her and holds her. Location with doubles.

7

Sc. 185H Madeleine and Scottie play scene. The wind blows and the waves dash up against the rocks throwing up a curtain of spray. Transp.

8

ing roads turn this into a two-hour drive. Why did Hitchcock choose Big Basin over Muir Woods, which is much more convenient to San Francisco?

Leonard South recalled that when Hitchcock first visited Big Basin "he loved it. He thought it was great. We didn't care for it, though. We felt the light wasn't as good as the Muir Woods—we had to bring in brutes [large studio lights] to make it work." Herbert Coleman, on the other hand, remembers choosing Big Basin for the opposite reason: that the light was too poor in Muir Woods.

The Spaniards "discovered" the Big Basin redwood forest not long before building missions Dolores and San Juan Bautista. Located about twenty-three miles northwest of Santa Cruz, the basin isn't a true basin, but a slight depression in the Santa Cruz Mountains. The 2,500-acre area became California's first state park in 1902, after a photographer's interest in the trees began to call attention to the awesome landscape. The park now comprises more than sixteen thousand acres.

Sequoia sempervivens is the classic redwood that gives this forest its beauty, and its ancient splendor would of course have attracted Hitchcock. The stand of trees through which Novak and Stewart wander is more than a thousand years old. The Latin name and definition is prominent in all the literature connected with Big Basin; the film's explicit reference suggest the same was true even in 1957.

No one at the park has any recollection of the *Vertigo* filming; nor does any park record remain of the two-day visit. The crew's shooting days were shorter than usual—under five hours.

On October fourteenth, most of the time was spent on the conversation just prior to the redwood cross-section scene. Judging from where the Jaguar is parked and where the redwood cut is positioned, the scenes were filmed on a trail known today as the Redwood Trail. The two-and-a-half-page sequence was completed in a number of setups, the most difficult one requiring seven takes; in the final cut of the film, only a page of this material remains. Though Big Basin had (and still has today) a cross section like the one in the film, all of the dialogue surrounding the cross section itself was shot later on a soundstage, then integrated seamlessly with the location footage.

The sequence at Big Basin is, in pace and atmosphere, one of the film's most haunting. Apart from a few circumstantial details, it remains remarkably similar to the look of the final film—right down to Novak's stance as she leans against the tree.

1

2   3

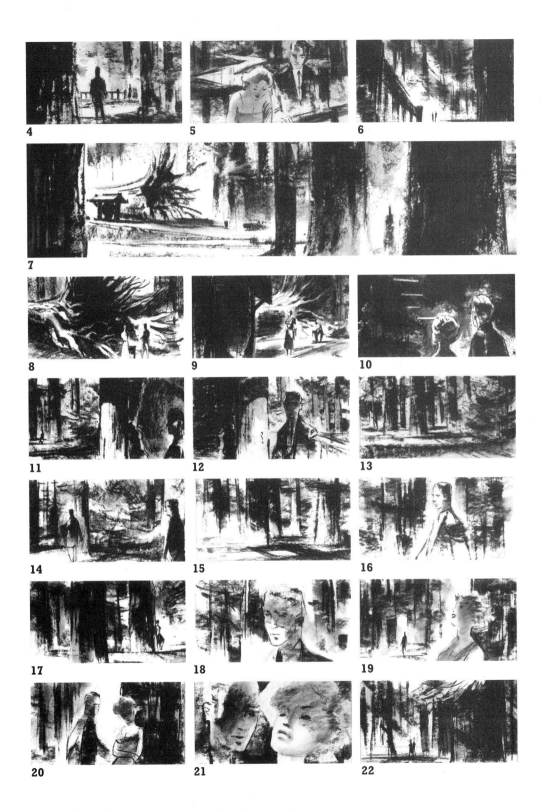

VERTIGO: The Making of a Hitchcock Classic

The cast and crew returned to Big Basin early the next day to film Novak and Stewart walking through the trees—the shots seen just before Madeleine seems to disappear behind a large redwood. The conversation itself, like almost all the other significant dialogue scenes at this location, was filmed back at Paramount.

The location shoot ended at 2:48. The entourage packed it in for Los Angeles and Paramount Studios after filming sixteen days without a break. But there would be no rest for the weary: At eight o'clock the next morning, shooting commenced on Stage 5, to film the scene set in Gavin Elster's office. Hitchcock, Stewart, and the crew faced three more days of shooting before their first weekend off.

According to Donald Spoto, Hitchcock so liked Henry Bumstead's design for Gavin Elster's office that he had the director redesign his home office in the same style. This is not strictly accurate, according to Bumstead: What Hitchcock was impressed with was his choice of paneling for the office, not the office itself, and the director asked Bumstead to purchase similar paneling for his Bel Air home, believing it would go well with some rugs he had purchased in Marrakesh during the filming of *The Man Who Knew Too Much*.

Elster's office—one of the film's many elaborately decorated interior sets—was filled conscientiously by Henry Bumstead with San Francisco memorabilia: old maps and posters, a prominent glass case holding a model of a

ship. An entirely separate section of the room, complete with raised floor and a visible ceiling, gave the shorter Tom Helmore a chance to tower over the sitting Stewart. Coleman called Elster's office the "seven-walled set."

The set featured a large bay window that overlooked the shipbuilding cranes. All of the shots that contain the view out Elster's window were shot using transparencies: The window, in other words, was a film screen upon which the scene with the cranes were projected. In the finished film, the background plate appears in only a few shots. Most of the sequence is filmed so that the window does not show, leaving the Foley track—the soundtrack of ambient sound; in this case, introducing subtle hints of shipyard noise—to remind watchers what's outside the window.

The crew began to set up on that first day a little before 9:00 A.M.; the first take rolled at 10:20, and, with an hour break for lunch, the day did not finish until 6:10 P.M.

The soundstage work reveals a slightly different Hitchcock. Now, with everything at his control, he was able to push more surely for what he wanted: Setups took longer, and on average Hitchcock called for a greater number of takes. On the first day, there were seven takes on some dialogue from Elster as he sat at his desk. Line problems, camera-movement problems, and a director willing to push a little further for perfection made for longer days. Compared with many of his colleagues, Hitchcock was almost frugal with his footage: Outside the studio, Hitchcock rarely took more than two or three takes, and even inside, he generally limited himself to seven to eleven at most.

Herbert Coleman had worked with far less efficient filmmakers. "I assisted Willy Wyler on a couple of pictures," Coleman remembered, "and the contrast between Hitch and Willy Wyler was: Willy Wyler would do forty, fifty, sixty, ninety takes. Yet he knew exactly what he liked. I think on *Roman Holiday,* if he did fifty, sixty takes, he would say to the script clerk to print so-and-so, hold so-and-so."

One difference between Hitchcock and many of his fellow directors had to do with what came later, in the editing room. Since Hitchcock was involved from the start in the conception and writing of his films, the editing was essentially in place before filming began: His scripts were designed to be shot one way, and one way only. Other directors are often required to provide "coverage"—footage of the same scene from several angles—so that a sequence can be altered if necessary in the editing room. Except when he worked for David O. Selznick, the mature Hitchcock always had the final say in the assembly of his footage: He had the power and freedom to shoot with the economy that total control provided.

The sequence in Elster's office— where Scottie's old school acquaintance offers the bait and Scottie reluctantly takes it—dominated early scripts, and it remains an important scene in the film. This scene, and the one with Midge that precedes it, are the only "normal" moments in the film—the only sequences not overly influenced by the haunting of Carlotta/Madeleine or the sense of vertigo (certain elements do foreshadow this: the tall cranes, the swiveling chair, and the yearning for a freer time). Hitchcock took great care in establishing the mood of the film. As in many of his pictures, he created the real danger not in the dark, wet streetscapes of film noir, but in carefully appointed offices and beautiful surroundings.

Two separate sketches for the brief but important second meeting between Elster and Scottie: Though the pencil-wash illustration appears more finished, the primitive pencil sketch is much closer to the composition of the final shot—and suggests how carefully Hitchcock and his crew planned even the posture of his seated actors.

• • •

Cast and crew moved to another part of the enormous Stage 5 for Elster's club after more than two days in his office. The day moved along without much incident; Tom Helmore's inability to pronounce the name McKittrick Hotel properly in the club scene cost some time, as a similar problem pronouncing Ernie's had in his office the day before.

Then, after nineteen days of shooting, Hitchcock, Stewart, and the crew finally got some time off. Kim Novak and Stewart would return Monday morning for a sequence that would bedevil the production: their long first meeting in Scottie's apartment.

Scene 151 of *Vertigo*, the couple's first encounter—in Scottie's apartment, after Madeleine leaps into the bay—is nine minutes long. It lasts from page 46 to 57 in the final script, and it was filmed as written, with only a few minor line changes. But to nearly everyone involved, from the technical crew to the young actress at its center, it would prove one of the most daunting.

The scene begins with a slow pan from Scottie, seated on the sofa by the fireplace, toward his bedroom across the apartment; in passing, we see Madeleine's clothes drying in the kitchen. The camera stops on his bedroom; through the open door, we see Madeleine sleeping, and we hear her murmuring something about "her child."

It is a terrific shot, connecting Scottie's gaze to Madeleine. It also offers a good introduction to Henry Bumstead's design work. Hitchcock never came to "approve" a set, Bumstead recalls. "There was an assumption that because you were working with Hitchcock, you would do your absolute best." According to Robertson, Hitchcock liked to meet in the evening with the technical crew on the next day's set to discuss the work for the following day. There were seldom specific requests from Hitchcock above or beyond what the script required.

In his eighties, Bumstead is still one of the top art directors in the industry (his work for Clint Eastwood is his most notable), and his philosophy has always been that location should realistically match character. He dislikes design work that gives a spectacular apartment or home to someone who could never afford to live in such a place.

"In the early days, we kept good set pieces to reuse, and I was building an apartment for this one character, so I was using three great-looking bookcases that we had in storage. When the director walked through, he didn't say anything critical—just, 'Hm, this guy must like to read.' And, in fact, he didn't. It wasn't in his character at all. That's when I began to realize that the set has to match what's happening with the character," Bumstead explained.

According to some accounts, Hitchcock had photos taken of several bachelors' apartments as research material. No such photos survive today (in fact, the only research photos that still exist were taken at San Juan Bautista and the rejected Muir Woods site), and, according to Bumstead, he really didn't check a lot of apartments. He does recall, though, talking to the Asian gentleman who lived in the apartment at 900 Lombard in an effort to convince him to change the ironwork that can be seen outside the door (although Bumstead could not remember why they wanted to change the ironwork).

But there were a few specific requests from Hitchcock. According to Bumstead, he asked that Coit Tower appear outside Scottie's large apartment window, despite the fact that the actual tower was down the street (it can be seen in the background as Scottie and Madeleine talk on his porch), and the window in question appears to face the wrong direction. Hitchcock confessed to Bumstead his purposes: "I was in Hitch's office and he asked if I knew why he wanted Coit Tower outside the apartment window. I confessed that I didn't. He smiled and said, 'Coit Tower is a phallic symbol.'"

Filming for the apartment scene began at 9:45 with the long pan, which was accomplished in four takes: one with a bra hanging on the line in the kitchen, followed by three more without a bra, to satisfy the censor. One of the braless takes was chosen for the final cut.

A later shot was more difficult. It was a short moment—the phone rings and Madeleine wakes as Scottie answers it—but it was originally envisioned as an elaborate crane shot. Nine takes were required; it was difficult to get the timing right on the crane, the phone, and Madeleine. Two of the takes were printed, but ultimately the shot was discarded in favor of a simpler version.

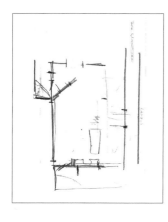

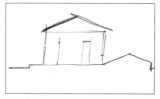

Scottie's bachelor apartment, sketched from every angle by Hitchcock himself. Coit Tower, Hitchcock's chosen phallic symbol, couldn't have been visible through the actual apartment's window, but a little careful transparency work made all the difference.

Similarly, the follow pan as Madeleine walks from the bedroom to the fireplace took six takes, with only the final two printed. Hitchcock spent time on this shot, eager that it should match in style the later shot of the remade Madeleine emerging from the Empire Hotel bathroom.

For Kim Novak, on her first day of studio work for the production, it wasn't an easy beginning. Not only did the apartment scene call for her first prolonged passages of dialogue; she had to begin the sequence lying naked in bed, and then finish it in only a robe. And, if Novak's own account is to be believed, the day began with one of the most famously harrowing on-set experiences in Hitchcock lore. When she reported to her dressing room in the morning of the first day, she has said, there was a plucked chicken hanging from her mirror; when she turned around, she found Hitchcock, Stewart, and the crew gathered at her door to see her reaction. Herbert Coleman could not confirm the story, but he wasn't inclined to deny anyone the right to add a little color to their memory of making the film.

Otherwise, her account of the shoot seems almost willfully charitable. "A lot of people said Hitchcock was difficult to work with," Novak has said, recalling those first few weeks. "But, partly because I knew nothing about technique, I loved working with him. You know, Harry Cohn didn't like the *Vertigo* script, but he said, 'It's Alfred Hitchcock—you'd better do it.' Hitchcock knew exactly what he wanted technically and helped me out with that, while allowing me to bring my own interpretation to the role." There was an immediate closeness with Stewart. "Jimmy made me feel like I belonged. He had a wonderful way of making you feel that he'd never met anybody like you before. In the weeks

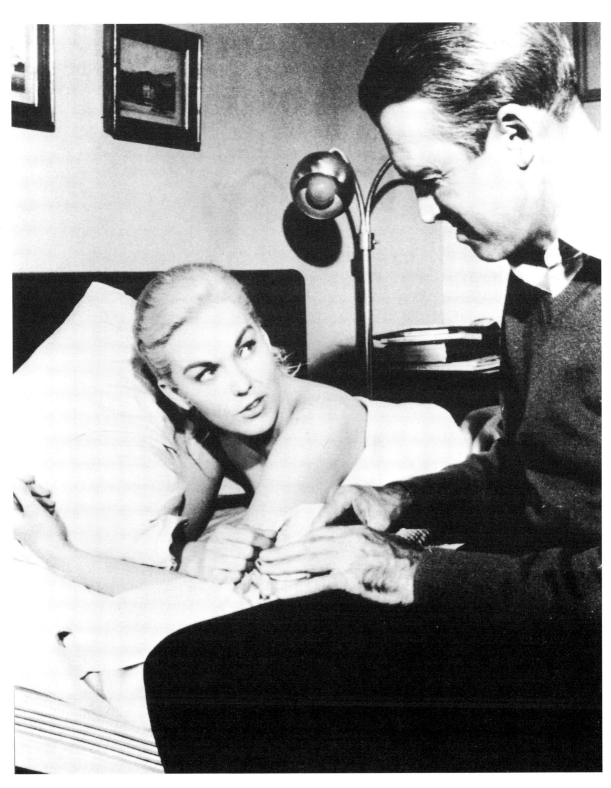

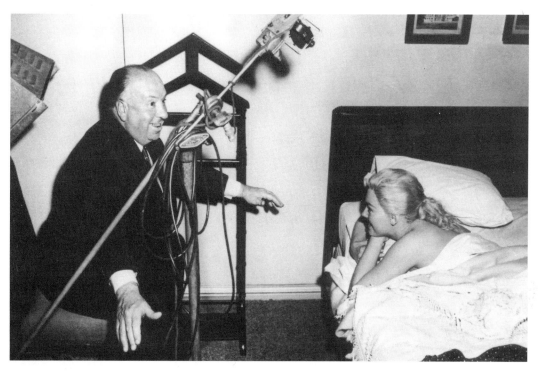

The actors may have appeared content for the cameras (and Hitchcock seemed positively ebullient), but scene 151, between Stewart and Novak in Scottie's apartment, was among the film's most difficult.

ahead, he looked after me. He was like the boy next door, my father, and the brother I wished I had. He had a natural kindness and sensitivity. And that stutter. Perhaps I identified with it because I have always had a stutter of sorts, too. I was nervous at first with Hitchcock. I kept saying to Jimmy, 'What do you think he wants me to do?' Jimmy put a gentle arm on my shoulder and said, 'There, there now, Kim. It will be fine. Now, if Hitch didn't think that you were right for the part, he wouldn't have signed you to do it in the first place. You must believe in yourself.'"

After this first week of studio work, Novak would not return until October thirtieth, when part of the bell tower sequence was filmed. Barbara Bel Geddes was on the lot during this time, filming her first scene with Stewart—Scene 16.

For all that's been written and rumored about Kim Novak's difficulty on the set, it's interesting to note that the greatest number of takes occurred on the Bel Geddes scenes. Yet Bel Geddes and Hitchcock got along extremely well.

Midge's apartment was vintage 1950s San Francisco, and a marvel of set design; in the final film it looked even more intricate and colorful.

She came prepared and had few pretenses; when she asked Hitchcock what he wanted, all he said was, "Don't act." "He and Edith Head gave me clothes that looked very well on me—little sweaters that I love, with little collars and little simple skirts, and I felt very secure. It was just the way I felt Midge should look."

The first day with Bel Geddes was long, beginning at 9:00 A.M. and ending close to 6:00 P.M. To bring the scene from Scottie's "ouch" as he reaches for the falling cane to the line "I had to quit" took eight long takes, with only the last printed. This was trumped by the eleven takes required for a later moment in the scene, again with only one take printed.

Bel Geddes returned after the weekend to continue the scene, this time averaging fewer takes; maybe she had taken Hitchcock's advice and stopped acting.

After the weekend, Henry Jones spent two problem-free days as the coroner in the inquest scene, which had caused so much trouble for the censors. No shot took more than four takes. For the inquest set—an exact replica of a room at the Bautista mission—Hitchcock made another special request: He asked Bumstead to secure the ceiling to the walls on the set. The customary film set had removable ceilings ("wild," in stage terms), which gave the crew greater flexibility in positioning cameras and lights; when Bumstead asked about the change, Hitch explained that he didn't want Burks lighting it like a studio, but like a location. This put Bumstead in a bind—he was good friends with Burks, for whom the fixed ceiling would make life more difficult—but this was Hitchcock. Bumstead still remembers the look on Burks's face when they visited the set the day before shooting, but in retrospect, he concedes that Hitchcock was right: In the film, it is difficult to tell that the inquest scene wasn't shot on location. And further to the air of authenticity the ceiling gave the room, Hitchcock must have known that he would need a visible ceiling to pull off the extreme camera angle he wanted to use to open this scene of judgment—and that a sense of enclosure could only add to our feeling for Scottie, as Madeleine's death itself hangs over his head.

The first of the bell tower scenes filmed was the murder sequence from Judy's flashback, in which Elster throws his wife from the tower as Judy runs

The final moments between Gavin Elster and Scottie at the inquest reappear later in the film, during Scottie's nightmare—this time with the figure of Carlotta Valdes (played by Joanne Genthon) interpolated into the scene.

Henry Jones, in his memorable turn as the judgmental coroner.

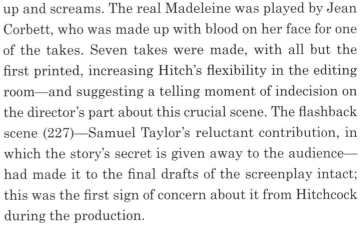

up and screams. The real Madeleine was played by Jean Corbett, who was made up with blood on her face for one of the takes. Seven takes were made, with all but the first printed, increasing Hitch's flexibility in the editing room—and suggesting a telling moment of indecision on the director's part about this crucial scene. The flashback scene (227)—Samuel Taylor's reluctant contribution, in which the story's secret is given away to the audience— had made it to the final drafts of the screenplay intact; this was the first sign of concern about it from Hitchcock during the production.

When the troublesome bell tower footage was safely in the can, the crew moved to Stage 16 to shoot Scottie and Madeleine's morning-after meeting outside

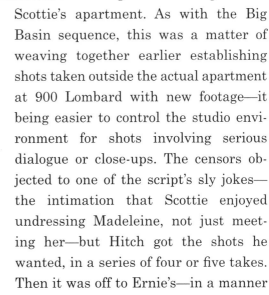

Scottie's apartment. As with the Big Basin sequence, this was a matter of weaving together earlier establishing shots taken outside the actual apartment at 900 Lombard with new footage—it being easier to control the studio environment for shots involving serious dialogue or close-ups. The censors objected to one of the script's sly jokes— the intimation that Scottie enjoyed undressing Madeleine, not just meeting her—but Hitch got the shots he wanted, in a series of four or five takes. Then it was off to Ernie's—in a manner of speaking.

Doc Erickson recalled that it was on impulse that Hitchcock decided to build the famous San Francisco restaurant Ernie's on the soundstage. After dining

The film's brief murder scene—shown only during Judy's flashback—in its original storyboard version.

in a number of restaurants in San Francisco while scouting locations, the director announced at the end of a meal that they would build their own Ernie's at Paramount. Even the exteriors of Ernie's were filmed in the studio, Bumstead remembers.

According to Peggy Robertson, owner Rolando Gotti and maître d' Carlo Dotto made quite a fortune off the traffic from people who associated *Vertigo* with Ernie's Restaurant. Ernie's is now gone, but as anyone who visited the San Francisco landmark before its demise would confirm, Henry Bumstead captured its essence on Stage 5 at Paramount. The duplication is astonishing, a testament to Bumstead's ability to replicate a location on demand. Of course, the pressure was on: Not only was the forty-by-sixty-foot set designed to Hitchcock's high standard (and he never missed a detail: Robertson recalled that during the Fairmont ballroom scene, the director glanced at an ashtray and said, "Oh, this won't do. We must have ashtrays from the hotel"), but Bumstead also had the owners of Ernie's to impress: To add that last gesture of realism, they were brought in to appear in the scene, as well. (They can be seen briefly in both the Madeleine and Judy scenes as the maître d' and bartender.)

The first day on the Ernie's set was October thirty-first. A great portion of the day's time was spent on setting up, rehearsing, and filming the challenging crane shot from the film's first Ernie's scene. The shot required eight takes, and nearly three hours to prepare and shoot. Later in the afternoon, it took far less time to film the close-up of Kim Novak and Stewart's point of view—six takes, printing the second and the last two—although this shot would be weighed in the balance, much later on, and found wanting.

The set was authentic down to the food, which was prepared by Ernie's itself. The menu that was set before the extras consisted of salad with Roquefort dressing, New York steaks, baked potatoes, vegetables, banana fritters, and zabaglione. Neil Rau's account of the filming in the *Los Angeles Examiner* gives a sense of what the mock "evening at Ernie's" was like:

> A half hour later, after Hitchcock has indulged his craving for realism by trying take after take, it is beginning to be noticeable that the extras have had their fill. They're having to act, now, to make it appear they are enjoying their food.
>
> Hitchcock either has sensed this or he has obtained what he considered just the exact footage he needs. He looks at his wrist watch and beckons me over to the camera.
>
> "Watch what happens now," he whispers. And there is an audible groan from the roomful of extras when Hitchcock, his eyes twinkling, calls out in a serious voice:
>
> "That was a good morning's work, folks. Now you can have an hour for lunch!"

Cast and crew returned to the Paramount soundstage on November first to film the Judy scenes in Ernie's. They had few difficulties, and when they were finished, they spent the remainder of the day on a number of retakes for scenes they had already worked on: Elster's club, the notorious Scene 151 (Scottie's apartment), and the brief scene outside the apartment.

The next day, it was back to Scottie's apartment for another difficult passage: Scene 189, in which Madeleine returns to Scottie's apartment early in the morning, tormented by the dream of the church in San Juan Bautista. The going was not easy: Seven takes were required on the first setup and eleven on the next, which began with Scottie's line "It was a dream, you're awake, you're all right now." This scene, which lasts about two minutes, took twenty-five minutes to film.

But now there was evidence of trouble: They returned the next day to try again on Scene 151. But even on this round, Hitchcock remained unsatisfied: Looking at the rushes the next evening, he resolved to return to Scene 151 yet again, despite the delay and expense.

The bad luck continued. After shooting a brief scene on the Fairmont ballroom set, the crew returned to the set for Midge's apartment to shoot the quick scene just before she and Scottie leave for the Argosy Book Shop. The camera setup was a simple track forward and pan—as Scottie begins to fix a drink, Midge charges out the door to Pop Liebel's—but nothing seemed to work. Eleven takes clicked by and not a single take was printed.

They returned to continue the battle, retaking not only this scene but also the first scene with Midge. Then they moved on to the portrait scene in Midge's apartment, but after numerous takes, once again nothing was printed. The frustration level must have been high, with the pressure weighing especially hard on Bel Geddes, whose scenes seemed to be the hardest to get right.

Once more into the breach the next day: Stewart did seven takes on the line "It's not funny, Midge" (the last printed), Bel Geddes six of "Stupid, stupid, stupid." With so many takes, are we to draw the conclusion that there was a problem with Bel Geddes? There's no strong evidence either way. Peggy Robertson remembers Hitchcock liking the actress, but she does recall them having to do the scene over and over again. We do know that Hitchcock liked her enough to cast her again several months later for his television series, in the episode "Lamb to the Slaughter."

Barbara Bel Geddes; at left is the "revolutionary uplift" brassiere that gives Scottie so much amusement.

What is clear is that both performers were having bad days with difficult scenes. The proof is in the film. Only a cynic could walk away from a screening without a great deal of sympathy for Midge as Bel Geddes portrays her.

The next couple of days were spent on the effects stage, with Farciot Edouart and Wallace Kelley shooting the Argosy Book Shop scene and the car interiors with Midge. It's no secret that Hitchcock used transparency (or rear-screen projection) work for such scenes. The director described rear-projection in his interview with Peter Bogdanovich:

> For rear-projection shooting there is a screen and behind it is an enormous projector throwing an image on the screen. On the studio floor is a narrow white line right in line with the projector lens and the lens of the camera must be right on that white line. The camera is not photographing the screen, and what's on it; it is photographing light in certain colors; therefore the camera lens must be level and in line with the projector lens.

Though somehow car work is always obvious, the projection shots in *Vertigo* are of the highest quality—and a slight difference in quality can make all the difference in preserving the audience's suspension of disbelief (as some of Hitchcock's more awkward efforts of the 1960s would prove). To incorporate rear-screen footage successfully into a shot, the director of photography and the effects specialist must work together to match the lighting of what was shot by the second unit and what's being shot by the director on the effects stage. There is no better work in any film than what Burks and Edouart achieved in the Argosy Book Shop scene.

One of the persistent questions about the film has to do with this scene, in which the interior and exterior of the shop darken as Pop Liebel tells his story. It was a technical challenge for Hitchcock and crew to get the studio set to darken in perfect timing with the complicated transparency work. The gradual darkening is at first imperceptible. Within moments, though, the ambient lighting has dimmed severely enough that the actors are no longer clearly visible. Nice film work, but the real magic occurs when Scottie and Midge step outside: The effects specialists exceeded themselves, projecting the transparency footage so that it was reflected behind the actors on the exterior glass of the Argosy Book Shop; in the background, Pop Liebel turns on the interior lights. It's impossible to tell that the scene wasn't shot on location.

Robert Burks was a specialist at this kind of work, according to Bumstead. Burks and Leonard South had begun their careers together in the Warner Bros. special effects department, and their expertise in using lighting renders all these tricks invisible.

Hitchcock's preoccupation with the red, gold, and green color palette while making *Vertigo* made for a number of memorable scenes, but not every attempt was successful. During the simple process shots in the Scottie-Midge car scene that immediately follows the Argosy sequence, Hitchcock experimented with a green filter on the projector used for the transparency. They shot twenty minutes of film—ten takes, in the last three of which, the green filter was used. The choice of the filter was later abandoned for that shot, but Hitchcock tried it again on the following over-the-shoulder shot when Scottie, sitting alone, looks at *Portrait of Carlotta* in the museum catalog. The first take was shot with the green filter, the second without—and it is the second that was circled as Hitchcock's choice.

Later that afternoon, using a stand-in for Kim Novak, the crew shot test footage of the green-light effect in Judy's bedroom—the effect inspired by the original Empire Hotel's neon sign. They did nine takes, with the light varied slightly each time to create the striking green silhouette effects that became a highlight of the Judy-Scottie scenes.

After the effects-stage work, the production moved to what was expected to be Bel Geddes's last day of work: the brief, poignant scene in the sanitarium. The exteriors had been filmed in February and March 1957 at St. Joseph's Hospital at Park Hill (which has now been converted into luxury apartments).

Midge with Scottie at the sanitarium.

The day did not start well. The actor cast as the doctor was unprepared. The first shot in the doctor's office was set up at 9:59 A.M., but by 10:15 Hitchcock had shut down work and called for a replacement.

"Hitchcock would do this sometimes, which could be very embarrassing. But he knew what he wanted. I remember that we filmed quite a bit with a major character in *Family Plot* when Hitch decided he wasn't working—so we had to go back and do it all over again," Bumstead recalls.

While they waited for a new doctor, the crew moved to Midge's apartment on Stage 11 and retook part of Scene 136, the "Stupid, stupid, stupid" scene. They shot a new close-up of Midge saying, "What have you been doing?" while waiting for Jimmy Stewart to come in to shoot a scene that wouldn't make it to the finished film: the brief, wordless tag ending that found Scottie returned to Midge's company at the conclusion. The setup for this shot was extensive—the crew began close to noon and finished a little after three. Robertson describes the scene in her notes:

> Sc:276. Int: Midge's Apartment. 50mm [lens size]. Variable diffusion [referring to filters used in takes]. Midge listening to giant radio [recording] CRANE FORWARD & JIB DOWN as Scottie enters & goes to window. She gives him drink and sits. Tag end.

The shot required nine takes; Hitchcock printed the fifth and ninth, and they were off again by 4:00 P.M., moving back to Stage 6 to shoot the doctor's scene. Raymond Bailey (who'd later become well known as the banker on TV's *The Beverly Hillbillies*) was at least some improvement over the previous actor, though the short scene that marked Midge's farewell seemed doomed to lifelessness. The first shot was recorded at 5:25, the last shot at 6:15.

Weekend screenings revealed problems with some of the exterior Argosy Book Shop scenes, so Bel Geddes returned for an additional morning's work on Monday; by lunch, the actress was finished and free to return to New York.

After lunch, the entire afternoon was spent on the kiss in the livery stable—Scene 199. There were five basic setups required for this scene, ranging from standard two-shots to big-head close-ups of the kiss. Six takes were made of the big-head close-up—one set favoring Madeleine, another three takes favoring Scottie.

Back in the corporate offices, meanwhile, the battle over the title was coming to a head. On October twenty-second, Hitchcock and Coleman had been cabled from the New York office: "No execs like *Vertigo* and believe it handicap to selling and advertising picture whether potential customers know what word *Vertigo* means or not—believe decidedly better title would be "Face in the Shadow."

Hitchcock remained adamant: *Vertigo* was his preferred title. (It's hard to blame him; among all the memorable images in the film, faces hidden in shadow weren't exactly paramount.) Another cable was sent on October twenty-fourth: "I understand that you are still seriously interested in the title *Vertigo* for your current production and that you have also indicated that you are thinking of other possible titles. We are checking for you the title *Fear and Trembling*. Please reconsider list." The cable was signed by Paramount's Sam Frey, who included a new, longer list of possibilities:

Afraid to Love	**The Mask Illusion**
Alone in the Dark	**My Madeleine**
The Apparition	**Never Leave Me**
Behind the Mask	**Night Shade**
Carlotta	**Nothing Is Forever**
Checkmate	**Now and Forever**
Conscience	**Past, Present and Future**
Cry from the Rooftop	**The Phantom**
The Dark Tower	**The Second Chance**
Deceit	**The Shadow**
Deceitful	**Shadow and Substance**
Deception	**Shadow on the Stairs**
Don't Leave Me	**Shock**
Dream Without Ending	**Steps on the Stairs**
The Face Variations	**Terror**
Footsteps	**To Live Again**
For the Last Time	**Tonight Is Ours**
The Hidden Life	**Too Late My Love**
In the Shadows	**Two Kinds of Women**
The Investigator	**The Unknown**
A Life Is Forever	**Wanted**
The Lure	**Without a Trace**
Malice	**The Witness**
The Mask and the Face	

Hitchcock had no intention of changing his title, and the list was ignored. By the end of the month, there were signs of fatigue on the executives' part: "Have serious doubts—but will go along if insist—just make your name same size as title." The same day, the lawyers began a title search to make sure *Vertigo* was clear. The title was declared available on November seventh, Production 10344 became *Vertigo* on the nineteenth on all internal paperwork, and Sam Frey made it official to the world two days later.

The first day under the official title was spent on the effects stage; cast and crew shot more livery-stable footage, the dialogue at the mission's cloisters that precedes Madeleine's suicide (murder) and the shots inside her Jaguar as she and Scottie drive to San Juan Bautista. The work proceeded with few problems—the highest take count was five.

The next few days, on the Ransohoffs department-store set, were a different story. The work was slow, some setups requiring seven or nine takes. One complicated setup began with a close-up of Scottie.

> Big Head Scottie seated from (off screen) "I think I know the suit you mean" down to (off screen) "I won't do it." CRANE ROUND & FORWARD as Scottie rises and joins Judy at mirror for dialogue: from "It can't make that much difference" to "You've got to do this." Reflections in mirror—backs to camera.

This is the shot that is in the film, but what looks relatively simple on screen was indeed complicated to mount. Most of the takes were spoiled by crane problems or focus problems. One take was blown because one of the crew's makeup kits could be seen in a mirror. Only the first and last takes (one and nine) were printed.

The day ended in Judy's room at the Empire—a simple shot over Judy's shoulder as she opens the door and sees Scottie for the first time, accomplished in a single setup and single take. The next few days would focus on the scenes in Judy's room, Friday and Monday on this first scene (227) between Judy and Scottie.

The most interesting work came during the scene that would cause so many problems after the film was completed: the moment when Judy writes

Judy's letter-writing scene—which gives away the film's secret two-thirds of the way through the film—was hotly debated until the very last minute.

the letter to Scottie, then tears it up as she decides to pursue him instead. This was a bravura performance for all involved, from the actress herself to the camera and lighting crews who captured it. Two distinct choices were filmed. The first began with a close-up of Judy's left hand as she begins to write, then craned back and around. The camera then panned up to a close-up on her face and tracked back as she rises, following her as she crosses to the closet.

The second version began with a close-up of her face, not her hand, then followed the action of the previous take. Each option took four takes, but the entire setup, with its elaborate crane movements, required more than two hours. Only one take was printed on the second option, but this was what Hitchcock chose for the film—though he did insert a moment of Judy's hand as she writes before beginning the crane shot around the desk.

The production team had accomplished all of the first scenes in Judy's hotel room—as well as the brief scene in Scottie's apartment where he convinces her to change her hair—by the end of November. Beyond dozens of brief connection shots, there remained the scene that included Judy's reemergence as

Madeleine (the green-fog shot for which the crew had been preparing) and the 360-degree kiss (known to the crew as "the roundy-roundy shot." All of their work that Friday, November 29, was devoted to the sequence that includes her entrance: The morning was spent on the shots of Scottie waiting, then watching as Judy approaches, her hair now the right color but not yet the right style.

After a lunch break, the crew took care of the business that gets Judy into the bathroom to fix her hair, in six takes—one lost to a line fluff—take four (the director's favorite, Robertson noted dutifully) and six were printed.

The next moment—the instant of Judy's transformation into Madeleine's image, and Scottie's vision—is one of the film's most stunning. Yet a careful reading of the shooting script reveals a major difference from the finished film. Here are the script's instructions for the scene:

246. SCOTTIE

Judy—please—

(Judy doesn't answer for a moment, then she draws a deep breath, and turns resignedly away. She crosses to the mirror over a chest of drawers. Scottie watches as she picks up a couple of pins from a glass tray, and scoops up a handful of hair.)

(Scottie stands watching in silence. His eyes follow every move. We hear the tinkle of pins on the glass tray.)

247. FROM SCOTTIE'S VIEWPOINT

(Judy slowly turns from the mirror to face him. She looks exactly like Madeleine—her hair pulled back and done in a bun at the back of her neck. She stands there looking at him.)

(Scottie looks at her in wonder, his eyes shining.)

(Judy takes a step towards him, rewarded by his expression.)

(Scottie moves over and takes Judy in his arms.)

In the original, then, the change took place in Scottie's presence, and ours: "His eyes follow every move" as she pins her hair back, completing the illusion. For the final film, though, Hitchcock changed strategies, conceiving of the scene so that the final transformation happens off-screen—heightening the mystery of the change, and giving the director the opportunity to realize her reemergence in a single breathtaking shot. Here is the new version as described in Peggy Robertson's notes:

> Sc:247. Int: Judy's Bedroom. 50mm Shooting from the center. Scottie stands at window back to camera: turns. Turns back to window—hands on jamb. Hears door click and turns back. TRACK FORWARD to CU as he recognizes her.

The longing and expectation on Stewart's face are painfully visible and real. The moment was accomplished in a single take. A second setup was done with just a close-up in the same moment—the second was necessary only because the first went too quickly. After filming Scottie, they got on film three takes of what they had longed to see—the emerging Madeleine "bathed in green." All three takes—two with the full green effect, one with less green as an alternate—were printed. (Later, in December, they would return to try the shot with the green haze again.) With remarkable ease, some of cinema's finest moments were accomplished that late afternoon, and filming concluded for the day.

Scottie's morbid pleas are answered as, cloaked in an ethereal green haze, Judy pins up her hair and becomes Madeleine.

Novak remembers that important day's work: "It was so real to me, the coming out and wanting approval in that scene. It was like, is this what you want? Is this what you want from me? My whole body was trembling. I mean I had chills inside and goosebumps all over just because it was the ultimate defining moment of anybody when they're going to someone they love and they just want to be perfect for them. And that's what I think makes it contemporary. It's about that thing that goes wrong in love, when you're attracted to someone and then suddenly you need to change them."

The next two days, alas, took the crew back in time as they endeavored to reshoot the dreaded Scene 151 of Madeleine and Scottie in his apartment after her suicide attempt. Nearly a week had already been spent on this sequence; by this point, the production was nineteen days behind schedule (only four of which were due to bad weather) and nearly a quarter of a million dollars overbudget. Almost all of the delay can be ascribed to this one stubborn scene. But now, out of desperation or familiarity, or a little of both, they got it right: In these two days, the scene was at long last finished.

Scene 151 was finally completed in November, after countless retakes and almost a week's worth of shooting.

The production still faced the final tower sequence, the special-effects work for the vertigo shots, and all of the process work for the opening rooftop sequence. Next on the agenda, though, was the ultimate kiss: Scottie and Judy (now become Madeleine) in the room at the Empire Hotel.

This kiss—the "roundy-roundy" shot—was one of the film's daring gestures, a bold way to suggest Scottie's psychological maelstrom without resorting to expositional dialogue: As the couple kiss, the camera begins revolving around them—and the background that surrounds them transforms as surely as Judy had, becoming for just a moment the livery stable where Scottie and Madeleine had shared their last moments together. Among film students, this

is one of the film's most widely discussed shots, but differing accounts of how the trick was accomplished have led to widespread misunderstanding.

Over the years, some of the crew members have seemed to recall that a special circular set combining the hotel and livery scenes was built and filmed as a process-shot background—which has led some to believe that the entire shot was filmed on such a combination set. But Bumstead (who would have had to design any such thing) remembers that the entire scene was done using process footage put together from the two locations—the livery stable and the studios set for the Empire Hotel room.

"As I remember, it was all process. We had them on a turntable. The rest was on a transparency," Bumstead recalls. "The turntable can make you dizzy, though." The footage film in San Juan Bautista faded into a slow pan of Judy's hotel room to make the final process shot that was projected behind Stewart and Novak; the background resolved into a solid neon green as the shot ended. The impression thus created was that the camera was moving full circle around the lovers, when in reality it was the rear-projection image and the actors who were turning. The camera's movement is limited to a gentle track backward, then forward once again.

The celebrated revolving kiss—contrary to popular belief, it was achieved using specially shot transparencies, not a full stable set.

The tricky portion for Novak and Stewart was the final moment of the shot, where they were supposed to slide down and out of the shot. Since the camera was not actually circling, the actors were forced to lean farther and farther forward during this embrace, making it appear that they are going to lie down together. (This implication had been present since the very first story outlines, when Coppel had merely written "He lays her.") This sort of uncomfortable movement during a kiss was a popular technique for Hitchcock. He had used a similar awkward movement with Cary Grant and Ingrid Bergman in *Notorious,* and he did again in his next film, *North by Northwest,* with Grant and Eva Marie Saint.

The kiss was filmed on December sixteenth, three days before the picture wrapped. On the first take, Hitchcock called "Cut" in the first moments: The timing of the turntable was off, throwing their positioning out of whack. The second take went quite well until the final moment: As Stewart leaned into Novak, he slipped and fell, hurting himself seriously enough to require an hour's break while Stewart visited the studio doctor.

VERTIGO: The Making of a Hitchcock Classic

But there was no serious damage, and Stewart returned to shoot three more takes. The fourth and fifth were printed, and it is the fifth take that appears in the film; but the couple never quite got that final descent right, and in the end, the scene fades out with their two faces still filling the scene.

The day took an emotional toll on the actors. "Jimmy was deeply involved—more than anything else I've known he's done," Novak remembered.

"He'd go deep inside himself to prepare for an emotional scene. He was not the kind of actor who, when the director said, 'Cut!,' would be able to say, 'OK,' and walk away. I was the same way. He'd squeeze my hand and we'd allow each other to come down slowly, like in a parachute. He had this sensitivity I'll never forget."

The final days on the *Vertigo* set were full of activity: retakes in Scottie's apartment; the Elizabeth Arden inserts (where Judy gets her hair dyed); the steps of the bell tower; more interior Jaguar work; and the infamous water-tank shoot—all were dispatched in record time.

Some of the legend surrounding *Vertigo* has it that Hitchcock shot take after grueling take of Kim Novak jumping into the Paramount tank, but this is a myth, not truth. As mentioned earlier, a double had done the jump into the real bay some months earlier; Novak was obliged only to float in the tank, waiting for Stewart to save her, for four takes (approximately forty minutes). The first take was ruined because Stewart's hair looked wrong; in the next, he paused too long on the dive; the third didn't match the previously shot footage of Scottie lifting her out. And in the fourth take, only camera A ran (there were two cameras covering this shot—one shooting from the top of the dock, looking at Madeleine floating in the water, while the second covered Scottie diving into the water). Between the two cameras, the four takes were sufficient to cut together the scene, and Novak returned safely to dry land.

The last days of principal photography focused on the film's opening, and the signature shot of every Hitchcock film—his brief cameo appearance.

Jimmy Stewart spent December eighteenth hanging around—quite literally, on Stage 5, as they filmed the rooftop chase that brought about Scottie's crippling vertigo. Most of the long-shot work was handled by a double, but Stewart himself appears in the shot where he slips and must grab onto the edge. All of the shots took only one take (except for the first angle on the fall, which required two because Stewart's face was hidden in the first).

The latter part of the afternoon was spent sitting in Scottie's DeSoto, doing process work for some of the following scenes. This was worlds different from slipping and hanging on to a ledge: All that was required of Stewart was to sit in a parked car with a projection screen behind and steer the car in accordance with the direction indicated by the footage. Shooting two of these sequences took only about twenty minutes of Stewart's time; after he went home,

The staircase into the bay at Fort Point—which doesn't exist—had to be fabricated by Paramount; these early pencil sketches show two views—seen from above (top) and from the water.

Hitch and crew returned to the rooftop set to film the cop's dialogue and fall, using a double for Scottie's hands.

Thursday, December nineteenth, was the last day of principal photography on *Vertigo,* but it was hardly a slow finish. This is the list of setups for the last day:

Elizabeth Arden
Judy's Apt.
McKittrick Hotel, front door
Tank
Dark Passage
Rooftops
Ext. Shipyard
Ext. Ernie's
Int. Tank
Closet
Ext. Dolores Mission (process)

Some of this footage was shot by a second-unit team, under the direction of Herbert Coleman and Danny McCauley. Most of the shots involved were brief, but they included an important shot, "Judy's Apt." (her hotel room), a retake of Scottie waiting for Judy to emerge from the bathroom with her new Madeleine look complete. It is this version (again done in only one take) that is in the final film:

Sc:247. Int.: Judy's Bedroom. 75mm Variable RETAKE PF 491 Scottie in front of green window. Facing cam.: Turns & sits on arm of chair. Looks around. Rise. TRACK FORWARD as he stands looking camera left.

Around lunchtime on the nineteenth, this important moment was filmed near the paint shop on the Paramount lot:

Sc. 21. Ext.: Shipyard. Mr. Hitchcock walks camera left to right & out passing Scottie entering. Scottie pauses to speak to Gateman who gestures & Scottie walks on & out.

Needless to say, only one take was required.

It was the end of principal photography but not the end of work for most of the crew. Additional second-unit work was to be done during postproduction, some of which would require further work from Stewart—including the all-important "vertigo shots" and the dream sequence.

But now, it was time for Christmas vacation. Within forty-eight hours of the production's last shot, the Hitchcocks and the Wassermans were on their way to a month's vacation in Jamaica.

| # POSTPRODUCTION

**Only robbers and gypsies say that one
must never return where one has been.**

—Kierkegaard

The time he spent in Jamaica gave Hitchcock occasion to evaluate what he had accomplished during the filming. He had to admit that Novak had improved during the production. Her attitude may have been difficult, and her personal life was undoubtedly a mess: Even during this short vacation, she managed to focus the nation's attention on her affair with Sammy Davis, Jr. Hitchcock couldn't have been sad to realize that soon she would be Harry Cohn's problem again, not his. Yet neither could he have failed to realize that, on-screen, Novak had the look. Moreover, as an untrained actress, she seemed able to tap dimensions that Vera Miles (who was much more skilled) could not have reached. The reality of the box office forced the director to use big-name stars, yet he could accomplish so much with the unseasoned. He was Grace Kelly's

teacher. Unwilling as she was, he had also brought something real out of Kim Novak. Who would be next?

Bel Geddes intrigued him. She was smart and interesting. He'd cast her for an episode of his television show, and he must have considered how else to use her. But he could sense the same independent streak that had tarnished his grooming of Miles. Bel Geddes had no interest in being groomed by anyone.

Novak, for her part, was too unpredictable—and she was under contract to Cohn, who would never relinquish her completely for any reasonable price. No, the future Hitchcock blonde was still waiting to be discovered: someone new, who wanted a teacher and mentor, who came with no difficult baggage. He would keep waiting.

Back in New York, Hitchcock watched the first rough cut of *Vertigo* with Lew Wasserman, Herbert Coleman, editor George Tomasini, and Peggy Robertson soon after he returned from Jamaica in early January.

Robertson remembered that there were few problems of any importance. But there was work to do: Hitchcock was very unhappy, for instance, with Madeleine's run across the yard in San Juan Bautista. "I had talked to Hitch and he asked me to tell George to cut part of the run even though it wouldn't quite match. I remember when I [ran] into George, he took one look at me and with his deep, charming laugh, he said, 'He doesn't like Madeleine's run.' George knew Hitch well enough that I didn't have to tell him."

Tomasini was well loved by Hitch and the crew. A large, friendly man, he was nothing like what one might expect an editor to be. He was an outdoorsman with a deep, booming voice—the opposite of the quiet, sedentary Hitchcock—yet editor and director got along extremely well. After seeing his work on *Rear Window,* Hitchcock refused to let anyone but Tomasini touch his films (with the exception of *The Trouble with Harry,* which was already in production), and the two worked closely together for a decade. (During these years, Tomasini was also the editor on John Huston's *The Misfits* and J. Lee Thompson's *Cape Fear,* and he was nominated for an Academy Award for his work on *North by Northwest.*) Tomasini's death after *Marnie* would be a tough blow for Hitchcock personally and creatively.

An uneasy alliance: Novak and Hitchcock.

During that first screening, Hitch made extensive notes on the editing of the film and the dubbing. As of January 6, 1958, Bernard Herrmann was on contract and at work on the film's score—Hitchcock had been discussing the film with him for some time beforehand—but the focus in mid-January was still on the shape and sound of the film itself.

As we've seen, Hitchcock's films were generally shot to an existing cutting plan; this enabled Tomasini to start building this first rough draft during the filming, and he finished assembling it in the few weeks after the production wrapped. Many films spend months in this phase of postproduction, but *Vertigo* took little work before it was ready to score (that is, close enough to final form that music could be written to fit the timing of each sequence).

Thirty-five-millimeter prints, reduced from the VistaVision originals for editing purposes, were separated into ten-minute reels (or approximately one thousand feet); notes that Hitchcock made at the time used individual reel numbers (1, 2, etc.) for reference. With the exception of *Rear Window* and *Psycho,* the Paramount films were shot in VistaVision, Paramount's proprietary widescreen process, and released nationwide in either anamorphic or standard 35mm prints (see Appendix B for a full description of VistaVision).

Most of the first batch of notes concern Hitchcock's ideas for lengthening or shortening specific shots, and they highlight some of the director's larger concerns on his first viewing. Not unusually, after seeing this first cut, Hitchcock was primarily concerned with tightening the film. In the second reel, he tightened the long dialogue scene between Elster and Scottie. He asked Tomasini to keep the pace when the film gets to Ernie's: "Start on Ernie's straightway—i.e. rhythm outside and inside without a stop." Further time was saved when Scottie follows Madeleine in his DeSoto: "Lose all downhill shots. Straight on Grand Ave. Try without a dissolve. . . . Drop whole of California Street. As Madeleine turns to go down California Street dissolve to car turning into street with railing—left turn—right turn—Grand—pick up at Stockton— thus losing all hill shots. Ignore geography—consider length only regardless of turns." This sequence would still take considerable time in the final film; it must have been long indeed in the rough cut.

The notes also touch on more serious problems. For example, Hitchcock had specific, lengthy instructions for the flower-shop scene: "Podesta's Flower Shop sequence. Put in establishing shot of flower shop. He opens door slowly in his CU [Scottie's close-up shot]. As light appears on his face we then reveal the shop. The screen is black: we see it unfold and then establish flower shop. When completely revealed—then go to mirror shot which is secondary and should be used only as an occasional snip—used when he backs away as she comes forward. We must see her buy the posy. Do we have enough footage on Scottie so we could eliminate the mirror? Anyway, only use it when Madeleine comes forward and turns."

Later, in reel 6, Hitchcock returns to tightening. The car scenes are too long: "Get the cuts shorter and shorter on car ride. Build it up so it gets more comic. Snap-snap. Increased tempo. Need rhythm. Pick up shot later of Jaguar down street and turning. In the straight her shots are dull."

In the very next reel, however, when Scottie and Madeleine visit Big Basin, Hitchcock takes the opposite tack. "Lengthen opening shot into Woods," he wrote. "The dissolve to Woods must be very slow. . . . Delay when Scottie comes up to Madeleine leaning against tree. . . . Lengthen fade out—Scottie and Madeleine walking into sun." Lingering on scenes like this helped the director achieve just the dreamlike aspect he wanted for Scottie and Madeleine's forest encounter.

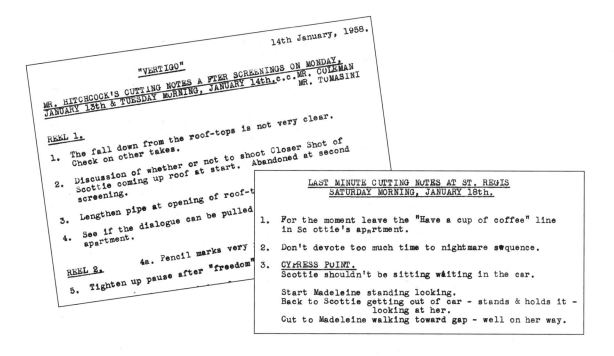

14th January, 1958.

"VERTIGO"

MR. HITCHCOCK'S CUTTING NOTES AFTER SCREENINGS ON MONDAY, JANUARY 13th & TUESDAY MORNING, JANUARY 14th.c.c.MR. COLEMAN
MR. TUMASINI

REEL 1.

1. The fall down from the roof-tops is not very clear. Check on other takes.

2. Discussion of whether or not to shoot Closer Shot of Scottie coming up roof at start. Abandoned at second screening.

3. Lengthen pipe at opening of roof-t

4. See if the dialogue can be pulled apartment.

4a. Pencil marks very

REEL 2.

5. Tighten up pause after "freedom"

LAST MINUTE CUTTING NOTES AT ST. REGIS
SATURDAY MORNING, JANUARY 18th.

1. For the moment leave the "Have a cup of coffee" line in Scottie's apartment.

2. Don't devote too much time to nightmare sequence.

3. CYPRESS POINT.
Scottie shouldn't be sitting waiting in the car.

Start Madeleine standing looking.
Back to Scottie getting out of car - stands & holds it - looking at her.
Cut to Madeleine walking toward gap - well on her way.

At other times, though, Hitchcock was far less certain of what he wanted. In his notes concerning reel 11, for example, there are two points labeled "debate"—both having to do with the crucial question of when the audience should suspect that Judy is actually Madeleine. "Debate: Scottie waiting outside Empire hotel. Question of amount of time he spends there gives more importance to the girl—must be very careful until we see her—not to spoil the big surprise." Then, concerning the dialogue in this scene, he wrote: "Debate, 'You've got to prove you're alive these days.' His question here is so persistent it might be a tip-off." The line was cut from the final film.

Then these provocative instructions about Judy's letter-writing scene appear in the notes: "Cut the three murder scenes over Judy's CU." Hitchcock was still worrying over the effect of the crucial revelation in the scene: Did he mean to cut the flashback? Or was he just calling for a change in approach—from superimposing the scenes to dissolving into them? "I remember there being some question about this scene. I don't think we wanted it in at first," Robertson remembered.

One note was no surprise: "101. Drop Tag." Hitchcock had never seriously intended to include the film's tag ending in the final cut—it was shot only to placate the censors—and it was cut after this first viewing.

After seeing this version of the film, Hitchcock also dictated fourteen pages of dubbing notes. Much of the transcript is repetitive, but it does provide a window as to Hitchcock's intentions in several scenes—and a testament to his overall commitment to the use of sound (in addition to music) to achieve the effect he was looking for.

Hitchcock's notes for sound on the first reel read:

Over the opening scene we should hear some shouts and the metallic sound of feet climbing the rungs of a steel ladder. These sounds come while the screen is empty and before the first hand comes over to grip the railing. Naturally, these sounds will increase in volume as the three reach the top. Over all, we could have faint sounds of the city, mostly automobile horns and truck noises. Perhaps even the faint clang of a cable car bell. These faint sounds will continue, but should be dominated by the running feet of the three men across the rooftops.

Now we come to the leaping part of the chase. Naturally, of course, the sounds we now have in the picture should be eliminated entirely and fresh ones substituted. [This refers to the temporary track Tomasini had included in this first draft of the film.] In addition to the feet leaping onto the tiles, we should hear the clatter of a few broken ones as they fall into the alleyway below. It is very important that the timing of the broken tiles reaching the alleyway below should correctly indicate the depth they have fallen. They should also have an echo quality. We must also bear in mind the quality of the running feet, both on the part of pursued (whose footsteps should be heard running into the faint distance) and the policeman and the detective (whose feet will be heard approaching), because all of these are off-screen sounds but very important for the continuity.

When the policeman falls, we should consider a long cry which dies away as he falls to his death. After he has reached the ground we should hear faint sounds of alarm and the patter of running feet to his rescue.

In Midge's Apartment: There should be first the overall faint sounds of the city again; perhaps not exactly the same as the rooftop sounds. Here, for example, we could eliminate the cable-car sounds.

"VERTIGO"   1/15/58

Reel #1

Over the opening scene we should hear some shouts and the metallic sound of feet climbing the rungs of a steel ladder. These sounds come while the screen is empty and before the first hand comes over to grip the railing. Naturally, these sounds will increase in volume as the three reach the _all, we could have faint sounds of the city, mostly _ noises. Perhaps even the faint clang _ill continue, but across

"VERTIGO"   1/15/58

Reel #1 - (Continued)

of running feet to his rescue.

In Midge's Apartment: There should be first the overall faint sounds of the city again; perhaps not exactly the same as the rooftop sounds. Here, for example, we could eliminate the cable-car sounds.

The music to be played on the phonograph in this sequence should be discussed with Mr. Herrman.

It might be a good idea toward the end of this sequence, that is, when Scottie is climbing up the kitchen steps, to

The music to be played on the phonograph in this sequence should be discussed with Mr. Herrman[*sic*].

It might be a good idea toward the end of this sequence, that is, when Scottie is climbing up the kitchen steps, to increase the traffic sounds, because we are nearer the window, and it will also make us more conscious of the proximity of the street and high buildings outside.

(Note to Mr. Coleman: I did not mention it above, but presume that the sound of the gun will be changed to give it a more out of doors effect.)

In the second reel, Scottie's first look at Madeleine is dealt with in an entirely different way:

As Madeleine approaches toward Scottie and becomes a big head, we should take all sounds of the restaurant away so that we get a silence, indicating Scottie's sole impression of her. As Madeleine is joined by her husband, the sounds of the restaurant should be renewed, right up until her exit. I don't know what Mr. Herrman [*sic*] has in mind for music here, but if he should decide upon NO music, for fear it might sound like restaurant music, it would be better to avoid it in order to get this moment of silence, when Scottie feels the proximity of Madeleine.

Hitchcock asked for silence again when Scottie enters the dark passage behind Podesta's: "After he has passed through the mysterious door and comes into the dark passageway, our traffic sounds should become fainter, almost to the point of silence."

To contrast this dark moment with the next, in the next reel Hitchcock instructed Tomasini: ". . . when the door opens and reveals the flower shop, we should hear pleasant sounds of voices; perhaps a little laughter also, so that the sound matches up to the lightness of the flower-laden atmosphere."

An effect that is later integrated into Herrmann's score is the bell toll from Mission Dolores. One of the takes listed on the first day of shooting was a sound recording of the tolling bells, and Hitchcock wanted this track at a very specific point in the Dolores graveyard scene: "When Scottie looks at the headstone and reads the name 'Carlotta' we should hear the bong of the big bell from the basilica next door. It should ring about three times while Scottie is taking down the name."

In the Argosy Book Shop scene, Hitchcock softened the background noise to underscore the tragic story told by Liebel. His first instructions are to match the street sounds with the realism of the scene—softer in the store and slightly louder outside. In this moment, Hitchcock seemed to be thinking out the scene, with Robertson taking the notes:

> I think perhaps that we ought to take a certain amount of dramatic license in the latter part of this book shop sequence, that is: When Pop Liebel tells the story of Carlotta, and we see the dusk descending, it might be a good idea to slowly keep down the traffic sound as well, so that by the time he has reached the lines— "by her own hand . . ." we can let the faint traffic noise creep in again, then building it right up to when Scottie and Midge come out onto the sidewalk.

The darkening light in this scene matches the darkening mood. Hitchcock gave specific instructions for the Fort Point scene:

> We should be careful not to make water noises here. Actually, when we were down there, we never really heard a great deal of water noise—perhaps the breaking of waves over the rocks, and I think this could be kept to a minimum. Perhaps some wind noises could be used judiciously. Our real water sounds should come when Scottie dives in. This should be kept going until he staggers out with Madeleine to the car. I imagine the music going to take over here, but naturally, ordinarily, sounds will be subordinated. I would like, however, to make sure that both musical and soundwise we are subdued enough in the background, so that the words—"Madeleine, Madeleine"—can be dramatized.

Silence is as important as sound: "Once we are among the trees it calls definitely for silence, and it should be silent. We might have a little wind noise now and again, but very faintly, especially when Scottie is searching for Madeleine. At Cypress Point the sound of wind and sea is self-evident, and the sea noise should build up at the climactic kiss." Other scenes receive similar treatment, but the notes from this point on are fairly obvious or duplicated from previous scenes.

There are several moments he left to Bernard Herrmann. Hitchcock, it is clear, was expecting the composer to create a special moment for the 360-degree kiss:

> When Judy is in the bathroom changing—we just hear faint traffic noises, and when she emerges and we go into the love scene we should let all traffic noise fade, because Mr. Hermann [*sic*] may have something to say here.
>
> For the rest of the sequence we will hear faint traffic noises, except when we go away to the portrait (when Mr. Herrman [*sic*] will be the one to take over).

For the final scene, Hitchcock indicated that once the camera had moved inside the tower, there should be "no external sounds, just the sound of the clattering feet up the tower, and when there appears the nun at the end we should hear just the last footsteps as she comes into the tower, but they must be very faint or we may be accused of cheating here.

"When Madeleine falls we should hear a wild cry, echoing in the night, which is suddenly cut short, but we MUST NOT hear any thud."

By Friday, January seventeenth, the four legal-size pages of editing notes have been reduced to two by George Tomasini. The notes from the Friday cutting session give the timing of the film as two hours, five minutes, and thirty-two seconds—and the effort to shorten this time was on. "Shorten. . . . Shorten. . . . Trim. . . . Trim. . . . Cut in half"—this is the mantra on the final cutting notes.

The most extensive notes are on the first vision of Judy as Madeleine: "37. Judy's room—ghost effect. Scottie turns—POV Judy stationary in fog (half the present amount). Back to Scottie. Back to Judy. She walks—immediately she comes out the fog—i.e. on the step forward then lift the fog filter."

Saturday morning, Hitchcock generated another page of details on three specific scenes: Cypress Point, Mission Dolores, and the murder scene.

CYPRESS POINT

Scottie shouldn't be sitting waiting in the car.

Start Madeleine standing looking.

Back to Scottie getting out of car—stands and holds it—looking at her.

Cut to Madeleine walking toward gap—well on her way.

OR

In her cut—instead of being stationary—she can be on the move already—getting near the gap.

i.e. Everything in movement.

MISSION DOLORES

Trims as already mentioned.

Also cheat Scottie way down the aisle ["cheat" means to cut away, then back to what would be a later moment]

Leave her exit from Chapel as is.

Trim Scottie's exit from chapel and also outside as mentioned before.

Drastic all way through.

MISSION DOLORES GRAVEYARD

Trim Scottie's first look.

Trim all walks.

Trim all her cuts.

Speed all Scottie's looks and walks.

Take a look at taking his walk to corner at start (shot ends in Scottie walking forward to CU shooting up).

MURDER

Dissolve in on Elster holding the woman's dead body—long before Madeleine come [sic] thru trap-door so that we establish him holding the woman,

Then Madeleine comes up thru trap door. Check other takes to see if there is a slower one.

Try to double-cut.

Body falls (new Fulton* shot)

---

* John Fulton, Paramount special effects.

Back to her (double cut)

Body on ground (shot we have now)

Shot of Judy's face darkening does not come off. We must see the outlines of her face thru the flashback. When the lights goes [*sic*] down on her—Dissolve while the light is going down—stop-frame with her face there—enough to recognize her and know that these are her thoughts.

Hitchcock returned to Los Angeles from the St. Regis in New York on February third. That same afternoon, he screened *Vertigo* in Paramount's Room 7, then met with Bernard Herrmann to discuss the music. They met again on February sixth; Herrmann, who had been at work during Hitchcock's vacation, was already close to finishing the score.

On the seventh Jimmy Stewart screened the film for the first time. He created his own list of editing notes; though they are brief and sometimes difficult to interpret, they offer a rare look at a Hollywood studio actor contributing to the creation of his films—and reveal a marked concern for the quality of *Vertigo* as a whole, not just his performance.

JIMMY STEWART'S NOTES

REEL 1

1. Roof-tops CU hanging earlier.

REEL 3

2. Podesta's flower shop. Not like a mirror. Have Paul Lang fog mirror or put some dirt on mirror.

REEL 7

3. Cypress Point. Dialogue to be tightened.

REEL 8

4. Union square shot—put back last part of shot?

REEL 10

5. Exterior Sanitarium—shoot?

REEL 11

6. Outside Empire Hotel—too rushed.

7. Other takes of Jim [Stewart] at door of Judy's room. Where he takes longer at door

Slate 466 Take 3 printed and used. 170'

Take 1. Too long before Judy's eyes closed. 175'

Take 2. No landing light. 175'.

8. Flashback. Have Judy run in first to Tower as it is her POV.

REEL 13

9. Scottie in chair after Big Kiss scene.

REEL 14

11. No vertigo shot "I made it."

With these changes, the film took on a shape not far different from what would eventually be released. All that remained was to record the score, which was nearing completion. But events on the horizon would soon conspire to create yet another delay.

There is little documentary evidence to indicate how involved Bernard Herrmann was with the production of *Vertigo* before his contract began on January 6, 1958, but it's known that he knew enough to have begun composing three days earlier. Herrmann watched the first rough cut of the film in Los Angeles in early January before Hitchcock saw it in New York. But did the composer spend much time on the set to get a sense of what Hitchcock was up to? He must have visited at least once, but the evidence suggest he wasn't too impressed: There's a well-known photograph of the composer asleep on the *Vertigo* set, with Hitchcock looking down at him implacably. As Herbert Coleman recalls, it wasn't a staged shot: Coleman noticed the snoozing Herrmann and quickly set it up as a lark.

Herrmann's composing speed was remarkable. His complex, haunting score was completed by February nineteenth. He was paid $17,500 for ten weeks of work. Hitchcock intended that next Herrmann would conduct the orchestra for the sound-track recording sessions, but this was not to be.

Hitchcock and Herrmann: It was a legendary, if not always smooth, collaboration. Steven C. Smith reveals in his excellent biography of the composer that Hitchcock had wanted Herrmann to compose for him as early as 1942 (more than likely for the Universal production of *Saboteur*). He was the first choice for *Spellbound,* though in the end Miklos Rozsa did the famous score. Selznick wanted him for Hitchcock's *The Paradine Case.* James G. Stewart, the sound engineer on *Citizen Kane* and other RKO films, as well as on *Paradine,* gave biographer Smith this account of Herrmann's reaction upon being shown only a few scenes from the film: "He came in, and I ran the picture for him; Selznick was not present. All Bernie did during the screening was complain—about the picture, about the way it was shot, about the way it didn't adapt to music." Not an auspicious beginning.

It was not until Lyn Murray (who scored *To Catch a Thief*) suggested Herrmann for Hitchcock's 1955 black comedy, *The Trouble with Harry,* that the two would finally pair up. Herrmann had relocated to Los Angeles four years earlier and was working full-time as a film composer. Once they got started, the two worked so well together that they would not separate (although he served only as a consultant on *The Birds*) until a disagreement over *Torn Curtain* eleven years later. Orson Welles, later in life, said that 50 percent of the success of *Citizen Kane* was owed to Herrmann's music. It may be fair to say that Herrmann's music played just as significant a part in the Hitchcock success story.

The two men could not have been more different in personality. While Hitchcock was quiet and went to extremes to avoid conflict, Herrmann thrived on it. Sidney Gilliat, who worked with Hitchcock as the screenwriter on *The Lady Vanishes* and *Jamaica Inn* just before Hitchcock left for the United States, recalled in a recent interview how avidly Hitchcock would avoid direct confrontation: "He was a very complex character. . . . But he always had the pose of the inscrutable Buddha, which he liked to play up. He used to do a lot of that rather odd standing against the wall business when he was rehearsing certain scenes."

Herrmann was Hitchcock's temperamental opposite. When he felt a musician or a fellow composer wasn't meeting his own standards of perfection, Herrmann was capable of flying into fits of rage. As the head of MGM's music department recalled to Smith: "I think Benny Herrmann committed suicide. Unwittingly; not with drugs, not with a pistol, but with a four-letter word called hate. I'm convinced that he filled his life with unneeded stress and tension."

But somehow, the artistic sensibilities of these two artists was enough to bridge their emotional differences. Perhaps it was Herrmann's respect for Hitchcock's abilities as a film director. Perhaps it was Hitchcock's working style, which allowed fellow artists to work at their own pace and on their own, leaving Herrmann to contribute without confrontation.

Herrmann once wrote, in defense of film music, that "music on the screen can seek out and intensify the inner thoughts of the characters. It can invest a scene with terror, grandeur, gaiety, or misery. It can propel narrative swiftly forward, or slow it down. It often lifts mere dialogue into the realm of poetry. Finally, it is the communicating link between the screen and the audience, reaching out and enveloping all into one single experience." It isn't known whether Hitchcock read this piece in *The New York Times,* written in 1945 in response to an attack on film music by world-famous conductor Erich Leinsdorf; but whether he did or not, the sentiments expressed match Hitchcock's.

In an interview published in the 1930s, Hitchcock gave his impression of the underlying purpose of film music:

The first and obvious use is atmospheric. To create excitement. To heighten intensity. In a scene of action, for instance, when the aim is to build up to a physical climax, music adds excitement just as effectively as cutting. . . . Music can also be a background to a scene in any mood and a commentary on dialogue. . . . It is in the psychological use of music, which you will observe, they knew something about before talkies, that the great possibilities lie. It makes it possible to express the unspoken. For instance, two people may be saying one thing and thinking something very different. Their looks match their words, not their thoughts. They may be talking politely and quietly, but there may be a storm coming. You cannot express the mood of the situation by word and photograph. But I think you could get at the underlying idea with the right background music. It may sound far-fetched to compare a dramatic talkie with opera, but there is something in common. In opera quite frequently the music echoes the words that have just been spoken. . . . The basis of cinema's appeal is emotional. Music's appeal is to a great extent emotional, too. To neglect music, I think, is to surrender, willfully or not, a chance of progress in filmmaking.

Here are two men, then, committed to creating emotional impact by wedding sound and image in a powerful alchemy.

Their relationship extended off-screen as well; like other friends and coworkers, Herrmann and his family were often guests at Hitchcock's Bel Air home. As Herrmann's third wife recalled, after dinner "Benny used to wash dishes with Hitch, and they'd talk about what they'd do if they weren't in the film business. Benny wanted to run an English pub, until somebody told him you actually had to open and close at certain hours. Benny asked Hitch what he would want to be. There was a silence. Hitchcock then turned to Benny, his apron folded on his head, and said solemnly, 'A hanging judge.'"

"I could never work from a script when scoring a Hitchcock film," Herrmann once told an interviewer; "it's Hitch's timing that creates the suspense. You can't guess his musical requirements ahead of time." But Hitchcock did provide Herrmann with one early guidepost for his work: A recording of the music for J. M. Barrie's *Mary Rose*—the play he'd mentioned to Maxwell Anderson so early in the creation of *Vertigo*. He had gone to great lengths to find a recording of the music, which had so impressed him as a young man attending the London theater.

Mary Rose intrigued Hitchcock throughout his career. When he hit a dry spell, he would occasionally turn to it as a film candidate; Universal, which did not think the play could ever make a good movie, allegedly went so far as to write into Hitchcock's contract that he could film anything *but* Barrie's play. *Mary Rose* has a vague similarity to *Vertigo*—they both feature haunting women as main characters—but Hitchcock's inspiration seemed to have more to do with the play's atmosphere, one of "eerie music, angels singing and low moaning wind."

Other than what exists in the previously discussed dubbing notes, no specific notes seem to survive from Hitchcock to Herrmann, save one set tantalizingly titled "Mr. Hitchcock's Additional Music Notes"; if there were more, they have yet to be located. Even these notes, though, contain their share of insight:

REEL 1

1. Midge's Apartment. An important factor is the contrast between the dramatic music over the Rooftops and the soft, totally different quality of the background music in Midge's apartment.

Remember that the Rooftop's music is background music and Midge's apartment music is coming from the phonograph and is, therefore, quite small and reduced in volume: it is small, concentrated music coming out of a box.

REEL 6

2. The car ride from Exterior Brocklebank down to Exterior Scottie's apartment. This music should start off quite dramatically and, by degrees, get more comic—developing when Scottie starts to throw up his hands.

REEL 14

We should not have crescendo music in the Tower so that we have to take the music down in order to hear the dialogue.

By and large, though, it seems that Herrmann was given a free hand. And the result is arguably the best film score ever written.

Herrmann's score is rendered in an intense mix of deep romantic colors that allude to dark leitmotifs of Wagner's *Tristan und Isolde,* and Latin rhythms that lend the Wagnerian romanticism a new-world feel. Swirling harps and blaring brass provide an aural equivalent to the vertigo effect Hitchcock committed to the screen. And a steadily ascending and descending scale drives forward the anticipation and eroticism of the final transformation of Judy into Madeleine.

The music's dynamics alone suggest the course of the story in all its mounting passion. After the three-minute title music, a swirl of noise matched to the title designs, the rooftop sequence begins *allegro con brio* and ends with the shrill musical vertigo effect. When Scottie sees Madeleine for the first time, Herrmann provides a lush 6/8 *lento amoroso;* the orchestration is all strings, harp, and contrabassoon. In the following scenes, the music is driven by a habanera rhythm, which gives the music an old California feel. When Scottie and Madeleine kiss at Cypress Point, Herrmann's instructions are *molto appassionato;* at the tower, *allegro furioso.* The entire score is a bravura work, with subtle orchestrations, subtly integrated layers of leitmotif, and a clutch of melodies that resonate with longing and desire.

Herrmann considered the score his best work. Curiously, though, after watching the film in January and February, he questioned two of the core components of Hitchcock's production: "They should never have made it in San

```
                    "VERTIGO"

                                      Hollywood, 4th February, 1958.

          MR. HITCHCOCK'S ADDITIONAL MUSIC NOTES.


     REEL 1.

     1.  Midge's Apartment.  An important factor is the contrast
         between the dramatic music over the Roof-tops and the
         soft, totally different quality of the background music
         in Midge's Apartment.
         Remember that the Roof-tops music is background music and
         Midge's Apartment music is coming from the phonograph and
         is, therefore, quite small and reduced in volume:  it is
         small, concentrated music coming out of a box.


     REEL 6.

     2.  The car ride from Exterior Brocklebank down to Exterior
         Scottie's Apartment.  This music should start off quite
         dramatically and, by degrees, get more comic -- developing
         when Scottie starts to throw up his hands.


     REEL 14.

     3.  We should not have crescendo music in the Tower so that we
         have to take the music down in order to hear the dialogue.
```

Francisco, and not with Jimmy Stewart. . . . It should have been an actor like Charles Boyer. It should have been left in New Orleans, or in a hot, sultry climate. When I wrote the picture, I thought of that."

But the sultry overtones Herrmann brought to the *Vertigo* score would, in the end, be brought to the screen under another's baton. As the time for recording the film's sound track neared, a musician's strike destroyed Herrmann's chance at conducting the score in the United States. To release the film on time, Hitchcock was forced to commission an overseas recording. By late February, Hitchcock and Herbert Coleman had arranged to travel to London in March to record the score, and Muir Mathieson was hired to conduct. Herrmann, meanwhile, continued composing right down to the wire: One cable refers to Herrmann scoring the music for the Elizabeth Arden sequence over the weekend before the London recordings.

The London recording session, though, was almost equally doomed. The London Symphony hadn't quite recorded half the score when its musicians walked out in support of the American strike, throwing Hitchcock and Coleman into a panic. Coleman wired executive Frank Caffey at Paramount, Hollywood:

Completed sequences one AA, one BB, five CC, seven CC, seven DD, thirteen BB, fourteen BB, fourteen BB1, nine BB, ten AA, nine A1, ten CC, ten DD, thirteen AA, two BB today. Thirty-eight minutes in three sessions before international musicians European in Zurich withdrew all men in sympathy Hollywood musicians. Hitch considers most important sections finished. We are checking rest Europe for possibilities continuing. Mathieson conducting and must receive full card after Herrmann with credit "Conducted by Muir Mathieson." Will keep you advised. Would appreciate your advice Mexico, South America, Canada IMMEDIATELY. Regards. Herbie

The Vienna orchestra negotiated quickly for the opportunity. The Viennese music community was eager to capitalize on film business from the United States during the strike, and they were able to participate in the recording with a clear conscience, since the job was being farmed out by Paramount London and not Paramount Hollywood.

The complement of the recording sessions were held in Vienna, from the fourteenth to the eighteenth of March. Hitchcock returned to Hollywood from London on March sixteenth, disappointed that a hometown orchestra would not be providing the recording. Ironically, it was not until April third that Hitchcock received a letter from the London musicians explaining their action. On that same day, Hitchcock drafted this response (the italicized sections were edited out of the final letter):

April 3rd, 1958

Thank you for your letter of March 19th, which I received today: it was forwarded on to me by Claridges. Unfortunately, it arrived there after I had left London [*on March 13th*] to return to California. Thus you will see why I [*did not comply with your request*] was unable to meet with you and the Assistant General Secretary of the Musicians Union.

The picture, to which you refer, is a Paramount picture, and it was their decision to record the music in London. This decision was reached after assurances from the Paramount London office [*that*] there would be no opposition to the work being done there [*and, as a matter of fact, the second day's scoring was in progress before the English Musician's Union agreed to support the Hollywood musicians*]. When this occurred, Paramount, of course, agreed to stop work that evening, and the picture was immediately shipped out of England.

Herrmann was never happy with the Mathieson recordings. At the time, Coleman wrote to the director of the Vienna orchestra that Hitchcock and Herrmann were happy with the results, although the letter hints that

PARAMOUNT PICTURES CORPORATION
WEST COAST STUDIOS

5451 MARATHON STREET ☐ HOLLYWOOD 38, CALIF.
TELEPHONE HOllywood 9-2411 CABLE ADDRESS "FAMFILM"

April 3rd, 1958

Mr. George Elvin
General Secretary
Association of Cine &
Allied Technicians
2, Soho Square
London, W.1., England

Dear Mr. Elvin:

Thank you for your letter of March 19th, which I received today: it was forwarded on to me by Claridges. Unfortunately, it arrived there after I had left London on March 13th to return to California. Thus you will see why I ~~did not comply with your request~~ to meet with you and the Assistant General Secretary of the Musicians Union. *(was unable)*

The picture, to which you refer, is a Paramount picture, and it was their decision to record the music in London. This decision was reached after assurances from the Paramount London Office ~~that~~ there would be no opposition to the work being done there. ~~and, as a matter of fact, the second day's scoring was in progress before the English Musicians Union agreed to support the Hollywood musicians.~~ When this occurred, Paramount, of course, agreed to stop work that evening, and the picture was immediately shipped out of England.

Kindest regards.

Sincerely yours,

Alfred J. Hitchcock

there may indeed have been complaints—among them a certain dissatisfaction "about the heavy bowing sound from the strings." But the letter goes on to assert that that was exactly the effect Herrmann had been after. "I'm very relieved that the bowing sound from the strings has not posed a problem," the orchestra's director responded in April. "I guess luck was on our side, though on the spot I would not have given a nickel on a bet that this was the effect Mr. Herrmann wanted."

Later, though, Herrmann would contend that the recordings were sloppy and full of mistakes. Newly restored and rereleased in 1996, the recording does reveal some sloppiness on the part of the musicians—a quality that may not be readily apparent when listening to the sound-track recording by itself, but which becomes more obvious when played against a recent recording of the score.

For years, the *Vertigo* sound track was available in only a severely truncated form, the result of an older trade agreement that prevented film companies from exploiting Viennese recordings; this created an enormous problem for Paramount, which consequently could release only the recordings made in London. Today, the aficionado can discern which tracks were recorded in London and which in Vienna by comparing the older release (still available in CD) with the newly restored version.

There was one interesting sidebar to the music for *Vertigo:* a pop song called "Vertigo," written for the film by Jay Livingston and Ray Evans but never released. The team had provided to the somewhat reluctant Hitchcock and Doris Day the hit song "Que Sera Sera" for *The Man Who Knew Too Much* (Hitchcock told the team he had no idea what he wanted for a song, and when he heard "Que sera" said that was what he had in mind. Doris Day refused at first to record the song, saying it was childish. After pressure from Paramount, she relented, but quipped at the end of the recording session that they would never hear her sing that song again. The song went on to become her television series' theme song). According to the songwriters, Hitchcock approached them for *Vertigo,* hoping that they would help familiarize audiences with the concept. "Gentlemen, the studio thinks that no one knows what the word 'vertigo' means," Hitchcock explained to the team. "But that's what my picture is about, and if you will write a song explaining what the word 'vertigo' means, it will help me a great deal." They wrote the song—with references to dizzying heights—and recorded a demo. Jay Livingston asked the singer at the demo recording session if he now knew what 'vertigo' meant. The singer replied, "It's an island in the West Indies, isn't it?" The team submitted their work, but may well have been relieved when Hitchcock decided not to use it. Paramount, on the other hand, was plugging the song on all the advance theater advertisements for *Vertigo;* they couldn't have been happy about its demise. Paramount did release another *Vertigo*-related song, arranged by Jeff Alexander and Larry Orenstein, after the film's release. Set to Herrmann's love theme, the song, entitled "Madeleine," was not a success.

One of the typical aspects of any film production is how unpredictable the sequence of events can be. Working in the interest of economy, production teams often treat the most important sequences as undertakings distinct from the

September 4th, 1957

NIGHTMARE SEQUENCE

At a meeting held today in Mr. Hitchcock's office at Paramount Studios, a discussion on the Nightmare Sequence for the picture, "FROM AMONGST THE DEAD" took place. In attendance - Herbert Coleman, John Ferren, Hal Pereira, John Fulton, Dee Erickson, and Henry Bumstead.

SUBJECT:
Sketch for scene #215, "FROM AMONGST THE DEAD".

CENTRAL IDEA:
The scene is played nearly exactly as written with no addition of sets, or vistas or landscapes.

There is imposed on the entire sequence a Color Throb or Pulsation. This is a rhythmed beat of colored light which swells from and recedes to darkness. This pulsation is rhythmed to begin at a normal heart beat and gradually increase to a flutter in the final sequence where it stops and is held in the glare of the final revelation. The color changes in hue from indigo blue through the spectrum as the sequence progresses, in psychological and emotional cohesion with each scene, ending in a pure white and black at the end.

With the exception of the inquest section, Scottie's head, Carlotta's, the nosegay, the necklace, the falling body, etc., are kept at dead center of the screen. This increases the hypnotic effect, centers the spectators attention and makes the apparent reality unreal.

COLOR SCORING FOR SEQUENCE 215

Scottie's face - relatively colorless on a gray pillow. His head turns and centers on the screen as the color beat begins *as the pillow appears.* Color for color beat is indigo blue. The indigo blue starts in a light tone, and gradually deepens until it is like sample - when his eyes open. When he turns his head and centers it, the angle of the camera should be eye level. Scottie's eyes stare intensely, but with no facial expression (he is in the dream world). Throughout this sequence the color beat is used as the illumination for the subject matter, and as it recedes we go momentarily into black screen. This takes care of the first shot.

NIGHTMARE SEQUENCE
Page T w O

SECOND SHOT
Revealing the portrait of Carlotta. When Scottie's head leaves screen, Carlotta's head appears. Do not show frame, just her head of the painting, and just as Scottie's head was isolated so is Carlotta's. During the dissolve, the color beat changes from indigo blue to a clear blue. Then, a chromatic change to yellow green takes place as indicated on Card #2 as the flowers replace the face.

The nosegay goes on in its natural colors with the light yellow green beat upon it. While this yellow green beat is going on, the individual colors of the flowers begin to change to deep blues, violets, magentas, and lemon yellows. As this is happening, the yellow background dissolves into a black background while the beat changes to a clear white light (which will show the pure colors) on the flowers only.

The white beat continues over flowers until the explosion, even though it might be almost indiscernible.

Quick break - shock transition to final scene of inquest. Exact decor as in original sequence, but illumination very clear and detailed, like a still, with the actors motionless. Color has changed to clear orange (like cellophane over entire scene). The pulsation is there but is toned down and unobtrusive. I suggest that, while the original beat is no light and then full light, this should be full light to one-half light or even two-thirds light and then up again. Play scene as written.

We start on her face, when it turns, and pan to necklace - in lap dissolve to insert of necklace, the same size as the original shot of Scottie's head. While on necklace, the beat has changed from orange to clear red. The unobtrusive beat on background also. The unobtrusive beat should intensify slowly on the necklace. That means slowly going back to original light to dark beat. Colors for scene of inquest are shown on Mr. Ferren's Card #4.

Lap dissolve to Scottie's head with eyes still open, but now with an inquiring alive expression. We have returned to the heavy pulsation with light on his face only. The beat on Scottie's face becomes a deeper red (blackish), as shown at the bottom of Mr. Ferren's Card #4. The background is solid black. His body becomes discernible, profiled by some light behind. We are now aware that he is walking. Camera retreats as he advances, always keeping Scottie's head dead center. While he is walking, we see the background change from black to the graveyard set. He pauses at the brink of the open grave looking down.

From Scottie's point of view, we see the black depths of the grave with the headstone to mark it. The red beat continues over this shot.

bulk of a film's production—as was true of a number of *Vertigo*'s most celebrated visual effects.

An instructive example is *Vertigo*'s animated nightmare sequence, which began its production phase in August of 1957, before principal photography began. The director had turned to the art world before, most memorably with the dream sequence designed by Salvador Dalí in *Spellbound.* Now he invited contemporary artist John Ferren to design the dream. A fan of Ferren's work, Hitchcock had first commissioned the artist for another particularly personal project, *The Trouble with Harry;* for this dark comedy—like *Vertigo,* only recently recognized as one of the director's best—Ferren contributed the paintings John Forsythe's character has painted, and he gave the actor some lessons in technique. The Ferrens became friendly with the Hitchcocks and Colemans during these years, John's widow, Rae, recalls; they relocated permanently to Long Island, New York, after completing the design work for *Vertigo.*

NIGHTMARE SEQUENCE
Page T h r e E

Break to black screen for a few seconds. Quick shot of Scottie's face looking down, pure white (not natural coloring - possibly shot in black and white) on black background. The beat is white light.

The beat continues to increase. Reverse shot of grave. Return to the same red beat on the ground. The pit grows larger.

Now shooting up on Scottie's full face, (as shown on Card #5) the pit takes over entire screen as strips of deep red color on what would be the sides of the grave appear around Scottie's windblown head. These strips stream back in animated fashion, giving the illusion of terrific speed. The scream starts. At the start of this shot, there is a mustard color (dirty yellow) pulsation on Scottie's face only (not on background). The receding red strips change through purple to dark steel blue as the face color changes from mustard yellow to sharp acid green yellow. (These are deliberate dissonant colors). The yellow becomes brighter, loosing its green tinge as the pulsation tempo increases. The face, now with a pure yellow beat on it, enlarges, takes over the screen, blurs unrecognizably.

Reverse angle, as shown on Card #6, showing Scottie falling as a pure, unshadowed, black, profiled mass from the Dolores Mission, which is clearly seen in the light yellow light. The roof background toward which Scottie is falling looses its identity and becomes a background of deep black red which comes up rapidly from darkness to a blinding white light at the moment of impact. The beat turns to red as the background changes to red, and changes again to white, as the background lightens. Scottie's body, still dead center of the screen, should be pure black on a pure white background at the final moment. The color beat has now increased to a fast flutter which stops and holds just before the moment of impact, during which time the scream increases to its final volume.

FOOTNOTES
First or Final Notes

1. Concerning the color snatches: These are correct in hue - but they are paint and not the transparent light of the final effect.

2. Once the color pulsation effect is achieved, the essentials are:

NIGHTMARE SEQUENCE
Page F o u R

FOOTNOTES (Cont.)

a. Keying of the color changes at the psychologically proper time.

By this, I do not mean the keying according to the script - but the duration of each color scene to permit the spectator to absorb the effect.

b. The rhythm of the pulsation. The increase in tempo must be slow and deliberate (uninterrupted) throughout the sequence. If possible, this should be mechanically controlled.

c. All dissolves, from one image to another, are lap dissolves.

On August twenty-seventh, Ferren submitted his sketch for the nightmare; it was adapted with few changes at a meeting a few days later attended by Hitchcock, Coleman, Ferren, Hal Pereira (Paramount's lead art director), John Fulton, Doc Erickson, and Henry Bumstead.

Subject: Sketch for scene #215 "From Among the Dead"
Central Idea:

The scene is played nearly exactly as written with no addition of sets, or vistas or landscapes.

There is imposed on the entire sequence a Color Throb or Pulsation. This is a rhythmed beat of colored light which swells from and recedes to darkness. This pulsation is rhythmed to begin at a normal heart beat and gradually increase to a flutter in the final sequence where it stops and is held in the glare of the final revelation. The color changes in hue from indigo blue through the spectrum as the sequence progresses, in psychological and emotional cohesion with each scene, ending in pure white and black at the end.

With the exception of the inquest section, Scottie's head, Carlotta's, the nosegay, the necklace, the falling body etc. are kept at dead center of the screen. This increases the hypnotic effect, centers the spectators [sic] attention and makes the apparent reality unreal.

COLOR SCORING FOR SEQUENCE 215

As Scottie rolls restlessly the camera watches and then catches him completely full face, asleep but finally expressionless and static, like a still. The face is dead center the screen, framed by the pillow only, which is a gray white expanse covering the screen and showing no borders. There should be a minimum of color (all grays) in this shot. The natural color changes to indigo blue (blue purple) Scottie's face remains unmoved and unchanged but the pillow background becomes a pure color area. As this is being affected the color pulsation begins. This is color rising out of black and receding with a defined and calculated rhythm. The initial rhythm should be that of the normal heart beat or throb. Scottie's eyes open and stare intensely but with no facial expression. (He is in the dream world.)

Superimpose Carlotta's portrait head on Scottie's in same dead center position. There is no decor of any sort around the heads, just the pulsating color. Do not show picture frame. Color changes to adulterated blue. Pan to flowers—or rather lift picture so that flowers rise to dead center position.

This sequence should be slow and deliberate—in silence, or a drum heart [sic] beat—with only the rhythmic color pulsation.

Slightly faster beat. Color changes from blue green slowly to yellow green. The flowers come alive, grow and fade, become florescent [sic], change color, start whirling in a dizzy maze—like pinwheels—and enlarge rapidly to cover screen. Quick break—Shock transition to final scene of inquest. Exact decor as in original sequence, but the illumination very clear and detailed, like a still, with the actors motionless. Color has changed to clear orange (like cellophane over entire scene). The pulsation is there but is toned down and unobtrusive, although there is a slow imperceptible building up of tempo. Play scene as written. Pan to necklace (is it a Lavelliere [sic] type? It should be red) which grows to fit the original size of Scottie's head in the first sequence. Superimpose Scottie's head with eyes still open but now, with an inquiring expression. Color beat now becomes red. Return to heavy pulsation with light on his face only. His body becomes discernible, profiled by some light behind. We are next aware that he is walking. Camera retreats as he advances always keeping Scottie's head dead center, showing he's in graveyard.

Break to black screen for a few seconds—no beat. Quick shot of Scottie's face looking down, pure white on black background. A dark red beat starts on face. Reverse shot of grave. The same red beat on the ground, the pit grows larger. Scottie falls. Faster beat. The pit takes over entire screen as strips of color on what would be the sides of the grave appear [around] Scottie's windblown head. These strips stream back in Disney fashion, giving the illusion of terrific speed. The scream starts. The strips begin, colored deep red. At the same time there is a mustard color (dirty yellow) pulsation on Scottie's face. The receding red strips change through purple to dark steel blue as the face color changes from mustard yellow to sharp acid green yellow. (These are deliberate dissonant colors.) The yellow becomes brighter loosing [sic] its green tinge as the pulsation tempo increases. The yellow face enlarges, takes over the screen, blurs un-recognizably. Reverse angle showing Scottie falling as a pure, un-shadowed, black, profiled mass from the Dolores Mission [actually San Juan Bautista] which is shown briefly in the clear yellow light. The roof background toward which Scottie is falling turns deep black red which comes up from darkness to a blinding white light at the moment of impact. Scottie's body, still dead center of the screen, should be pure black on a pure white background at the final moment. The color beat now increased to a fast flutter which stops and holds just before the moment of impact, during which time the scream increases to its final volume.

In the notes to the September fourth meeting, Ferren included footnotes explaining that the color changes reflected the viewer's psychological shifts, not Scottie's. "The duration of each color scene [acts] to permit the spectator to absorb the effect," Ferren wrote. Ferren's strength as an artist was with color: His work found its most frequent home in Abstract Expressionism (although his work was sometimes called not abstract enough), and his work hangs today in the Metropolitan Museum of Art, the Museum of Modern Art, the Guggenheim and Whitney museums, and the Los Angeles County Museum. According to a 1979 retrospective catalog, his turn to explosive, expressive color was triggered by an early visit to a Matisse exhibition. "Treatment of color in the paintings . . . embodies this expansiveness of light—a light that not only pervades the work itself, but envelops the viewer. Such a treatment has many European antecedents (Delaunay and Klee [another Hitchcock favorite] come readily to mind), but the driving force behind it in Ferren's work can be traced to a . . . sense of Taoist tranquility. The restraint of that light contrasts with his vivid, highly energized drawing, or with the sensual, audacious, often strident and demanding color that explodes in the works"—as, indeed, it does on-screen in *Vertigo*.

There are no surviving records that outline when the dream sequence was filmed. Nor were records kept for any of the other special-effects work on the film, which would certainly have been completed during this postproduction period.

Polly Burson, the stunt woman who performed the falls from the tower for Kim Novak, recalls filming in late December or early January. Ms. Burson, now retired, remembered doing a number of jumps from nearly sixty feet into

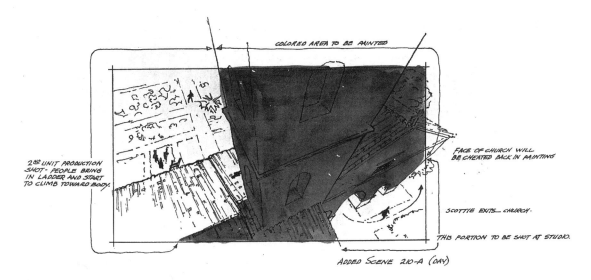

COLORED AREA TO BE PAINTED

2ND UNIT PRODUCTION SHOT - PEOPLE BRING IN LADDER AND START TO CLIMB TOWARD BODY.

FACE OF CHURCH WILL BE CHEATED BACK IN PAINTING

SCOTTIE EXITS CHURCH.

THIS PORTION TO BE SHOT AT STUDIO.

ADDED SCENE 210-A (DAY)

A fascinating production sketch illustrates just how live footage and matte paintings were combined to create the film's memorable overhead shot—from the perspective of a tower that wasn't there.

a circus net Paramount had purchased, and she recalled making three takes. She also described being strapped to a device that spun her in various directions while she threw her arms about as if she was falling, which must have been used in the shot of the fall during Judy's flashback. "I got seasick," she says. "When they called lunch, I said, 'Forget me.'"

Herbert Coleman remembers shooting a number of scenes while Hitchcock was in Jamaica. One in particular was especially difficult:

"Hitch didn't like the way Novak looked directly into the camera during her close-up at Ernie's," he recalls; it was a profile shot, and her look broke the fourth wall. "So he had me reshoot it. This was a problem, because the Ernie's

set was dismantled immediately after we were finished with it. So I cheated a little. We had one of the walls left, so to match the other shot, I used a smaller lens, which didn't show so much background. Hitch was furious. For years he was upset that I didn't match the original shot. But it was the best we could do." A careful look at this scene reveals the

difference between the two lenses: When Tomasini cuts to Scottie, then cuts back to Madeleine, there is much less background visible than in the previous cut (the original shot can be seen in the film's original trailer, which is included in the restoration's video release).

In early December, before wrapping the production phase, Hitchcock met with a hot young graphic designer to discuss the film's title sequence. Saul Bass had executed a series of eye-catching title designs for the opening credits of *The Man with the Golden Arm,* which had impressed the director enough that he asked Bass to go to work on titles for *Vertigo.* The original title concept had been simply to overlay the title cards over a shot of the San Francisco skyline, an obvious tribute to the city's visual appeal. But Hitchcock had something else in mind: a striking look that would draw the viewer immediately into the film's twisted psychological landscape. Bass eagerly accepted, and he set to work on what would become a stunning opening sequence.

"He seemed to like me for some reason," Bass recalled before his death in 1996. "Working with Hitch was a wonderful learning experience."

But Bass did not work alone on the *Vertigo* title sequence. The look he designed made striking use of Lissajous spirals animated for him by a little-known but influential avant-garde filmmaker named John Whitney. Bass had seen a set of designs Whitney had created as part of an architectural installation; in the building, a set of intertwining spirals had been etched into glass partitions. Was there a way to animate the spirals to that they would appear to spin? It was a question Whitney had already spent nearly a decade trying to answer.

John Whitney had attended Claremont College, in Pomona, where he studied classical music; there, he met John Cage, with whom he formed a lasting friendship. At roughly the same time, Whitney bought a 16-mm camera during a trip to Europe; the camera spawned Whitney's lifelong interest in creating cinematic visual effects that would match the aural effect of music—literally, to turn the invisible in music into the visible. This was beyond marrying music to image; this was an effort to make the image itself the music. Whitney's book *Digital Harmony,* a treatise on music, images, and computer animation, is a fascinating articulation of his experiments with, and passion for, the combination of music and film.

John Whitney and his brother James had always been interested in art and technology, and the two spent hours tinkering with surplus war machinery to build animation stands for their experimental films. According to John's son John, the brothers continued to "collaborate throughout their lives. They were always talking about their work."

There were two challenges in creating the revolving spirals of the kind that ultimately found their way into the *Vertigo* credit sequence. The first was to create an animation stand that could rotate continuously without its interior control wiring becoming tangled. The second was to find a way to link the movement of the rotating base through the control wire to the floating pendulum that drew each Lissajous spiral. This may seem simple now, but nothing of the kind had ever been built for film work; the design John Whitney eventually settled on was the precursor of computer animation stands developed nearly twenty years later.

The Whitneys discovered that the machine-gun turrets built for airplanes during World War II were actually sophisticated analog computers that allowed the turret to spin 360 degrees without tangling wires. The rotating gun plate sat on a base that allowed for continuous electrical contact wherever the gun was pointed. Purchasing brand-new surplus turrets, Whitney removed their guns and machine-made a flat aluminum plate to hold the animation.

The machine that controlled the spinning base was connected to the pendulum, which allowed for the two to move in a controlled pattern, making it possible to create the spirals. The creation was a work of genius—and done purely for the love of invention: It was merely a happy coincidence that Bass saw the spiral-based architectural work when he did, giving Whitney the opportunity to transform his glass-etching machine into an animation machine.

Whitney's pioneering work had an impact on future films. His brother James continued tinkering with the machine once the spirals were finished, and his further alterations resulted in an extraordinary experimental animation film, *Lapis*—whose images would in turn later influence Douglas Trumbull's designs for the final moments of *2001: A Space Odyssey*. John Whitney, meanwhile, went on to do advanced design work in cooperation with IBM; he made some of the very first computer-animated films in the early seventies,

work that led directly to films such as to-day's *Toy Story*. Like Bass, John Whitney died in 1996. But John Whitney, Jr., has continued his father's work, as one of the founders of U.S. Animation, a 2-D computer-animation facility. He remembers fondly his father's gift—a singular ability to work with machinery and bend it to his purposes. "He had a natural gift for building equipment, for building things. He had an understanding of electronics and electrical engineering and mechanical engineering that was just completely innate. He had this gift, which showed from a very early age," John recalls.

According to the family, Whitney collaborated with Saul Bass on several occasions. And it is Whitney's spiral designs, in the end, that bring Hitchcock's vertigo theme to the screen in its purest form.

"I can't tell you how marvelous it was to see my work for *Vertigo* for the first time with the Bernard Herrmann score," Bass remembered. The titles are another example of the unique unity of vision shared between the film's artists.

John Whitney and the spiral-drawing machine he built from surplus war materials . . .

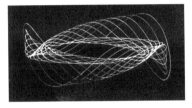

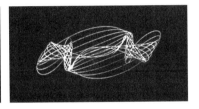

. . . and samples of the spirals themselves.

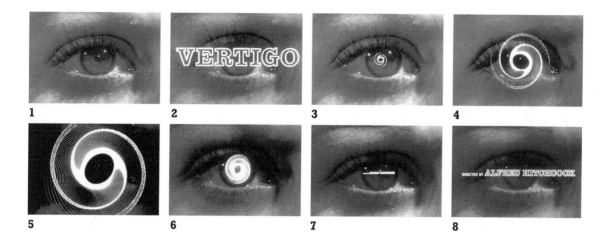

1 2 3 4 5 6 7 8

Bass's sequence begins with the left side of the emotionless face of a young woman (not Novak, but an anonymous actress whose features were both specific and universal): "Here's a woman made into what a man wants her to be. She is put together piece by piece and I tried to suggest something of this as the fragmentation of the mind of Judy," Bass explained. Then it pans down to her lips, then up to her eyes, which shift in both directions before the camera finally dollies in for a close-up of the right eye. Out of this eye comes the title VERTIGO, followed by the colorful Whitney/Lissajous spirals. "I wanted to achieve that very particular state of unsettledness associated with vertigo and also a mood of mystery. I sought to do this by juxtaposing images of eyes with moving images of intense beauty. I used Lissajous figures, devised by a French mathematician in the nineteenth century to express mathematical formulae, which I had fallen in love with several years earlier. You could say I was obsessed with them for a while—so I knew a little of what Hitch was driving at. I wanted to express the mood of this film about love and obsession."

As the credits continue, her eye fades away—the viewer is now within the eye—and Whitney's images spiral in, then quickly out again, and one is back to the eye. The final title card, "Directed by Alfred Hitchcock," is followed by a fade to black.

This sequence is quite different from the more purely graphic titles that Bass designed for *The Man with the Golden Arm, North by Northwest,* and *Psycho.* In these films, Bass used the actual typography, its positioning and movement, to create his provocative effects. The *North by Northwest* titles slide on and off the screen at sharp angles, integrated within the gridlike modern architecture of New York City; in *Psycho,* the titles schizophrenically break apart. *Vertigo* is unique in its stationary typography; except for the unobtrusive movement of the main credits, the considerable visual interest of the film's opening sequence rests entirely on the magnified face of this unknown woman—and on the undulating, spiraling patterns Saul Bass and John Whitney found within her.

The famous "vertigo shots" were also completed during postproduction. Years later, Hitchcock told François Truffaut of a personal event that had inspired the shot: "I always remember one night at the Chelsea Arts Ball at Albert Hall in London," he said, "when I got terribly drunk and I had the sensation that everything was going far away from me." John Fulton remembered himself and Irmin Roberts convincing Hitch that the best way to film the innovative reverse-track, forward-zoom point-of-view shots was in miniature: To use full-sized sets would have cost almost twenty thousand dollars, a scale model one-tenth the sum. Hitchcock told Truffaut that it was he who had suggested the model, but no matter: It was agreed, and Fulton went about building the set.

The miniature model of the tower's interior was built on its side; mounted on tracks, the camera moved back as the lens zoomed in. The effect is startling: The viewer's perspective is stretched in one surreal, dizzying motion, as if one is falling and rising simultaneously.

No record survives of the actual model used in the shot. At Universal Studios–Florida, a facsimile of the *Vertigo* setup is a feature of the "Art of Alfred Hitchcock" pavilion, but regrettably, not even a photograph of John Fulton's original set remains.

Throughout his career, Hitchcock used such trick shots to try to convey the mind losing control. In the original *The Man Who Knew Too Much,* the mother faints as the room rapidly spins around her. A similar technique appears in *Secret Agent,* when the character realizes that she has helped assassinate the wrong man. In *Notorious,* Hitchcock used this shifting point of view in two different scenes. In the film's beginning, we see Cary Grant from Bergman's hungover perspective: upside down and obscured by tousled hair. Then, as he

Vertigo's widely imitated tower sequence, as the storyboard artists envisioned it. ▶

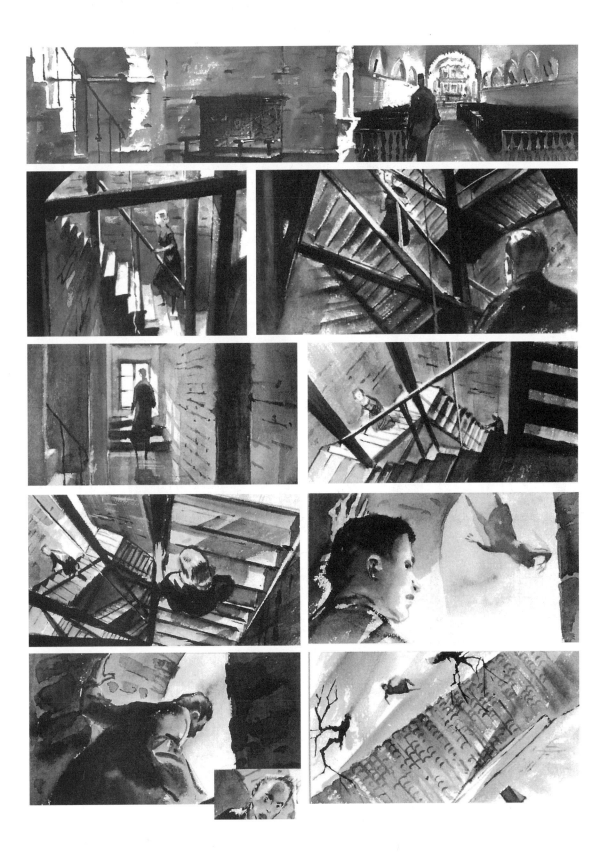

VERTIGO: The Making of a Hitchcock Classic

approaches her, the image slowly spins to the correct position. Later in the film, as Bergman realizes she's being poisoned by her husband, Claude Rains, the point-of-view shots of Rains pulsate and stretch away from her in a disturbing fashion. It was the refinement of the multiple-focal-point lens— the zoom lens—in the late fifties that made the "vertigo shot" possible. Hitchcock would use the technique once more, during Tippi Hedren's flashback in *Marnie;* in a bow to the Master, Martin Scorsese found a place for it in *Goodfellas.*

Health problems intervened again in the Hitchcock family as the film neared completion. During a routine checkup, it was discovered that Alma Hitchcock was suffering from cervical cancer. According to Donald Spoto's biography, "Hitchcock was beside himself with anxiety. While Alma was in surgery, he dined alone at a nearby restaurant. . . . After Alma's recovery, he not only never visited the restaurant again—he refused to go near it."

Alma's illness was diagnosed on April 12, 1958, and she was hospitalized April fourteenth; she would remain in the hospital until the twenty-fifth. During this extremely stressful time, Hitchcock was obliged to oversee the final preparations for *Vertigo*'s release, as well as wrapping up an *Alfred Hitchcock Presents* episode ("Dip in the Pool"). When not busy with these projects, he threw himself into the script of his next film, *North by Northwest.*

Herbert Coleman recalls that Hitchcock never submitted any of his films for public previews. There is no record of previews for *Vertigo*—no screening dates, no audience-response cards. Herb Steinberg, the head of publicity and marketing for Paramount and all of Hitchcock's Paramount films, said that there never was any reason to preview a Hitchcock film: "You knew what you were getting."

Yet with this delicate film, there still remained some question over one issue that involved the audience deeply: Whether to let on before the film's conclusion that Judy and Madeleine were one and the same. The details of this debate are almost lost to history. Yet, while examining the dialogue-cutting transcripts among the *Vertigo* archives, the author discovered a fact that throws new light on the decision-making process: Until April twenty-fourth, the film's running time was always given as two hours and three and a half minutes. Then, in the May first transcript—eight days before the San Francisco premiere—the film's length increased to two hours and seven and a half minutes. Somewhere, an additional four minutes had been added. But where?

Fortunately, the timings are indicated on each reel. Comparing the transcripts reveals that the only reel to change time was reel 11—the reel containing Judy's letter-writing confession scene. Before May first, reel 11 was 552 feet and fourteen frames long; after May first, it expanded to 924 feet and ten frames—nearly double its original length. Up until this final edit, the four-minute confession scene had not been a part of the picture.

"We were not sure whether we should let the audience know so much too early," Peggy Robertson remembers. "There was much discussion over that scene. And we screened it without the scene, but it didn't work as well."

Coleman remembers the debate well. It was the only time he could recall that Hitchcock ever gave him a direct order—and the only time Coleman refused. This film scene led to an unfortunate clash between the men at a screening.

"Well, there was quite a controversy," Coleman recalls. "I wanted it in the final cut and so did Sam [Taylor]. Joan Harrison, the producer of his television series, got to Hitch and talked him into running it without the scene, and at that running it started a real fight with Hitch and myself.

"Hitch and I stood face-to-face, arguing like hell about the film in front of everybody in the theater. They knew that Hitch was wrong, because Harrison jumped up and said, 'This is the only way you should show it, Hitch.' I took Hitch off to one side and continued to argue about it with him. Finally, our voices started rising, and everybody was sitting in the theater in absolute silence. Just the silence alone should have told Hitch it was wrong. We went to great expense to take it out; in the end, though, I won and it was put back in.

"I was the producer of the film, but he was the owner of the film, so I had to approve everything that went on and we had to agree on everything. When he released the picture this way [without the confession], I had to call all the prints back that we had sent all over the country and recut the scene and redo the music and everything and send those out. In the meantime, Barney Balaban, the president of Paramount, who had seen the picture in its original form with the scene in, had gone back to New York and told everyone it was the greatest Hitchcock film.

"Just before the release date, between that time and the actual release date, Balaban, not knowing it was out, had a run-in with the critics in New York. They told him he was crazy—it was the worst Hitchcock film ever made.

"He called us up in the studio and I thought we were all going to get fired—I thought the studio was going to get burned down. And he ordered that scene be put back, so I had to call everyone back in again and redo the whole damn thing."

Robertson doesn't recall the confrontation between Coleman and Hitchcock, but she does agree that there was a great deal of argument about the scene. Asked whether Hitchcock wanted the scene in or out, Robertson pointed out: "After all, he had written the scene into the script, so he must have wanted it in."

Years later, at a screening in New York, Samuel Taylor confessed how much he disliked that scene. In retrospect, he said, he would have preferred to have conveyed the revelation in the way he'd initially imagined—through a scene between Elster and Judy after the murder, the kind of scene he'd ultimately rejected because it seemed to "rob" Scottie of his central place in the film's viewpoint. Instead, "we did it in a very inept way. That letter scene startled me. How bad it is!" Taylor said.

But whether to include the confession at all was a different issue, and it haunted the film until its very release. Taylor (and later Hitchcock) had long argued that the story was not meant to be a mystery in the classical sense. As Taylor said, "With this story, it's absolutely essential that the audience know, because this is a suspense story, not a mystery."

The timing of the final decision to keep the confession scene is interesting. The decision was made during the week of April twenty-fourth; Alma returned home on the twenty-fifth. It is no secret that, in story crises like this, Hitchcock would often turn to his wife for guidance. Did Alma argue to keep the scene? As happened so frequently in their working relationship, it may well have been her judgment that Hitchcock followed.

Finally, the tinkering was over. Herrmann met once more with Hitchcock on April twenty-ninth for a final look at *Vertigo* and a discussion about *North by Northwest*. The San Francisco film was now complete; all that was left was to prepare for its premiere, in that city, on May ninth.

CHAPTER 5

PREMIERE AND BEYOND

I go but I return: I would I were
The pilot of the darkness and the dream

—Tennyson

With Alma so recently home from the hospital, Hitchcock may not have been in the mood for the rigors of promoting *Vertigo*. The cancer scare may have taken much of the joy out of the prospect of showing his film to the media; on the other hand, it may have provided a much-needed distraction. Whatever mix of emotions Hitchcock had to deal with, this part of the filmmaking process, the selling of the film, was one of the most important parts—and one that a filmmaker neglected at his peril.

As a young man, at a meeting of the Hate Club (a loose organization of filmmakers united by their dissatisfaction with the popular cinema of the time), he had created a stir by admitting that he made his films for the press. "The critics were the only ones who could give one freedom," he recalled, "direct the public what to see."

They had all laughed at him then, but few of those Hate Club members were around to laugh at him by 1958. Hitchcock's success had vindicated his attitude: He had gained the freedom and power he wanted, in large part through his wise use of publicity. Over the course of his career, it was never so much a question of garnering good reviews—although they were important, and, for Hitchcock, usually in plentiful supply—as of cultivating the well-placed feature story. Page after page of newspaper and magazine copy sold his films, his stars, and even himself as a director to the public. Hitchcock never ignored this aspect of the filmmaker's career; it was just as important as the filming itself—especially now that he had to compete against his own efforts on television. Why should people go out to the theater for a Hitchcock film when they could stay in and see one for free? So selling *Vertigo* was a responsibility not to be ignored; as demanding as his personal life may have been, he would be in San Francisco for the film's premiere.

"Hitchcock designated San Francisco as the place to premiere it," Paramount publicity head Herb Steinberg recalled. "He designated who he would like to have there for the opening, who would lend most to the publicity of the film, and he also was very, very helpful in the design of the advertising.

"When we finally had the premiere of the picture, we brought in newspaper people from all over the country to San Francisco. And among them were the syndicated columnists. We had coverage in most of the newspapers in the country and in some around the world."

Before the premiere, Paramount publicity released stories on the film almost every week. Most were puff pieces on the stars, and much was made of the supposed "feud" between Hitchcock and Novak. In one release, Novak denied there was a feud, and she claimed she was actually organizing a Hitchcock fan club on the set. Gossip columnists dutifully picked up publicity-fed stories about roses being delivered daily to Novak's dressing room from a mysterious admirer (allegedly Cary Grant).

In April, *The Hollywood Reporter* commented on an interesting gamble the filmmakers were making: allocating a large chunk of their advertising budget to college and high-school newspapers.

It is the first time any film company ever has allocated such a ballyhoo sum ($10,000) for campus media, completely distinct from magazines which have youth readership. Paramount and Hitchcock

are aiming at the broadening film going market comprising teenagers.

In making the school newspapers' buy, Paramount is after a package deal. In one issue appears the ad; in the subsequent issue appears a publicity plant dealing with the picture; the two are tied into one deal.

In addition to the school newspaper campaign, full-color ads announcing the film appeared in *Life, Look, Seventeen,* and *Fan List.* The ads alternated different tag lines; most were built around conventional-looking images of the stars, rather than on the Bass/Whitney poster graphic that has come to represent the film to modern audiences.

Anticipating the more structured and strict campaign for *Psycho,* ads for *Vertigo* flaunted the storytelling strategy that had so recently threatened to disrupt the production team: "When you have seen *Vertigo,* don't tell anyone the great secret of the story!" Other ads used the Whitney spirals as a motif: "Hitchcock creates a whirling, swirling vortex of suspense," they declared. "Alfred Hitchcock engulfs you in a whirlpool of terror and tension." In keeping with Paramount's high expectations for the film, Saul Bass posters for *Vertigo* boldly declared it "Alfred Hitchcock's Masterpiece."

TV spots also ran at the end of *Alfred Hitchcock Presents,* and there were print ads in the director's mystery magazine. And there were other, more specialized promotions: Theater owners were encouraged to give roses to Novak look-alikes, and they were promised a single with Jay Livingstone and Ray Evans's *Vertigo* song (recorded by Billy Eckstine) on one side and Herrmann's "Prelude" and love theme from the sound track on the flip. No opportunity, it seemed, was left unexploited.

Hitchcock planned an elaborate press tour for the film's May ninth opening. Journalists mingled with the actors and Hitchcock at a cocktail party in the Clift Hotel (where all of the out-of-town journalists were put up) in the afternoon. The menu for the cocktail party was printed in French, a nod to the film's source material.

After cocktails, the party moved to the Stage Door Theater, a 440-seat art house, for *Vertigo*'s first public showing; afterward, the journalists were bussed to Ernie's for a late dinner. After a dinner of "La Noisette de Boeuf Victoria avec

The Hitchcocks at the San Sebastian festival in Spain, where **Vertigo** *was showcased.*

sa Sauce Madere" and an appropriate wine, die-hards were invited to the Venetian room at the Fairmont Hotel, where Dorothy Shay entertained.

That was the official publicity. But there was more, no doubt to Hitchcock's annoyance.

The very next morning, Kim Novak held a special press conference of her own—the subject: a breaking scandal concerning her relationship with a Dominican Republic official.

With unfortunate timing, Novak had managed to become involved in an international incident on the eve of the film's premiere. According to newspaper accounts at the time, she had been dating Lt. Gen. Rafael Trujillo, Jr., son of the leader of the Dominican Republic. During this relationship, she received several high-priced gifts from the leader's son—including, allegedly, a Mercedes-Benz. A columnist from the *Los Angeles Times* described the morning:

Saturday I was rousted out of bed to attend the press conference with Miss Novak—of whom I'd already been advised that "Kim Novak's fondness for lavender will be fulfilled in her beautiful suite at

the Clift—lavender-scented, etc., etc." At the conference, devoted to the now famous unlavender foreign car, gift of Trujillo, Miss Novak looked unhappy. I have news for her—at least one person in the room was unhappier than she.

Over Dick Williams's Monday-morning column in the *Mirror-News* ran the headline KIM'S PEACEFUL WEEKEND SHATTERED. After describing the lavish opening activities on Friday evening, Williams described the next morning in some detail:

And on Saturday morning at 7 A.M., a curious wire service correspondent was banging noisily on the door of Kim's 13th floor Clift hotel suite. She wanted to confirm the Trujillo gift story.

But Kim's publicity girl wasn't buying any, thanks. No, Kim wasn't talking. She was sleeping. Finally, she got rid of the reporter by asking her to come back an hour later.

In the interim, the long distance wires were humming between the suite and Hollywood headquarters and Kim hurriedly arose. It was decided to hold a press conference at 10:30.

Kim looked very sharp in a red outfit at the conference and she handled the questions reasonably well. Every time she got off the party line, her publicist reminded her crisply, "Just a statement, Kim, just a statement."

And when prying reporters kept boring in and wanting to know how Kim thought that Mercedes-Benz was a temporary loan when she signed the bill of sale, her representative just cut the whole thing off and took her away.

It had been a busy year for Kim Novak. While Hitchcock was in Jamaica, a storm of publicity surrounded her alleged love affair with, and impending marriage to, Sammy Davis, Jr. Harry Cohn was so shocked that he left a party in New York and flew back to the studio to manage the crisis. Cohn used everything in his power to end their relationship; he threatened to fire Novak and use his influence to keep Davis from working anywhere in Vegas, and the couple's relationship ended almost immediately.

The Davis crisis may have been too much for Cohn, who was seen taking nitroglycerin tablets for his heart condition when he heard the news. He died of a heart attack at the end of February.

While Novak was fending off the scandal-hungry press, another contingent of reporters was spending the morning on a tour of *Vertigo* locations with Hitchcock and Jimmy Stewart, who was just as committed to his own publicity as the director was to his. The junket included stops at Fort Point and Mission Dolores, where the mock headstone of Carlotta Valdes still rested in the cemetery (according to several locals, the headstone would remain there for several years).

The *Los Angeles Times* writer described the scene during the tours, which had its share of technical problems:

> At noon Hitch, who is partial to travelogues, took us on a tour of the picture's location spots, from a florist's to the Mission Dolores and the Presidio. We rode in brand new cars (domestic), two of which broke down before we reached the top of Nob Hill. Hitch had set up a fake slab for a *Vertigo* scene in a quaintly picturesque cemetery adjoining the mission. There was one tiny tombstone (real) that I can't forget. It read, "Our Little Treasure—4 months and 16 days," and carried the name of a baby girl who died more than a century ago.

Another Los Angeles paper reported on Hitchcock's interaction with fans at the stops:

> When our caravan stopped at the florist shop where a number of the *Vertigo* scenes had been filmed, an elderly woman shoved her way through the crowd to Hitchcock's side.
>
> "Say Dearie, you look much better in person than you do on television," she told him. Later, I asked Hitch how he liked the publicity junket routine.
>
> The pudgy little director shrugged his shoulders.
>
> "You have to do it these days. It used to be that when you were finished filming your work was done—you were home safe. But today, you have to follow through. You have to go out and sell the picture with stunts like this. So, I guess I'll have to get used to people

asking me how much money I make and telling me how I don't look quite so bad in person."

But it was the Novak/Trujillo story that garnered most of the headlines. Monday morning's column about the film mentioned the scandal prominently, and the news sections devoted substantial space to the relationship between the actress and the general's son. The scandal lay not in the mere fact of the gifts—after all, Novak was no public official; it was hardly a crime for her to receive presents—but, at just the moment Congress was debating increasing aid to the Dominican Republic, reporters and politicians found it reasonable to wonder where the son of this tiny island nation's head of state was getting the money to give away expensive imported cars.

The scandal persisted until the eve of the New York premiere at the end of May, when the younger Trujillo finally said farewell to Novak. Amid waning rumors of marriage, the lieutenant general returned to the army's school at Fort Leavenworth, and the affair was ended as swiftly as the Sammy Davis imbroglio had been.

Despite all the distraction, the film did garner mostly positive notices from the local papers covering the premiere. One critic, Jack Moffitt of *The Hollywood Reporter,* published a particularly astute and prescient review on May twelfth:

Alfred Hitchcock tops his own fabulous record for suspense. Aside from being big box office, it is a picture no filmmaker should miss— if only to observe the pioneering techniques achieved by Hitchcock and his co-workers. . . .

The measure of a great director lies in his ability to inspire his associates to rise above their usual competence and Hitchcock exhibits absolute genius in doing this in *Vertigo.* . . .

Stewart gives what I consider the finest performance of his career as the detective. He portrays obsession to the point of mania without the least bit of hamming or scenery chewing. Miss Novak has become a fine actress. . . . Barbara Bel Geddes comes into her own. . . .

The skill with which Alec Coppel and Samuel Taylor constructed their screenplay . . . proves two things—1) that an audience will buy any startling change in human behavior if you give it time (with montages and subtle buildups) to believe the transitions and: 2) that a murder mystery can be the greatest form of emotional drama if one concentrates on the feelings of the characters rather than the plot mathematics. . . .

Vertigo is one of the most fascinating love stories ever filmed.

Moffitt singled out the contributions of most of the technical staff in this review, an exceptionally detailed and perceptive piece of trade criticism. And its tone was echoed by other organs: *Film Daily*'s reviewer wrote that "all in all, the picture is an artistic and entertainment triumph," scoring the direction as "excellent" and the photography as "tops." *The Motion Picture Herald* also rated the film as "excellent." The *Herald* made special mention of Novak, saying that the actress had found a "new plateau in her career through the expert guidance of the 'master of suspense.'"

But there was dissent, even from the beginning. *Variety* (5/14/58), which also predicted big box office for the film, praised the locations and "Hitchcock's directorial hand, cutting, angling and using a jillion gimmicks with mastery." But the *Variety* critic qualified his praise with one major complaint, the gist of which ran directly counter to Moffitt's analysis in the *Reporter:*

Unfortunately, however, even that mastery isn't enough to overcome one major fault, for plain fact is that film's first half is too slow and too long. This may be because Hitchcock became overly enamored with Frisco's vertiginous beauty, and the Alec Coppel-Samuel Taylor screenplay . . . just takes too long to get off the ground. . . .

By [the film's climax] *Vertigo* is more than two hours old, and it's questionable whether that much time should be devoted to what is basically only a psychological murder mystery.

The reviewer concluded that the film "looks like a winner at the box office," but he had settled on an objection that would dog *Vertigo*'s nationwide reception—its languorous length and pace.

The word outside the trade presses tended to follow *Variety*'s lead. The Los Angeles newspapers held their reviews until the film's general release at the end of the month. In the May twenty-ninth *Los Angeles Times,* Philip K. Scheuer sounded the tone that most popular critics would take with the film:

Someone has described the latter-day Alfred Hitchcock film as a thrillorama. This is as handy a way as any to sloganize Hitchcock's *Vertigo,* which is part thriller and part panorama (of San Francisco). Except for a few startling dramatic moments the scenery has it. . . .

In plot outline it is fascinating—Hitchcock has dabbled in a new, for him, dimension: the dream—but he has taken too long to unfold it.

The twice-told theme, hard to grasp at best, bogs down further in a maze of detail; and the spectator experiences not only some of the vertigo afflicting James Stewart, the hero, but also—and worse— the indifference. [Was Scheuer really characterizing Stewart's character as "indifferent"?]

Blonde or brunette, Kim is not a remarkable actress, but she does manage a creditable physical differentiation between Madeleine and Judy. I was bothered by the fact that I could catch almost nothing that Madeleine said (Stewart was guilty of some mumbling, too). I had no trouble understanding the more raucous Judy.

The *Los Angeles Citizen-News* (5/29/58) concurred, but felt the picture had more serious problems in the story department:

Unfortunately, the story, as adapted for the screen comes off less praiseworthy, for most of the time the picture is not a little confusing. The story line is not easy to follow. . . .

Vertigo is technically a topnotch film. Storywise, little can be said. Hitchcock does as well as he can, considering the script, in a directorial capacity. *Vertigo* is not his best picture.

Hazel Flynn, critic for the *Beverly Hills Citizen,* characterized the film as "middling Hitchcock." She wrote, "It has some extraordinary items in it but, once the plot has begun to 'round, not even the director himself, apparently, quite knew how to get off the treadmill." She added, however, that even minor Hitchcock was "head and shoulders above the photoplays of many other directors."

The reviews weren't all bad. The *Los Angeles Times*'s main competitor, the

Los Angeles Examiner, found no fault in the film, although Ruth Waterbury conceded that "you may feel it starts slowly. . . ."

She continued: "There are two vivid stars in *Vertigo,* and both of them are displayed at the top of their form. One is Kim Novak, the actress, and the other is Alfred Hitchcock, the director. In their quite different styles neither of them has ever been more intriguing. . . . *Vertigo* may well make you dizzy, but it surely won't bore you—if you like excitement, action, romance, glamor [*sic*] and a crazy, off-beat love story."

Vertigo premiered in New York at the Capitol the same weekend it opened in Los Angeles at the Paramount. Sam Taylor remembers the screening—especially the red-carpet treatment he received:

"This was in 1958, and when we approached the Capitol we had to slow down to a crawl because there were a lot of limousines in front of us, obviously with famous people, and there was a whole crowd, naturally, of people who are always at premieres with autograph books and things.

"People would come out of the limousines, there would be a great cheer, and they would be attacked, and there was a red carpet. Finally our limousine drove up in front of the Palace and the red carpet and the crowd of autograph people surged forward and somebody opened the door for us and one of the crowd stuck his head in and looked at us and said, 'Nobody!' So there you are."

Cue panned the film severely on the thirty-first of May:

There was a time when Alfred Hitchcock did nothing but turn out 70-80-90 minute movie masterpieces. They were taut, terrifying exercises in suspense-manhunt melodramas, eerie tales of murder done and detected, killings thwarted, dangers evaded, and horrifying flights into the miasmic maze of disordered minds.

As director Hitchcock grew more successful, his producers grew more generous. They put more footage in his films, and greater production values. Hitch broke the rhythm of his melodramas to make side excursions into scenic beauties and romantic bypaths, elaborately dwelling on lavish settings, costumes and similar appurtenances. He became entranced by method rather than mood, style rather than substance, gimmicks rather than grim melodramatics, and his pictures became elaborate chess problems—in which frequently the beauty of the pieces rather than their moves seemed to fascinate him.

. . . *Vertigo* is a two-hours-and-eight-minutes case in point.

The New Yorker, whose review ran on June seventh, was equally unimpressed. John McCarten summarized his review: "Alfred Hitchcock, who produced and directed this thing, has never before indulged in such farfetched nonsense." This same contempt was echoed later by *Time* magazine's memorable label for the film: "another Hitchcock and bull story."

But not all the East Coast coverage was bad. And the bad reviews were, for the most part, attributable to the critics' confusion over the admittedly complex plot.

Richard Griffith, in a June seventeenth *Los Angeles Times* story headlined VERTIGO PLEASES NEW YORK, wrote that the critics "don't want to spoil audience enjoyment by tipping off any of the master's little surprises—but since a Hitchcock film consists almost exclusively of said surprises, there is little else for reviewers to say than see it for yourself."

Griffith summarized the majority opinion on the film as "a treat for all of his fans and for many who do not even know his name."

Those involved in the making of the film also found the finished product to be everything they had expected. Taylor, who hadn't done much film work before *Vertigo,* remembered being pleased by what he saw. "I thought the film was very good and I was pleased with it. But I didn't go around saying that I had just written a masterpiece or anything like that—and neither did Hitchcock, for that matter; at least he didn't say so. It was a normal reaction—I thought, It's a good picture and I'm pleased with it. As Hitchcock would say, 'It's just another movie.'

"But I don't remember any jumping up and down, and as a matter of fact, you know very well it wasn't hailed with hosannas. I think a lot of people were puzzled by it. It was just a Hitchcock picture that seemed to be a little different for Hitchcock."

Herbert Coleman liked the film, though, like many others on the Paramount team, he admitted that it wasn't his favorite Hitchcock film: *To Catch a*

Thief, doubtless a more exotic filmmaking experience for those involved, remained the close-knit group's favorite.

In a note to Hitchcock sent during the summer of 1958, animator John Ferren praised the movie:

> I liked *Vertigo,* both as a picture and my sequence. I saw it twice. The first time I was put out by some technical roughnesses, the second time I thought that it had a real kick and was fine in and for the story. Incidentally Bob Burks photographed the thing (I mean the entire picture) beautifully. My home town never looked so good. . . . My feet are clay enough to have enjoyed seeing my screen credit up there bigger than life.

Saul Bass, who later won an award for his design work on *Vertigo,* wrote: "I'd like to take this opportunity to thank you for providing me a framework within which I could produce something of worth. I do hope I may have the opportunity to work with you again."

If grosses are any indication of success, *Vertigo* was neither winner nor loser. It finished twenty-first in 1958 ticket sales, with $3.2 million—the equivalent of approximately $7 million in 1997 dollars. This was about $2 million off what Hitchcock had made on *Rear Window* ($5.3 million) and what he would take in on *North by Northwest* ($5.5 million), but better than *The Wrong Man*—a ranking that accurately reflected each film's relative commerciality.

The 1958 figure does not account for overseas sales. The final cost of making *Vertigo* ran to $2,479,000—which means it garnered something like $1 million in domestic box-office profit on its first outing. Of the final price, Paramount picked up $2,004,722.49 and Hitchcock Productions paid $443,307. None of these figures include Hitchcock's or Stewart's salaries, which were based on an undisclosed percentage of the film's grosses.

The real money was in the ownership of the film. Hitchcock's contract gave Paramount an eight-year lease on five of the films, after which the rights would revert to Hitchcock. Paramount rereleased *Vertigo* and *Rear Window* in 1963 to play off the release of *The Birds,* but no figures are available for this second run. There was another release after the rights reverted to Hitchcock in the late sixties, through Universal, and then a sale to television. After the early seventies, the film was pulled from release, along with the other Paramount films Hitchcock owned (*The Trouble with Harry, The Man Who Knew Too Much,* and *Rope,* which Hitchcock had financed through his own short-lived company, Transatlantic Pictures). *Psycho,* Hitchcock's last Paramount film, was sold to Universal in 1968, when the rights returned to Hitchcock.

Vertigo had very limited availability in the early seventies, then disappeared completely from distribution in 1974. Why? There was no compelling legal or financial reason. According to Herman Citron, Hitchcock's agent, the decision was personal. Hitchcock refused inquiries from colleges and film societies that requested it for screenings. He wasn't so restrictive with the other titles (two of which he donated in 16mm reductions to a prominent eastern university), but with *Vertigo,* he was far more protective.

If Hitchcock's intention was to set aside a nest egg for his family by keeping *Vertigo* and the other films off the market, the decision was wise. The director's career may have been on the wane in the sixties and seventies—certainly his last great film was *Marnie,* which has deeply divided critics over the years—but his critical reputation was approaching its zenith.

There is an odd parallel between the period of the director's critical rise and the decline of his new work. In 1958, Hitchcock was an economically successful director. His pictures turned profits and his personal recognition skyrocketed with his popular television series. But despite his artistic pretenses as a young director in England, Hitchcock was never considered a "serious" filmmaker by American critics. When their personalities lent themselves to the enterprise, directors like Hitchcock were used as advertising labels for films, but that was as far as the auteur theory went in America's consciousness: There simply was no serious domestic critical community available to celebrate cinematic artists.

Nineteen fifty-eight, though, was a turning point for both Hitchcock and art cinema. In France, Claude Chabrol and Eric Rohmer had published in 1957 the first book-length critical assessment of Hitchcock—*Hitchcock: Classiques du Cinéma.* The book ended with *The Wrong Man* (what a difference a few years would have made); though it was unavailable in English until the late sixties (*Hitchcock: The First Forty-four Films,* translated by Stanley Hochman) their work was extremely influential.

One of Chabrol and Rohmer's fellow filmmakers, François Truffaut, was also a Hitchcock admirer. After a brief meeting with Hitchcock during one of the master's visits to France, Truffaut proposed conducting a series of interviews to discuss the genesis of all of Hitchcock's films. The celebrated Hitchcock/Truffaut interviews (comprising fifty hours in all) began during the postproduction of *The Birds* and the start of production on *Marnie*. Published in book form—first in France in 1966, then in 1968 in the United States—the interviews treated Hitchcock's career with a sense of continuity and purpose, with Truffaut insightfully tracing recurring themes and establishing core films (*The Lodger, The Man Who Knew Too Much, Shadow of a Doubt, Notorious, Rear Window*).

Surprisingly, both directors had remarkably little to say about *Vertigo*. Hitchcock acknowledged defects within the picture, and he groused slightly about Novak's performance (over which Truffaut enthused). The overall impression that Hitchcock gave was that *Vertigo* had failed him. But Hitchcock the auteur of 1962 was the same man who had worried over the box-office receipts for *The Wrong Man* just before mounting *Vertigo*—indeed, the same man who had shocked the Hate Club decades before with his pledge of allegiance to the critics—and he remained quick to criticize films that offered no box-office or critical satisfaction. After all, what other judgment was there to trust? To the entertainer, the audience and the critics have the final say: No matter how secure one may feel in a performance, it's the level of applause that determines success.

But years after the mixture of applause and complaint that greeted *Vertigo* had died down, Hitchcock's most personal film began to attract an extraordinary level of renewed critical interest. Among several books written during the director's last years that examined the Hitchcock canon, by far the most important—both in general and in the special attention it paid to *Vertigo*—was Robin Wood's *Hitchcock's Films* (1965).

Wood began his analysis with a fundamental question: "Why should we take Hitchcock seriously?" His response made well-reasoned comparisons to another great English entertainer: William Shakespeare. Wood argued that Hitchcock's films showed a "consistent development, deepening and clarification," that there was an overall unity to his work that transcended the merits of each individual film. "But within this unity—and this is something which rarely receives the emphasis it deserves—another mark of Hitchcock's stature is the amazing variety of his work . . . consider merely Hitchcock's last five

VERTIGO: The Making of a Hitchcock Classic

films, made within a period of seven years, *Vertigo, North by Northwest, Psycho, The Birds, Marnie*. . . . True, he never invents his own plots, but adapts the work of others: again, one cannot resist invoking Shakespeare. Hitchcock is no more limited by his sources than Shakespeare was by his. The process whereby Greene's romance *Pandosto* was transformed into the great poetic drama of *The Winter's Tale* is not unlike that whereby Boileau and Narcejac's *D'Entre les Morts* became *Vertigo:* there is the same kind of relationship. . . . Shakespeare's poetry is not an adornment for Greene's plot, but a true medium, a means of absorbing that plot into an organic dramatic-poetic structure; precisely the same is true of Hitchcock's mise-en-scène in *Vertigo*."

But it was a later pronouncement in Wood's book that led to the reawakening of interest in *Vertigo* in the seventies and eighties: "*Vertigo* seems to me Hitchcock's masterpiece to date, and one of the four or five most profound and beautiful films the cinema has yet given us." He supports this large claim by examining the film's treatment of themes "of the most fundamental human significance." And, like its creator, Wood spends considerable time debating the significance and reasoning behind the decision to include Judy's confession two-thirds of the way through the film. "Our immediate reaction to the revelation, I think, is extreme disappointment. This can exist on a purely superficial level: we have come to see a mystery story and now we know it all, so what is the use of the film's continuing? Why should we have to watch the detective laboriously discovering things we know already? Much popular discontent with the film can be traced to this premature revelation, and in terms of audience reaction it was certainly a daring move on Hitchcock's part."

Vertigo, according to Wood, ultimately represents the world as "quicksand, unstable, constantly shifting . . . into which we may sink at any step in any direction, illusion and reality constantly ambiguous, even interchangeable."

He concludes that *Vertigo* "seems to me of all Hitchcock's films the one nearest to perfection. Indeed, its profundity is inseparable from the perfection of form: it is a perfect organism, each character, each sequence, each image, illuminating every other. Form and technique here become the perfect expression of concerns both deep and universal. Hitchcock uses audience involvement as an essential aspect of the film's significance. Together with its deeply disturbing attitude to life goes a strong feeling for the value of human relationships. . . . Hitchcock is concerned with impulses that lie deeper than individual psychology, that are inherent in the human condition. . . . In complexity and subtlety, in emotional depth, in its power to disturb, in the centrality of its concerns, *Vertigo* can as well as any film be taken to represent the cinema's claims to be treated with the respect accorded to the longer established art forms."

It was this kind of evaluation that increased public demand for the film— just as Hitchcock was tucking it away for more than a decade. Wood's book was followed by others, including Donald Spoto's *The Art of Alfred Hitchcock* (1976), more an approach for laymen to the master's films. Spoto agreed with Wood in his assessment of *Vertigo,* but by the time his book was published, the film was gone—which only added to its allure. The film that once had drawn audiences only slowly to neighborhood theaters was now hoarded jealously in clandestine prints held by fans and collectors; these prints ranged from the good (pristine IB Technicolor 35mm or 16mm reductions) to the awful (including black-and-white versions and primitive video dupes).

Since the film returned to the screen—at first as a part of a major 1984 Hitchcock rerelease program, then in the glorious 1996 restoration—*Vertigo* has served as mirror to the critical perspectives of our time: feminist, Marxist, and deconstructivist critics regularly issue new readings of its meaning, while others offer close readings that sketch Hitchcock the filmmaker as Svengali, as necrophiliac, even as confused loner.

Even the quality and place of *Vertigo* in the canon is still hotly debated. There are still academics who see the film, with its narrative and structural weaknesses and its occasional technical shortcomings, as a failure; but the majority opinion places the film among Hitchcock's most important, and often at the top of the list—and maintains, moreover, that it is the key to understanding Hitchcock, the artist and the man.

Are the original creators surprised at the renewed interest in *Vertigo*? Herbert Coleman is not surprised at Hitchcock's popularity, but he is bemused by the attention lavished on this film. For Coleman and other crew members, it was just another Hitchcock project.

Sam Taylor is pleased that after so many years the film has a following. "I am very proud. Not surprised, because it does have the depth that is fairly unusual for a picture of that sort. I watch with a great deal of pleasure the growth of the legend of *Vertigo.*"

Novak still sees the film as a very personal one for herself and Hitchcock.

"It was almost as if Hitchcock was Elster, the man who was telling me to play a role . . . here's what I had to do, and wear, and it was so much of me playing Madeleine . . . but I really appreciated it. In hindsight, I think he's one of the few directors who allowed me the most freedom as an actress. That might seem hard to believe because he was so restrictive about what he wanted. But even though he knew where he wanted you to be, he didn't want to take away how you got to that point. He wouldn't tell me what to be thinking to get to a point. Today, I'm very proud of *Vertigo* because I do think it's one of the best things I've ever done."

For Stewart it was the character's fear that still resonated with him. That, and Hitchcock's own personal involvement. "After several years, I saw the film again and thought it was a fine picture. I myself had known fear like that, and I'd known people paralyzed by fear. It's a very powerful thing to be almost engulfed by that kind of fear. I didn't realize when I was preparing for the role what an impact it would have, but it's an extraordinary achievement by Hitch. And I could tell it was a very personal film even while he was making it."

Hitchcock never matched the zenith of the period that ran from *Rear Window* through *Marnie* (and many would contend that that film is a disaster). His films of the late sixties, *Torn Curtain* and *Topaz,* were weak; only the last two Hitchcock films, *Frenzy* and *Family Plot,* showed anything like the special quality that marked his finest work.

By the 1970s, time had caught up with Alfred Hitchcock. He was an artist who had never planned to retire—yet, though he went through the motions of writing a new script, it was clear to everyone around him that his filmmaking days were over. His confidante, friend, and co-creator, Alma, had suffered a series of strokes. Letters he wrote during the period reveal the director in his final role: as a husband caring dutifully for an ailing wife. Given his concern for and attachment to Alma, it is doubtful that even Hitchcock himself entertained any serious notion of shooting another film after *Family Plot* in 1976. Planning and writing had always been Hitchcock's great pleasure—he often said that after finishing a script he dreaded having to go on and commit it to the screen, for the film was already complete and perfect in his mind. Yet he surely missed the days of total involvement in crafting challenging shots with a well-tuned crew.

After much lionizing in the final years of his life—months before his death, he was awarded a knighthood—Sir Alfred Hitchcock died at his home in Bel Air in April 1980, certainly aware that his reputation was intact with the only audience that counted: posterity.

> **The death of Hitchcock marks the passage from one era to another. . . . I believe we are entering an era defined by the suspension of the visual. . . . I don't think we'll have the strength to make cinema much longer.**
>
> —*Jean-Luc Godard, 1980*

Allusions to *Vertigo,* in today's culture of cinema, music, and television, pop up everywhere. Certainly many are unintentional—after all, every murder mystery features scenes of detectives following their objects of pursuit—but just as many are by way of intentional and direct homage to the film. Even before its initial release, Kim Novak and James Stewart had their lives affected by *Vertigo,* choosing for their next project a story that profited directly from the mysterious atmosphere Hitchcock created around them. *Bell, Book and Candle* comes nowhere near the sophistication of *Vertigo,* but its proximity to the film in release date, and its vague thematic similarities—Stewart is bewitched again by Novak—often confuse moviegoers.

Hitchcock reworked the themes and daring construction of *Vertigo* in his last film for Paramount, *Psycho.* Norman Bates, too, suffers from an obsession—his after the death of his mother—though, in his case, of a far more deadly variety: Unable to accept her death (due to his own actions, just as Scottie felt that his inaction had led to Madeleine's death), he develops a psychological problem far more complex and unhealthy than Scottie's. Rather than remaking women into his mother, he keeps his dead mother preserved and kills off any woman who threatens her dubious reality.

Hitchcock's daring strokes in the con-

struction of *Psycho* overshadowed the groundwork he had laid in *Vertigo*. Killing off the story's lead actress in the film's first half hour had its own disorienting effect on 1960 audiences. The effort to keep audiences from revealing the "surprise" (as the advertising campaign had attempted for *Vertigo*) was doubled: The *Psycho* ad campaign was built on the premise that no one would be seated after the film started. Hitchcock made a special film for the distributors of *Psycho,* explaining the policy and why it should be enforced. Pinkerton guards were hired for the major theaters in New York, Chicago, and Los Angeles to assist in enforcing the "no late seating" policy. And, in the end, what had had a questionable effect on *Vertigo* ticket sales was a major success with *Psycho:* The film earned more than $8 million in its first release.

Psycho came at an important moment for Hitchcock. The last of his Paramount films would also be his final unquestioned box-office winner, and his work seemed to grow more impersonal as that of younger filmmakers grew more personal. But *Vertigo,* if not in its first release, then certainly in its 1963 rerelease, began to have a slow and methodical influence on the very artists whose success—whose power and freedom—Hitchcock envied.

Hitchcock stood in a unique position to these filmmakers: His films influenced the experimental and independent filmmakers more profoundly than the work of any other major studio director. *Psycho* certainly revolutionized the horror genre and the production process, proving to the studios that a very profitable film could be made for under a million dollars. The studios for the most part ignored the lesson, but the sixties saw an enormous growth in small production companies whose sole purpose was to turn out low-budget horror fare.

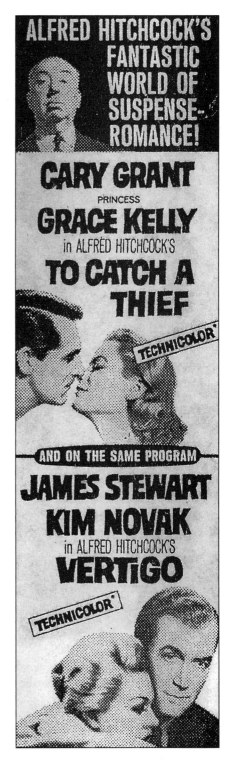

In the four decades since its initial release, the generation of moviemakers who grew up on Hitchcock and *Vertigo* has grown into maturity. And as a result much of the director's work finds its way into popular films by way of allusion—through either images or film construction that owes a debt to the Master's style. The director himself seemed not to mind this homage, no matter how absurd: When *Vertigo* turned up as the focus of Mel Brooks's 1977 Hitchcock parody, *High Anxiety,* Hitchcock himself wrote Brooks a complimentary note and sent a case of expensive Bordeaux wine as a gift.

Other than the obvious spoofery of *High Anxiety,* the most overt absorption of *Vertigo* is in Brian DePalma's 1976 *Obsession*. But that film is less an extension of Hitchcock's work than, quite simply, a mess. It exhibits none of the structural bravery of Hitchcock's film; worse yet, the very thing that makes *Vertigo* work—our uncomfortable identification with its lead character—is missing. DePalma's film never gives us the opportunity to share Cliff Robertson's feelings for his lost wife, who dies in the film's first twenty minutes; what's left is not an engaging mystery—despite its provocative Bernard Herrmann score—but a series of long scenes of pursuit without any momentum behind them. DePalma later reworked *Vertigo* in a tawdry enterprise that mixed it with *Rear Window* in a prurient blend, but *Body Double,* intended as an angry assault on DePalma's critics, never generated the kind of interest the director had hoped for.

There are better filmmakers whose work owes much to *Vertigo*. Martin Scorsese, for all the differences between his typical subject matter and Hitchcock's, has done far more to earn comparisons with the director of *Vertigo* and *Psycho*. Few other filmmakers have taken the kind of risks Scorsese has. The obsession of De Niro's taxi driver in the film of the same name is the dark portrait of a working-class Scottie in a world far more nightmarish than Hitchcock ever imagined—a connection assisted by Herrmann's last, truly great score.

Certainly Scorsese's lushly romantic 1993 film, *The Age of Innocence,* owes much to *Vertigo*. Think of the lingering camerawork over the flowers in the title sequence, designed by Saul and Elaine Bass; the attention to art and the past; the passionate obsession of the male character with a forbidden woman; the psychological breakdown of that character under the grip of social standards. *Vertigo* echoes in this film's every frame.

The real value of a great work of art is reflected less surely in the necessary evil of imitation (think of the poor imitations of Shakespeare's plays pulled together by competing theaters) than in how the work influences other artists as they add their own creations to the dialogue. Martin Scorsese is an excellent example of the artist as synthesist—as, for that matter, was Alfred Hitchcock.

Hitchcock liked to portray himself as the uninfluenced artist, but he screened movies weekly, sometimes daily, during the months he spent between projects. Ken Mogg, editor of the Hitchcock publication *The MacGuffin Journal,* has done brilliant work in linking *Vertigo* with possible predecessors: the two versions of *Le Grand Jeu* (1934 and 1953); *Carrefour* (1938); *The Uninvited* (1944); *Portrait of Jennie* (1948); and even *I Remember Mama* (1948, costarring Barbara Bel Geddes and set in San Francisco)—all bear signs of having made strong impressions on Hitchcock.

Among the recent wave of independent filmmakers (and *Vertigo,* despite its development at Paramount, was almost an independent film in both conception and execution), there are many directors who come to mind as keepers of the flame. Gus Van Sant, the director of *My Own Private Idaho* and *Mala Noche,* has done thought-provoking work within the obsession genre that Hitchcock helped create. His imagery and rich colors evoke the sensuality of colors that the restored *Vertigo* reveals. Danish director Lars von Trier's *Zentropa* is a stunning film that appears to owe much of its imagery to *Vertigo.* Von Trier uses transparencies in a stylish and imaginative way, and the film's spiraling images lead the viewer into the fractured world of postwar Germany in much the way they led *Vertigo*'s audience into Scottie Ferguson's twisted inner world.

And *Vertigo*'s influence has extended in other directions besides the thematic. Often called "the filmmaker's film," over the years it has had a special influence on experimental filmmakers. Director Chris Marker was certainly affected by the film: His groundbreaking *La Jetée* (1964) is suffused with direct allusion. The twenty-nine-minute film tells the story through still photographs of a man who's obsessed by an image from his youth. When he meets the woman central to the image, they visit a Parisian garden. "They stop by a tree trunk with historic dates," the narrator tells the viewer. Then, "as if in a dream, he points beyond the tree and hears himself saying: That is where I came from. . . ." *Vertigo* was also an explicit part of Marker's film *Sans Soleil* (1982). *Sans Soleil* has a complicated narrative that moves all over the world, but a memorable sequence intercuts scenes from *Vertigo* with a visit to San Francisco.

Chris Marker recently wrote an interesting homage to *Vertigo* for *Projections:* "The power of this once ignored film has become commonplace," Marker wrote. "'You're my second chance!' cries Scottie as he drags Judy up the stairs of the tower. No one now wants to interpret these words in their superficial sense, meaning his vertigo has been conquered. It's about reliving a moment lost in the past, about bringing it back to life only to lose it again. One does not resurrect the dead, one doesn't look back at Eurydice. Scottie experiences the greatest joy a man can imagine, a second life, in exchange for the greatest tragedy, a second death."

Marker described his first experience with Hitchcock's film: "I saw *Vertigo* as it was shown in France. I could hardly tell the year, but the rule in those times was approximately one year after the US release, so we can say 1958/60. The impact was immediate and didn't cease, even though I deepened my understanding at each new screening. But the emotion was and still is intact. When they presented part of the trailer on TV to announce the 1996 release of the 70mm version, seeing Novak in the green light of the room after her final transformation gave me the same goose flesh as ever."

There is "something of *Vertigo*" in a CD-ROM Marker is currently creating, entitled *Immemory.* "I use as the gatekeepers of the Memory sequence the two gentlemen who [made] the best use of the name "Madeleine," Mr. Alfred Hitchcock and Mr. Marcel Proust. It is through a digitized Novak the user will gain access to different layers of my Memory machine."

Vertigo has also inspired artists outside of the medium. Much of this work was recently recognized in an exhibition at the Museum of Contemporary Art in Los Angeles. "Art and Film Since 1945: Hall of Mirrors" called attention to artwork connected to many of Hitchcock's films, most notably *Spellbound, Rear Window, Psycho,* and *Vertigo.* The exhibit included both art used in *Vertigo* and art inspired by the film; featured in the exhibit are the opening titles by Saul Bass and John Whitney, Marker's *La Jetée,* and other works that pay homage to Hitchcock's vision.

Cindy Bernard's photographic work is perhaps the most straightforward in the exhibit, yet startling on its own terms. In the series entitled *Ask the Dust,* Bernard revisited a group of famous film locations to shoot pictures using the same lenses and camera positions as the original films. The results are haunting—the locations are recaptured not as we know them, but like ghost landscapes, without actors or the context of a theater to animate them. Of the twenty-one films that Bernard selected, two were Hitchcock's: *North by Northwest* (for which she chose the site of the famous crop-duster scene) and *Vertigo,* for which she selected the view of the Golden Gate Bridge from Fort Point. "As an object or film," Bernard has said, "*Vertigo* is beautiful, an amazing piece, just on that level."

When she originally conceived the project in 1987, Bernard chose as her cultural window the twenty years between 1954's *Brown* v. *Board of Education* decision and Richard Nixon's 1974 resignation. "The films that I included either fit the idea—that of landscape and the effect that film has had in defining the landscape for us—[or were] films that I loved and wanted to include."

Vertigo fell neatly into both categories, although Bernard admitted that the fit didn't appear natural at first. But nevertheless, she was drawn to the film: "I think it was the depiction of impossible memory—Scottie's inability to let go, [his desire] to re-create the space of that experience, to create a simulacra of Madeleine. This was very powerful to me. I also think the attraction has to do with the film as a metaphor of the artistic process: Scottie's obsessive desire to make this thing/woman what it is he wants her to be."

Bernard's work demonstrates the power of location to evoke the memory of a film—perhaps most provocatively with *Vertigo,* a film itself concerned with the power of memory, and a film so linked to its location that it has inspired decades of pilgrimage.

Indeed, it's difficult to think of another film that has inspired this kind of devotion. Harrison Engle, the director of *Obsessed with Vertigo,* AMC's excellent documentary on the making and restoration of the film, may have been one of the first pilgrims to visit the Bay Area specifically to observe the locations from the film. The young midwesterner was on a school trip to the West Coast in June of 1958—no more than a few weeks after *Vertigo*'s release—when he went on his own to visit the San Francisco sites. "The film was mesmerizing and deeply affecting the moment I saw it," he says. "It touched that part in me that we all feel—that wants us to hold on to the past."

Chris Marker recalled his own visits to the locations: "My first move was to do something relatively original at the time, very common today: revisiting all the locations, doing the '*Vertigo* tour.' I did it again a few times, and especially in 1982 to shoot the footage for *Sans Soleil*. You won't be surprised to hear that when I relaxed at the little coffee shop on the San Juan Bautista plaza, the cookie on my plate was in the shape of a spiral," Marker remembered. He went on to note that "utopia" for him meant renting the apartment at 900 Lombard Street, which he did during his 1982 stay.

Over the years a number of articles have been published describing *Vertigo* tours; in fact, a map was recently published, listing the film's locations (among other Bay Area film locations). This author's own pilgrimage in 1986 was overwhelming in its effect: The work of Cindy Bernard may come closer to conveying the power those locations hold than words can.

Remembered lines and music were an important part of Christian Marclay's contribution to the MoCA exhibition. Using elements from *Vertigo*'s dialogue and score, Marclay's installation, *Vertigo (soundtrack for an exhibition),* plays snippets from the film at random lengths and at random intervals. The installation was described as a "new soundtrack" that "startles the unaware gallery visitor, conjures up iconic images from the film, but then creates from them a new film of the imagination."

Marclay, a sculptor and "sonic" artist, originally composed the installation for a 1990 Paris exhibition entitled "Vertigo"—an exhibition that had nothing explicitly to do with the film, though Marclay points out that this particular curator had a penchant for using Hitchcock films as titles for his exhibitions. "This installation was not meant to be ambient music," Marclay explained. "The volume is meant to be loud so that the museum or gallery visitor is startled and not allowed to ignore it. I took the film's soundtrack as raw material to work with—both the dialogue and the music. Once the dialogue or the music is pulled out of context, the abstract lines take on a significance that I didn't notice in the film.

"There are many moments in the film though where image and sound cannot be separated, where the two have become so connected in almost a cliché way that the music summons the image and the image summons the music."

• • •

Vertigo's unique appeal continues to draw artists and audiences back into the darkness of the theater to experience the wrenching obsession and loss that it conveys so deeply. Who would have ever imagined in 1958 that such a dark, unlikely story would have so much to say to audiences forty years later? No surprise, then, the comparisons between Hitchcock and Shakespeare—two masters skilled at selling such misery to a willing audience.

| # RECALLED TO LIFE: *VERTIGO* RESTORED

Lo no mori, e non rimasi vivo.
(I did not die, yet nothing of life remained.)

—*Dante*

Alfred Hitchcock left an enormous and diverse estate. When his wife Alma died, two years after the director, their holdings were inherited by their only daughter, Patricia Hitchcock O'Connell. Even before Alma's death, Herman Citron and Universal began discussing a new rerelease of the five films owned by Hitchcock. As early as July of 1980, Aljean Harmetz reported for *The New York Times* that Citron was expecting the films to go back into circulation.

Three years later, the rerelease of the five films was achieved through a deal with Universal Pictures. Though he revealed no specifics, one of the trustees of the estate, Leland Faust, said that

OPPOSITE: *James C. Katz (left) and Robert A. Harris, the restoration team who brought* Vertigo *back to life in 1996.*

the arrangement (orchestrated by the head of Universal's Classics division, James C. Katz) was just what the Hitchcock family had hoped for. *Vertigo* was not sold to Universal, as was *Psycho* (and the large *Alfred Hitchcock Presents* library), but leased to the studio for a limited time; the five films were rereleased within a few months of one another.

Vertigo was unveiled in December 1983. While domestically the film netted only a respectable $2.3 million, it did extremely well overseas, on video and on broadcast television. James Katz, of the film's restoration team, guessed that *Vertigo* and the four other films released in 1984 did over $50 million in business on this rerelease—a substantial figure under any circumstances.

But the film's financial success was insignificant in comparison with the major critical reception the film received. Janet Maslin reported in *The New York Times:*

> An astonishing burst of applause greeted the penultimate moments of Alfred Hitchcock's 1958 *Vertigo* at the performance I attended—astonishing because only seconds later, the film's real ending left the audience in gasping disbelief.
>
> If *Rear Window* seemed a pleasant surprise when it re-emerged last fall, *Vertigo* now seems shocking. For those who remember it fondly as Hitchcock's lost masterpiece, there are some surprisingly rough edges; for those to whom it's unfamiliar, it may seem unbearably cruel. What is sure to startle anyone is the spectacle of the film, especially so emotionally powerful a film, whose every element is precisely geared to the larger whole. No director today exerts the kind of unrelenting control that Hitchcock did. And Hitchcock, for all his remarkable powers of reason, never shaped a film as fervently or perversely as he did this one.

Many critics looked at *Vertigo* in the light of Donald Spoto's *The Dark Side of Genius,* the biography of Hitchcock he published in 1983. Virtually every critic responded to the "autobiographical nature" of the film—to the way Scottie's re-creation of Madeleine echoed the director Hitchcock's yearning to recreate the lost Grace Kelly. In this school of criticism, Stewart and Novak are reduced to Everyman and Everyblonde—if one can accept the idea of Alfred Hitchcock as anyone's Everyman, or Kelly as anyone's Everyblonde.

Even a critic like Peter Rainer, who admitted up front in his review for the *Los Angeles Herald Examiner* that he does not share the opinion that "Hitchcock was a great artist of dread and terror," ultimately admitted the power *Vertigo* has in its influence on other directors: To him, it was "the craziest of Hitchcock movies, even more so I think than *Psycho*—and that quality of personal obsession must be what grips these filmmakers. It still has the power to grip audiences, too."

Andrew Sarris, who originally panned the movie, had come around twenty-five years later:

> There is something very darkly, very deviously funny in the spectacle of Stewart's meticulous effort to remake the shop girl into the femme fatale. On the one level it is a directorial parable on Hitchcock's own efforts with Novak, on another a critique of the eternal search for the ideal woman. The cream of the jest, however, is in the casting of supposedly all-American James Stewart in the role of the pathological Pygmalion. . . . *Vertigo,* like all Hitchcock films, is an elaborate balancing act, and he has found the means of pouring all the inherent ambiguities of the cinema into our collective unconscious. I have barely scratched the surface of my own speculations. . . . For the moment, let us say simply that *Vertigo* looks and sounds magnificent after more than a quarter of a century. Of how many contemporary films will we be able to say the same in 25 years hence?

When the newly restored print of *Vertigo* was released in 1996, there was no question that this was Hitchcock's preeminent film. Maslin, under the *The New York Times* headline HITCHCOCK AT HIS DEEPEST, called the film prescient, "the deepest, darkest masterpiece of Hitchcock's career. . . . The lure of death, the power of the past, the guilty complicity of a clean-cut hero, the near fetishistic use of symbol and color: these Hitchcock hallmarks are all mesmerizingly on view. (Here's a film in which the heroine's twisting hairdo signals the hero's primal terror. And in which, as the restoration newly emphasized, there is ominous, alluring magic to a certain shade of green.)"

The film, nearly forty years later, had finally, securely lived up to its classification as Hitchcock's masterpiece, as Bass's poster had always proclaimed. Many reviews focused on the restored elements—the revelations that the restoration provided about Hitchcock's use of color, about the intense Herrmann score.

In the late 1970s, the *Village Voice* voted *Vertigo* the greatest American film of all time. At the time of the 1996 restoration, J. Hoberman wrote in its pages that the 70mm restoration matched the hype but that "when its drama is distilled to overwhelming desire (and the desire to be desired), when its narrative is vaporized by the force of mutual (and mutually exclusive) longings, this movie could cast its spell from a nine-inch black-and-white TV set."

The restoration was a difficult, exacting effort, but its reception more than justified the work involved. The restored *Vertigo* debuted as a sold-out special event at the New York Film Festival. Fans had been fed slices of the restoration work during the year as the restora-

The restoration premiere: After a celebrity-studded opening, the film ran for months at New York's Ziegfeld Theater.

tion team of Robert A. Harris and James C. Katz took sections, along with original scenes for comparison purposes, to other festivals. The October fourth opening night at New York's Ziegfeld Theater was a genuine event: Kim Novak and Patricia Hitchcock O'Connell attended the event along with Harris and Katz, and she spoke briefly before the screening. The Ziegfeld itself was a product of restoration (though not quite a finished product at the time—plastic covered some unfinished portions of the foyer), giving the film a perfect berth.

The audience paid seventy-five dollars a seat to be among the first to view the new print. Walter Cronkite and Douglas Fairbanks, Jr., were among the celebrities in attendance. And, though doubtless many had seen it before, the audience reactions were those of first-time viewers—startled gasps at Madeleine's suicide, whispered *aha*s at Judy's confession. The crowd seemed visibly unnerved in the final, shattering moments: As Stewart stands in the tower's arch, there was a stunned, deeply felt silence from the crowd.

In the opening weeks, the film averaged $34,000 per theater—a remarkable total for any film, let alone one first released four decades before.

•   •   •

The restoration team traveled with the film to Washington, D.C., Chicago, Los Angeles, and San Francisco for a series of openings. The film remained at theaters in these major markets through December.

For years, film aficionados had clamored for a quality laser-disc edition of *Vertigo;* the 1996 restoration was the version that finally made it to disc as well as video (while it continued its on-screen life in international release). Harrison Engle's documentary on the restoration, featuring interviews with the surviving filmmakers and actors, was broadcast with the film on the American Movie Classics network in the October of 1997, and was released on both tape and laser disc.

The Hitchcock family is committed to cycling the film through the theaters every ten years or so, guaranteeing that *Vertigo* will be with us on the small and big screen well into the next century. It is a strategy unique among adult films (only the Disney children's classics see a structured re-release pattern). Even standard-bearers like *Casablanca* and *Gone With the Wind* have seen their theatrical audience shrink with the ready availability of videotape.

Thirty years ago, when Hitchcock was asked what he wanted done with extra *Vertigo* footage stored at Technicolor's lab, the answer was obvious: It was to be destroyed. Only the 35mm and 16mm negatives and a set of prints were stored in the Hollywood Bekins storage facility. Alternative takes, the original sound track—everything else was destroyed. There was no malice in this course taken by Hitchcock's staff. Sadly, at the time it was standard operating procedure.

A decade later, as standards began to change, it is doubtful that Hitchcock would have so cavalierly destroyed this material. But in 1967, *Vertigo* was merely a nine-year-old film, a completed product—not yet a cinematic cornerstone, or even a subject worth any prolonged conversation (as Truffaut's interviews attest).

The story of *Vertigo*'s restoration starts much earlier—all stories of preservation begin with the collector's desire to preserve a beloved film in its original glory—but for our purposes, it can be traced to the late 1970s, as the preservation/restoration movement was beginning. The most heroic preservation story of all is Kevin Brownlow's work on Abel Gance's *Napoleon*. His interest began when he was a young boy collecting silent films on 9.5mm prints.

The first Brownlow restoration of the film was in this format, years before he was able to find the money and the materials for the full restoration that played to sold-out houses around the world.

The *Napoleon* saga is familiar: Initial prints of the film had later been cut up into smaller and smaller versions, until the film was no longer recognizable. Similar problems were faced on *Lawrence of Arabia* and *Spartacus*. These films were saved by individuals who remembered each film as it once was and worked to re-create it as it resided there—the madeleine evoking memory.

If *Vertigo*'s rescue did not happen in quite the same way, it is in part because it never suffered quite the fate of those other films. Hitchcock's film was not an epic that was a road show and then cut down for wide release. Nor did the director make any changes in the film once it was released; nor did the studio force changes or cuts in existing prints. The film from the outset reflected the artist's personal vision, and (except for a change of format that restorers discovered along the way) it was never tampered with by other people. What was happening to the film was that, like all films stored improperly and uncared for, it was being tampered with by time. The colors were no longer bright and true; the separate elements for the optical work were shrinking, making the job of matching them nearly impossible; more distressing, the sound track was lost altogether.

As James Katz and Robert Harris discuss in the interview that follows, the story of *Vertigo*'s renewal begins with its 1983 rerelease. Katz was head of the newly formed Universal Classics, which had handled the general release of Brownlow's *Napoleon* and was instrumental in gaining the rights to the Hitchcock films. But the 1983 release was not a restoration, or even a preservation; prints were struck from the 35mm reductions that were available. Katz knew then from looking at the prints that *Vertigo* was in bad shape.

But a serious mission to repair *Vertigo* fully did not begin for another decade. In 1993, while working on *My Fair Lady,* Harris and Katz found the original music recordings to *Vertigo* rotting away in Paramount's vault. At their own expense, they made a new recording of the badly damaged track—with the original element disintegrating as it passed through the sound heads. Galvanized by their find, the pair began to look into what could be done for the film itself.

What happened next moves beyond restoration into a new area of film preservation that does not have a ready title. Harris and Katz found themselves confronted with the film's original elements—which were in VistaVision, a process neither of them had ever worked with before (although the team had worked with the similar Technirama format). Part of the challenge of restoring *Vertigo* was in working with this process, which Paramount used exclusively as a competitor to other wide-screen formats. Hitchcock liked VistaVision—it provided a wide-screen ratio and much clearer images—but probably for reasons of cost *Vertigo,* along with all of Hitchcock's other Paramount films, was reduced to standard 35mm for release.

Katz and Harris, then, were able to restore *Vertigo* not only to its original visual splendor but to a screen width that tripled the size of the image—lending the film's images a breadth of view audiences had never before seen. This they achieved by printing from a 65mm negative to a 70mm negative, with limited loss of picture at the top and bottom of the image. The result was a *Vertigo* that represented not what audiences had originally seen but what Hitchcock had originally shot.

This decision (as well as some others discussed in the interview) was not without controversy. The restoration (or improvement) of *Vertigo* raised some of the same concerns as Ted Turner's colorization attempts: At what point does an improvement begin and the director's original vision end? At what point does the work of enhancing images and sound tracks (in *Vertigo*'s case, through extensive remixing and the recording of a brand-new Foley track) begin to corrupt the original work? Yet these questions, at least in the case of *Vertigo,* pale before the restoration team's achievement: There can be no doubt that Hitchcock's film benefited from the work of Harris and Katz.

As of 1998, the restored *Vertigo* is the best way to see Hitchcock's masterpiece. Anyone who knows the film well may have minor complaints about the restoration (the new Foley track, for instance, contains sounds that are not in the original, including seagulls at Fort Point and the loud creak of a door during the final moments in the tower). The quirks of the physical film itself are part of our memory of any special movie, so anything new is likely to jar careful viewers. But seeing the restored print will likely extinguish anyone's preference for the faded, dirty print of 1983. There may still exist, in someone's garage or storage room, a pristine IB Technicolor print of *Vertigo,* but even if one was discovered, it would hardly match the look of the restored 70mm version.

In short, Harris and Katz—through judicious decisions and careful work—have created a *Vertigo* that Hitchcock himself would have enjoyed watching.

[THE RESTORATION OF *VERTIGO*]: AN INTERVIEW WITH JAMES C. KATZ AND ROBERT A. HARRIS

DA: *Vertigo* had some unique difficulties when it came to the restoration?

JK: Well, there was a lot of fading. You know, we knew that it was a wide-screen aspect ratio on VistaVision, but it was an eight-perforation horizontal format—a double-framed 35mm—and you know it had never been projected in VistaVision. In fact, almost no VistaVision films had ever been projected in theaters for full distribution. I think the only ones that ever were were *Strategic Air Command* and *White Christmas*. They actually were not only shot in VistaVision but were shown in the theater in that format.

What Paramount would do with all other VistaVision was reduce them to 35mm, which reduced the image about one-third the size it was shot in. So, we had always wanted to go to 70mm—because it's almost a one-to-one transfer. That was really what our aim was. And then we decided to do it DTS [Digital Theater Sound], which we thought would add a dimension to Herrmann's score.

Once we found the sound track and had decided to use it with a much higher-quality sound system, we knew that we were going to have certain problems and certain decisions that we were going to have to make that might be controversial. We knew we would have to do a new Foley track [the ambient-sound track—footsteps, gun shots, bird cries, and other sounds added by the filmmakers in postproduction], for one. We were able to transfer the music off these original 35 mags [magnetic sound tracks] that we found. We managed to get about 90 percent of what was there; we weren't able to capture the scene in the cemetery at Mission Dolores, but that section we were able to get off a Spanish track for the film. Each country, you know, remixed their own music.

At the same time, we made a conscious decision to digitize the dialogue tracks. When you digitize the dialogue tracks, you lose the Foley effects—and we knew we would have to re-Foley the picture. We knew this would be a controversial decision, but we figured we could almost duplicate exactly the old Foley effects. We had voluminous notes and we had a lot of Hitchcock's comments, and the old prints, which would serve as a map of the old Foley effects. The only thing was, in some instances, when you're dealing with the high-quality technology we were dealing with, you have to embellish those tracks a little bit in order to cover the sins of 1958—the hisses, pops, and bangs. So there are maybe one or two effects that are basically camouflage.

DA: The first thought that comes to mind were the seagull cries in Fort Point?

JK: There were seagull cries before. I don't know, exactly—there may be an extra one in there. But there's a foghorn in there that wasn't there before. I mean, you can count the additions on one hand. At the same time, it was a choice of hearing a hiss or a bang, or hearing an effect. We thought it was more pleasing to hear an effect.

Our basic objective was to expose the audience to the dimensions of Bernard Herrmann's score through DTS. And then, when we finally showed it to the likes of Andrew Sarris and Kenny Turran and people who knew *Vertigo* really well, they said, "You know, whatever you did, even though you had to mess with it a little bit, it's so impressive—such a force in the picture—such a wonderful score." They thought we made the right decision. We were obviously happy to hear that, because we knew the purists would take us on. Yet the alternative for purists would be to hear the 1958 track with hisses, bangs, and pops and everything else. It was basically a question of philosophy more than a question of ethics.

DA: Were there complaints?

JK: We have had letters, stuff on the Internet. You're not going to please everybody. The Internet is a plus and a minus for us. When we're looking for material, it's a tremendous help. And then we get all the naysayers.

DA: This can put you in a difficult position.

JK: We have to make those decisions all the time. And there's also a fiscal aspect to this—a responsibility that we have to the studio. The more people who come to see this and the more they are exposed to it, the better the chance is of our doing another one. So we want it to be commercially successful, and there are always going to be compromises. When you are working with old materials, you try to make it as palatable as possible.

We got complaints about how Hitchcock had ended the movie. It's very hard for people to separate us from Hitchcock. They say, "Boy, you know, *Vertigo* was great," and we have to keep reminding them that we just restored the picture and put it in a state that would be attractive for them to enjoy.

The great thing is, we're showing it to audiences and they don't know how it's going to end. I think Bob and I had always thought, Wouldn't it be great if we could sit down and watch this movie never having seen it before. What that experience would be like seeing it now. It's just something we'll never know. We're showing it to people who have only seen it on television, with commercials. *Vertigo* is not a film you want to see interrupted. People have seen it on a ten- or twenty-inch screen; people have seen bad prints in the theaters. They never really appreciated the score.

So we have a real cross section of people who've seen it, then— people who think they saw it in 1958, but if you ask them what it's about, they can't tell you anything; people who have seen it twenty times or so and really have a point of view on it. It was very interesting seeing it in theaters across the country and also seeing it with people from Chicago, who were friends with Kim Novak, who knew it from the fifties and sixties. There was a long time when it wasn't available at all, from 1971 to 1984, and no one could see the picture at all, so there was a real gap in there.

DA: I remember that's when I became very interested in the film, because it was one of the few Hitchcock films I hadn't seen and I was very excited when it was first rereleased.

JK: I was speaking with someone once about it at a festival and I said, "It's really amazing how successful these films were, considering what terrible condition they were in." We didn't realize how bad the condition of the films was until we started working on them again. We really saw what the sound problems were, what the picture problems were. We're going through the same thing now in a strange way with *Rear Window*.

DA: Let me back up a minute. Some of the questions that have been raised are about VistaVision, and what the real size of the image is.

JK: Well it's not a full 65mm, but it's still a wide-screen ratio.

DA: It's the right ratio.

JK: It's 1.85:1. It's almost the same size as the 65mm frame, with a bit of room to spare. And we did a hard matte to cover the excess.

DA: So you didn't really increase the image size at all—you went straight 1:1?

JK: We did straight 1:1 printing.

And then we did a hard matte so that it went on to 70mm, exactly the size of VistaVision. We didn't blow it up or reduce it.

DA: So there's absolutely no loss of image?

JK: It was a pure transfer—conversion, let's call it. We also had a DTS track on.

DA: I take it VistaVision prints existed of the film?

JK: There were no studio VistaVision prints—just the original camera negatives.

DA: There was another moment in the restored *Vertigo* that I was curious about: the moment when Scottie leaves Judy at the hotel and she recalls the murder. During the flashback, there seems to be a drop in the quality of the image.

JK: There was, because there was one shot in particular—where it goes back and forth from Kim to Jimmy in the frame in that sequence—for which the negatives, the separation—everything was just gone.

That sequence was too far gone; we didn't think it was really worth spending the money to improve it. As a result, we left it as is. I guess it's sort of a warning to everybody as to the working conditions that the film was in to begin with.

RH: Are you talking about the flashback? Ninety percent of the damage was done early. We could have made it maybe 10 percent better for $100,000. The improvement would have been so negligible that anyone who knows anything about film might have really been able to see it, but the normal audience would not.

DA: What could you have done? What would this process involve?

RH: We could've worked with it digitally to lower the contrast. They have a wonderful digital process called "degraining." It's really quite extraordinary. What they actually do is knock it out of focus.

DA: Interesting—kind of smear the image.

RH: Right, you can't focus anymore, but they don't tell you that you're losing focus. We looked at it. We got in a test one day of just a few frames and looked at it under a ten-power loop and you could see that the detail was gone. The grains were soft overall. So they giveth and they taketh away, but mostly they taketh away the quality and your money at the same time.

DA: You're watching for an hour and twenty minutes or so of this extraordinary print and then bang, you see what must be the original. . . .

RH: At that point, it's ten generations away from the original.

DA: When you say ten generations away, what does that mean exactly to someone who doesn't work with restoration?

JK: Well, if you're starting with the original and duplicating it any number of times for any number of reasons, you're ten layers away from what you started with.

DA: There was another moment in the restored film—in the final moments in the tower, the darkness in the scene, and the soft focus—is that in the original print?

RH: You're talking about the long dialogue scene with Jimmy and Kim? That was Hitchcock. It was shot with the focus basically on the wall behind them. The focus was shot wide-open. It's basic depth of field. It was shot with the lens wide open. Consequently, you are either in focus or out of focus and the focus on that scene was not there and Hitchcock went for performance—and the performances are unbelievable—and he just let the focus go rather than take a lesser performance. The darkness—that's the way that it's supposed to look; that's the way it always did look, as a matter of fact.

JK: And the shot of the 360-degree turn—that's not really sharp either, and that was the only thing we could figure—that they went for performance as opposed to clarity. That's the way it was made to be— in fact, it was shot with a fog filter. People have asked us about that.

One of the interesting things was that when the reviews came out about the picture, Mike Clark of *USA Today* said that he thought the ending was much too dark, unlike it was in the original film. The problem is that he is a victim of the video generation, where people are constantly trying to go for detail as opposed to atmosphere. We sent him some clips from one of the prints from 1958, and it showed him that it was, in fact, dark.

DA: My first inclination was that maybe they had lightened the video slightly.

JK: Well, they did.

RH: That's exactly what they did.

JK: And had we not been involved in the transfer of this version, it would have been exactly the same thing. We always laugh because we see so many videos where people are carrying torches in broad daylight.

DA: What do you think of the film?

JK: It's probably in the top ten most important films, I would say.

DA: What about Hitchcock films in general—where would you rank his films?

JK: He's made good ones, bad ones, mediocre ones.

RH: Have you seen *Family Plot* recently?

JK: Not one of his best. But then you see *The 39 Steps* and you see some of the great old ones he made.

DA: Is *Vertigo* his best?

JK: I think so.

RH: One of them. You really have to go period by period. I think it's one of his best from the 1950s, certainly. I like *Shadow of a Doubt* very much; in that whole period, it's certainly the best of the films where he had a budget to work with. I think it's unfair to compare *Vertigo* to *Young and Innocent,* which is a great film. You know, it's a great film for different reasons and was made on a totally different budget. I think if you break it up between studio pictures and non-studio pictures, it's a little bit fairer.

JK: People say *Vertigo* was the most revealing of his personality. It's a layered picture—you see more in it each time you see it.

It's got a lot of shots and sequences that have been copied many times—one of the most imitated films in one way or another. You know, people have tried to take aspects of it and use it in their films. People have tried to remake it unsuccessfully. You think of Hitchcock films that are being remade, or that people are trying to remake, or that are in development, films like *Psycho, To Catch a Thief, Dial M for Murder.* I think if they didn't hold up, nobody would want to remake them—and if they hold up, why bother? You would think after *Sabrina* they wouldn't try to remake pictures anymore.

DA: You mentioned something earlier about restoring *Rear Window* next.

JK: We're doing tests on five Hitchcock movies, and then we will give a report to Universal and we'll see which is worth going theatrical with, if they want to do anything at all—whether they want to go theatrical with *Rear Window* and what our recommendations would be regarding the others. We may just take it to the extent of preparing preservation materials and video materials.

It just depends on what we think potentially their worth is in the marketplace, and whether a given film is going to be a theatrical release, video and laser disc, syndication and network—whether it's going to be good for any of that.

DA: If you could save one film for whatever reason—only one—what would your choice be? It could be this film or another.

RH: For me, it would be *Lawrence of Arabia*.

JK: But you've already done that.

RH: That's the whole point.

DA: Looking at the history—the last hundred years of film—you would choose *Lawrence*?

RH: I would say *Lawrence*—yeah, that was an excellent film. It's not done yet; we're still missing two and a half minutes.

DA: Any ideas as to where that footage might be?

RH: I know exactly where it is, and I know how to do it. It's just a matter of getting someone in charge at Columbia long enough to okay the project for me.

JK: There are a lot of films, though. Really, we're getting slowly into trouble. I think if we could've gotten to *Around the World in 80 Days* before it was by the boards—but we'll never be able to make a print of that again.

DA: That's too bad.

JK: There are a lot of films that have fallen through the cracks, ones that are not owned by studios. People are only talking about restoring films in studios for the most part, but there are libraries.

Just getting everybody to do something—maybe to put some money in to protect their own interest—is difficult. Everyone's interests are different. They don't think they need it—they just want their own films done.

DA: Has there been any preservation done as far as the raw material you worked with on *Vertigo*?

JK: Oh, yeah. What you see in the theater is a by-product. Our goal is basically to make a new negative, *and* to create preservation materials so that the picture can be shown as it was meant to be shown on the big screen in perpetuity. I mean, that's what we're trying to do. We stress separation of elements. We make sure that everything isn't in one vault—one on the East Coast, one on the West Coast.

We do a whole preservation program. Studios are somewhat savvy about that, but a company like CBS—with *My Fair Lady*—is basically a video setup. So we did a whole preservation program for them on that. We advised them on how to separate their elements, where to store x and where to store y, what materials they needed, what they should be making their videos out of, and so on and so forth. This is basically what we do. Whatever kudos we get because of the way *Vertigo* looks, that's just scratching the surface—that's just a by-product. That's really showing the film as it is meant to be seen. And hopefully we can continue, but the basis of our work and the foundation is preserving all of the materials we create, in order to show the film in perpetuity.

DA: Has Universal made a pretty strong commitment to doing this kind of work in their libraries?

JK: Universal in their own quiet way is doing more preservation and restoration than most studios. Universal and Disney are both doing a lot. We work on the big films, the high-visibility, large-format films in particular. Other studios are doing day-to-day work, but there are also studios, like Fox, that aren't doing anything. So it's just a question of time.

AFTERWORD

Too late, too late. There's no bringing her back.

—*Scottie Ferguson, in* Vertigo

The phenomenon that was Alfred Hitchcock in the 1950s was born of a curious mix of artistic independence and teamwork. Hitchcock's consistent, singular vision gives the impression of a true auteur at work, yet everywhere in his history, there is evidence of how many people worked together to create this seemingly personal vision. Hitchcock allowed incredible freedom of interpretation from his colleagues; yet—and this is the key—their interpretations all stayed true to the idea of what a Hitchcock film should be. The intertwining of Hitchcock's cinematic success, television success, and success as a personality made the man not just an artist, but a kind of cultural force.

In all of the interviews and conversations that went into the preparation of this book, those who worked with Hitchcock were consistent in the tone of their responses. Each of them projected an overall admiration for the man and the artist; the sense of true artistic freedom when it came to their roles was comfortably mingled with the knowledge that they were serving the Hitchcock vision in their work. In the collaborative art of the cinema, this is the only way an auteur can survive.

In his earlier films, Alfred Hitchcock had defined a set of themes that the public responded to; he had a set level of professionalism that was respected industry-wide; and he had established a cinematic style, creatively mixing subjective camera work and carefully timed montage to build suspense, that would influence generations of filmmakers.

The films of the fifties are the fruit of these years of labor: the work of the mature artist aided by a team of colleagues who instinctively understood the nature of the creation and the creator. It is such a rare, felicitous fact that, from this vantage point, it seems almost miraculous; in fact, there are few comparisons in the history of cinema. Bad luck or timing derailed most auteurs before their careers had run their natural course. The end of the studio system (Hitchcock's mid-fifties zenith came at its twilight; its death in the sixties coincided with his decline) has made such bursts of incredible creativity nearly impossible.

Vertigo, the apotheosis of this singular period, manages to invite responses on so many levels that the film, and interest in it, will endure for generations to come. I am drawn back continually by the personal qualities of the film—by its inherent passion and beauty. As much as any film buff, I enjoy arguing over the film's every detail—over Hitchcock's artistic influences, over the minor, irresolvable plot conundrums. But what connects *Vertigo* to my soul is the palpable sense that this story was connected, very deeply, to Hitchcock's own soul. Made during a very difficult time—when both his health and that of his beloved Alma were in crisis, when problems with writers and actors and even story daunted at every turn, when the entire industry was entering a twilight of declining ticket sales and competing media—it marked a moment when Hitchcock himself must surely have been longing to re-create the past.

Harrison Engle's sentiments, expressed earlier in these pages, speak to the heart of the film: *Vertigo* is an expression of longing for what we can never have again, whether embodied in a person, a location, or an emotion. Those of us who are "healthy" do not wander the old places, looking for ghosts. But the film expresses a truth that may be dark but is unavoidable: Health falters, time destroys as well as heals, and one day we find the living crowded by the dead. In that sense, we all stand with Scottie in the tower.

| # *VERTIGO* CAST AND CREW

CAST

Scottie—James Stewart

Madeleine and Judy—Kim Novak

Midge—Barbara Bel Geddes

Gavin Elster—Tom Helmore

Coroner—Henry Jones

Doctor—Raymond Bailey

Manageress—Ellen Corby

Pop Leibel—Konstantin Shayne

Older Mistaken Identity—Lee Patrick

SMALL PARTS AND BITS

Capt. Hansen—Paul Bryer

Ransohoffs Saleswoman—Margaret Brayton

Jury Foreman—William Remick

Flower Vendor—Julian Petruzzi

Nun—Sara Taft

Policeman—Fred Graham

Beauty Operator—Mollie Dodd

Salesman—Don Giovanni

Model—Roxann Delmar

Waiter—Bruno Santina

Middle-Aged Mistaken Identity—Dori Simmons

Attorney—Ed Stevlingson

Girl in Portrait—Joanne Genthon

Young Mistaken Identity—Nina Shipman

Maître D'—Rolando Gotti

Bartender—Carlo Dotto

Acting Double for Kim Novak—Jean Corbett

Man Escort—Jack Richardson

Miss Woods—June Jocelyn

Saleswoman—Miliza Milo

Salesman—John Benson

Gateman—Buck Harrington

CREW

Director of Photography—Robert Burks, A.S.C.

Camera Operator—Len South

Technicolor Color Consultant—Richard Mueller

Art Direction—Hal Pareira and Henry Bumstead

Special Photographic Effects—John P. Fulton, A.S.C.

Process Photography—Farciot Edouart, A.S.C., and Wallace Kelley, A.S.C.

Set Decoration—Sam Comer and Frank McKelvy

Titles Designed by Saul Bass (with designs by John Whitney)

Edited by George Tomasini, A.C.E.

Assistant Director—Daniel McCauley

Makeup Supervision—Wally Westmore, S.M.A.

Hair Style Supervision—Nellie Manley, C.H.S.

Sound Recording by Harold Lewis and Winston Leverett

Costumes—Edith Head

Nightmare Sequence and Carlotta Painting by John Ferren

Music by Bernard Herrmann

Conducted by Muir Mathieson with the London Symphony and the Vienna Philharmonic

Associate Producer—Herbert Coleman

Directed by Alfred Hitchcock

Screenplay by Alec Coppel and Samuel Taylor (with an earlier draft by Maxwell Anderson and additional work by Angus MacPhail)

Based upon the novel *D'Entre les Morts* by Pierre Boileau and Thomas Narcejac

Vertigo was nominated for two Academy Awards in 1958—one for Bumstead's art direction and the other for sound.

| # VISTAVISION

The process used to film *Vertigo* has created much confusion with contemporary audiences and writers. VistaVision was developed by Paramount to compete with Fox's CinemaScope. Widescreen formats were an attempt by studios to compete with television, which began cutting into ticket sales in the fifties. CinemaScope had been successful for Fox, but Fox owned the process, and so VistaVision was born.

The CinemaScope process was an anamorphic process—that is, the widescreen image was squeezed onto a standard 35mm frame during filming, using a special lens, and then projected through a similar lens that would "unsqueeze" the image. A theater needed only to increase the screen size and purchase a CinemaScope lens to project a widescreen movie. The screen size is expressed in ratios, so a

CinemaScope image was 2.55:1—meaning the screen was more than two and a half times wide as it was tall (standard films and television are approximately 1.33:1, that is, a third wider than it is tall).

There were problems, though, with CinemaScope: expensive lenses, and a limited depth of field. When Paramount decided to develop its own process it reached back to technology developed in the late 1920s. The basic principle was to run the film horizontally through the camera and projector, using frames twice the size of an ordinary 35mm frame. The genius behind this is that you get a larger frame without having to print wider film. By moving the film sideways through the projector/camera and using frames the size of two rather than one this essentially doubles the image size, providing a screen ratio of 1.85:1. The camera that was developed by Loren L. Ryder and John R. Bishop was called the Paramount Lazy 8 Butterfly Camera because the side-mounted film magazines resembled butterfly wings.

Paramount released the resulting films in three formats (hence the confusion today): As an actual VistaVision print (one that moved horizontally through the projector), as a regular 35mm print reduced from the VistaVision format, and as an anamorphic print. The last format was not compatible with the CinemaScope lens, so theater owners had to rent or purchase one from Paramount. The first VistaVision film was *White Christmas*.

According to Paramount records, *Vertigo* was never shown in the true Vista-Vision format (that is, projected through a projector moving the image horizontally). The restored version of *Vertigo* followed a similar route. The restoration was printed on 70mm stock—70mm projectors can be found in nearly every major city. The initial release at the New York Film Festival (followed by Washington, D.C., Chicago, Los Angeles, and San Francisco) was in 70mm (see the Harris/Katz interview), and then on regular 35mm prints in smaller cities, where 70mm projectors were harder to come by.

VistaVision is still used today by special effects production companies. The superior quality of image is important for most effects work that requires rear-screen and traveling matte shots.

SOURCES AND BIBLIOGRAPHY

The principal source for *Vertigo: The Making of a Hitchcock Classic* was the collection of Hitchcock's production files held at the Margaret Herrick Library of the Academy of Motion Picture Arts and Sciences. Author interviews with members of the film's creative team were another important source; they were conducted in 1996–7, with the exception of the comments from Charles Bennett, which were from interviews conducted in 1991–2.

For information on Hitchcock's life, the author's own research into Hitchcock's personal and production files, as well as the two biographies listed below, were the principal sources of dates and information. The files were not available to either John Russell Taylor or Donald Spoto, so their dates, particularly on the *Vertigo* production, were subject to the vagaries of memory. Taylor's dates tend to be more accurate than Spoto's—and both can be checked against Jane Sloan's authoritative *Alfred Hitchcock: The Definitive Filmography* (which has only the rarest lapse in accuracy—Sloan's work is a required resource for any Hitchcock scholar).

Dates for films in the text are release dates. The only exception here is the generalization for the 1983 rerelease of *Vertigo,* which is referred to by nearly everyone as the 1984 re-release. Rather than cause confusion, I've stuck with 1984, but for the record *Vertigo* was rereleased in November 1983, following the rerelease of *Rear Window* in October 1983 at the New York Film Festival.

BIBLIOGRAPHY

Bogdanovich, Peter. *The Cinema of Alfred Hitchcock.* New York: Museum of Modern Art Film Library/Doubleday, 1963.

———. *Who the Devil Made It.* New York: Alfred A. Knopf, Inc., 1997.

Boileau, Pierre and Thomas Narcejac. *Vertigo.* London: Bloomsbury, 1997.

Bouzereau, Laurent. *The DePalma Cut.* New York: Dembner, 1988.

Cardiff, Jack. *Magic Hour.* London: Faber, 1996.

Deutelbaum, Marshall and Leland Poague. *A Hitchcock Reader.* Ames: Iowa State University Press, 1986.

Dewey, Donald. *James Stewart.* Atlanta: Turner, 1996.

Eames, John Douglas. *The Paramount Story.* New York: Crown, 1985.

Ferguson, Russell, ed. *Art and Film Since 1945: Hall of Mirrors.* New York: Monacelli Press, 1996.

Gottlieb, Sidney, ed. *Hitchcock on Hitchcock.* Los Angeles: University of California Press, 1995.

Head, Edith and Paddy Calistro McAuley. *Edith Head's Hollywood.* New York: E. P. Dutton, 1983.

Hunter, Evan. *Me and Hitch.* London: Faber, 1997.

Leff, Leonard. *Hitchcock and Selznick.* New York: Weidenfeld & Nicolson, 1987.

Low, Rachel and Roger Manvell. *The History of the British Film, 1896–1950.* London: George Allen & Unwin, 1948.

McCarty, John and Brian Kelleher. *Alfred Hitchcock Presents.* New York: St. Martin's Press, 1985.

McGilligan, Pat. *Backstory.* Los Angeles: University of California Press, 1986.

———. *Backstory 3.* Los Angeles: University of California Press, 1997.

Perry, George. *The Films of Alfred Hitchcock.* New York: E. P. Dutton, 1965.

Rebello, Stephen. *Alfred Hitchcock and the Making of Psycho.* New York: Dembner, 1990.

Ryall, Tom. *Alfred Hitchcock & the British Cinema.* London: Athlone Press, 1996.

———. *BFI Film Classics: Blackmail.* London: British Film Institute, 1993.

Sloan, Janet. *Alfred Hitchcock: The Definitive Filmography.* Los Angeles: University of California Press, 1993.

Smith, Steven C. *A Heart at Fire's Center: The Life and Music of Bernard Herrmann.* Los Angeles: University of California Press, 1991.

Spoto, Donald. *The Art of Alfred Hitchcock* (second edition). New York: Doubleday, 1992.

———. *The Dark Side of Genius: The Life of Alfred Hitchcock.* Boston: Little, Brown, 1983.

Sterritt, David. *The Films of Alfred Hitchcock.* Cambridge: Cambridge University Press, 1993.

Taylor, John Russell. *Hitch: The Life and Times of Alfred Hitchcock.* New York: Da Capo Press, 1996.

Thomas, Bob. *King Cohn: The Life and Times of Harry Cohn.* New York: Putnam, 1967.

Thompson, David. *A Biographical Dictionary of Film.* New York: William Morrow, 1981.

———. *Showman: The Life of David O. Selznick.* London: Little, Brown, 1993.

Truffaut, François. *Hitchcock.* New York: Simon and Schuster, 1967.

Wood, Robin. *Hitchcock's Films Revisited.* New York: Columbia University Press, 1989.

INDEX